THE COMPLETE BOOK OF
Home
Environmental
Hazards

THE COMPLETE BOOK OF
HOME ENVIRONMENTAL HAZARDS

ROBERTA ALTMAN

☑ Facts On File

New York • Oxford • Sydney

THE COMPLETE BOOK OF HOME ENVIRONMENTAL HAZARDS

Facts On File, Inc.	Facts On File Limited	Facts On File Pty Ltd
460 Park Avenue South	Collins Street	Talavera & Khartoum Rds
New York NY 10016	Oxford OX4 1XJ	North Ryde NSW 2113
USA	United Kingdom	Australia

Library of Congress Cataloging-in-Publication Data

Altman, Roberta.
 The complete book of home environmental hazards / Roberta Altman.
 p. cm.
 ISBN 0-8160-2095-7 (HC)
 ISBN 0-8160-2419-7 (PB)
 1. Dwellings—Environmental engineering—Amateurs' manuals.
2. Pollutants—Environmental aspects—Amateurs' manuals. I. Title.
TH6057.A6A47 1990
640'.28'9—dc20   89-39982

British and Australian CIP data available on request from Facts On File

Facts On File books are available at special discounts when purchased in bulk quantities for businesses, associations, institutions or sales promotions. Please contact the Special Sales Department of our New York office at 212/683-2244 (dial 800/322-8755 except in NY, AK or HI).

Text design by Ron Monteleone
Jacket design by Levavi & Levavi
Composition by Facts On File, Inc.
Manufactured by the Maple-Vail Book Manufacturing Group
Printed in the United States of America

10 9 8 7 6 5 4 3 2

This book is printed on acid-free paper.

To Tillie Altman Salomon
who gave me life and Dr. Michael Sarg who
prolonged it

TABLE OF CONTENTS

PART TWO—ENVIRONMENTAL HAZARDS OUTSIDE THE HOUSE   195

INTRODUCTION

The Environmental Protection Agency estimates that over 26,000 deaths a year may be caused by exposure to hazardous substances inside the home. *Indoor* air pollution is considered to be a far more dangerous public health problem than *outdoor* air pollution. Dr. John Spengler, professor of public health at Harvard University, says that "concentrations of contaminants inside homes often exceed the maximum safe levels established for hazardous waste cleanup sites." The average American spends at least 90% of his time indoors; 65% of that time is spent at home.

Today, there is much more awareness and knowledge of what substances and circumstances can be harmful. Materials used innocently years ago, we now know cause cancer and other illnesses. Our industrial "progress" has led to a whole new range of problems: contaminated homes; bodies of water unsafe to drink, fish or swim in; soil that emits fumes that can kill; pollution of the very air we breathe.

Without a book like this, it can be very difficult to track down the information you need to make sure that your home is "healthy." It is virtually impossible to find all the information you need in one place. When I was looking for a house several years ago I could have used a book like this, but it hadn't been written.

Today it is probably impossible to have a totally healthy house in a completely safe environment. If you check out all the possible hazards in this book and your house emerges with a clean bill of health—that is great. If your home does have one or more of these problems, consider yourself lucky that you've found out, and then get to work.

Frequently, the solution is simple and is something you can do yourself. The worst case scenarios are rare. It is possible to eliminate, or reduce, just about any health hazard in or around your home. And while you may not be able to make your home completely risk free, you can get much closer to a zero risk factor.

Major and minor disasters, and life-threatening situations, are not common. What is common, however, are various pollutants in the home environment that can cause headaches, a runny nose, sneezing, coughing, difficulty breathing—any one of a number of different health problems. They may not be life-threatening, but they can be very annoying and make your life at home miserable.

Sometimes it is obvious that there is a problem in the house—you get headaches that disappear when you leave your home—but other hazards are not obvious at all. For example, radon has no smell or color. Without testing for radon in your home, you would have no way of knowing that you are inhaling this potentially deadly substance.

The Complete Book of Home Environmental Hazards is for anyone who lives in a house or apartment, or is shopping for a home, and is concerned everytime there is another story in the newspaper, or another report on TV, about a dump site leaking toxic fumes; contaminated drinking water; a "minor" accident at a nuclear power plant; leaded paint on the walls or a faulty heating system. It is for *anyone* who has some kind of health problem at home that magically clears up in a different environment.

In this book you'll find the latest information available on the environmental hazards that can affect your health. It will tell you what the problems are, how the different pollutants or environmental factors affect you, the signs and/or physical symptoms that signal a potential problem, how to find out if pollutants are present in your home and to what degree. It will tell you how to find the right authority if some further action is needed and, finally, how to get rid of, or reduce, the problem and the risk it poses. Cost estimates for various testing devices and procedures are included. Some of the costs may increase after publication of the book.

Virtually any phone number you may need is in this book, saving you a lot of time and aggravation, as well as costly phone calls. As a reporter I learned how difficult it can be to find the right official, the one who can give you the answer instead of another number to call. When I phoned I had the advantage of being able to say I was calling from a major news organization. And even then, it could take many calls to track down the right person to answer a question. You don't have to do any of that time-consuming tracking down. It's been done for you. Where appropriate, the specific phone numbers, by state, are at the end of the chapter. In addition, there is an appendix with more general numbers, which could be helpful, along with a list of toll- free 800 numbers.

The Complete Book of Home Environmental Hazards is written and organized to make as easy as possible *your* part of making your home healthy. It isn't a textbook, and every effort has been made to stay away from very technical language. Words that may not be all that familiar are in the glossary in the back. This is a *practical* guide with easy to follow steps so that you can figure out what you may be up against, healthwise, in the house you live in, the house you're planning to buy or renovate, or the apartment in which you reside.

This book is divided into three parts: environmental hazards inside the home, environmental hazards outside the home, and what to look for when buying a house to make sure it is environmentally sound. The section on buying a house is there to prevent, if possible, the need of ever having to use the first two sections of the book once you move into your new home.

Checking out your home fully can take quite a bit of effort, but it has some tremendous benefits. To buy and live in a house without inspecting it first can be very costly—for your pocketbook as well as your health. It's up to you to set your priorities, to decide how important it is to you to live in a healthy home; how much of an effort you want to make; what you can live with and WHAT YOU CAN'T LIVE WITH.

This book has been designed to help you make your home the safe haven that it was meant to be—as easily, as quickly and as inexpensively as possible. The house of your dreams *can* be the house of your dreams; it just takes a little more effort today.

ACKNOWLEDGMENTS

To acknowledge every individual who helped me on this project would take another book. The list goes on and on. I was pleased with the extensive cooperation I received from various local, state and federal agencies, including the Environmental Protection Agency, Department of Health and Human Services, Centers for Disease Control, Department of Energy and the Nuclear Regulatory Commission, the Consumer Product Safety Commission and the Federal Drug Administration.

Many professional, trade and consumer organizations were also very helpful, among them the White Lung Association, the National Cancer Institute, the U.S. Council of Energy Awareness, the Union of Concerned Scientists, the American Society of Heating, Refrigeration, and Air Conditioning, the National Asbestos Council, the Water Quality Association.

A special thank you goes to my editor, Deirdre Mullane, who was always supportive and encouraging and took what I thought was a "finished" manuscript and made it stronger—more readable and easily understood. And to Joe Vallely, my agent, who took more phone calls than anyone should be expected to take.

PART ONE

Environmental Hazards Inside the House

1

RADON

"Radon is one of the most serious environmental health problems today...the second leading cause of lung cancer in this country." That was what William Reilly, administrator of the Environmental Protection Agency, said in October 1989 as the Agency called on all Americans to test for radon in their homes, including detached homes, townhouses or row houses, trailers with permanent foundations, as well as basement, first and second floor apartments. At the same time, he released findings from the Agency's latest survey of radon levels in thirteen additional states, bringing to twenty-five the total number of states surveyed. In the survey, done in the winter of 1989, some of the highest radon levels to date were found. In addition to the EPA, others urging Americans to test for radon include the U.S. Public Health Service, the American Lung Association, the American Medical Association and the American Public Health Association.

WHAT IT IS AND WHY ALL THE FUSS

Radon is an invisible radioactive gas. You can't smell it, feel it or see it. When it is outside, it is virtually harmless. It dissipates into the air. It can become a BIG problem when it enters a home and becomes trapped there. As it accumulates it can reach dangerous concentrations.

Radon comes naturally from uranium, which is in the earth's soil and rocks. Black shale, phosphatic rocks and granites are some of the rocks that may have higher than average concentrations of uranium. As uranium decays it gives off radiation and transforms into a series of elements. Radon, a gas, is one of those elements.

Radon may also be found in areas that have been contaminated with certain types of industrial wastes such as by-products of uranium or phosphate mining.

Radon itself poses a minimal risk. It becomes dangerous when it decays—by undergoing a radioactive transformation. Elements called "radon daughters" or "progeny" are formed. It's the decayed radon (radon daughters or progeny) that is deadly. When the radon (gas) in your home undergoes the radioactive decay that produces the deadly radon progeny, the trapped progeny attach to dust particles in the air. When you inhale, the radon progeny on the dust particles attach to the surface of your lungs, damaging lung tissue. The more damage, the greater the risk of getting lung cancer. The amount of risk you face is primarily determined by a combination of the radon concentration in your home and the length of time you're exposed to it. The higher the concentration, the longer the exposure, the greater the risk.

Virtually every house in the United States has some level of radon in the air. Most homes will not have levels high enough to require reduction measures but a significant number will. In October 1989, the EPA estimated that at least eight million, or more than 10%, of the roughly 75 million homes in the United States could have levels above its guidelines.

According to the EPA, radon is the second leading cause of lung cancer deaths. It estimates that radon causes as many as 20,000 each year. Smokers exposed to radon are at a much greater risk. Tobacco smoke makes the lungs more susceptible to radon, according to Assistant Surgeon General Houk. In addition, the smoke attracts radon particles, which are then inhaled. Of the 20,000 suspected radon- related lung cancer deaths each year, 15,000 are smokers. Another study, by the National Academy of Sciences, says radon is responsible for about 13,000 deaths from lung cancer yearly. And there are some scientists who believe 20,000 deaths may be too low an estimate!

We know that exposure to radon can cause lung cancer because of numerous studies of underground miners who were exposed to radon for years. Studies of Colorado miners were used to establish projections of cancer risk due to radon exposure. Currently, studies are being conducted on the effects of exposure to household radon in a number of states and countries.

RADON'S "DISCOVERY"

Since the late '60s there has been concern about radon in homes. At that time, some houses in the West, built with materials contaminated by waste from uranium mines, were found to have high levels of radon. The concern in the '60s, and into the '80s, was always with man-made radon, radon that resulted from some action taken by man.

It wasn't until the mid '80s, that naturally occurring radon in homes became a concern. And its discovery came about in a bizarre way.

In December of 1984, Stanley Watras, an engineer working on the construction of the Limerick Nuclear Plant in Pennsylvania, went to the company Christmas party. When he entered the plant he set off alarms that had been installed to detect any worker leaving the plant with radioactive contamination. He was bringing radiation *into* the plant. A short time later his house was tested for radiation. His living room had the highest level ever found in this country. The level of radon in Stanley Watras's living room was 16 working levels! The EPA recommends levels of no more than two one-hundredths of one working level or 0.02. A person living with a working level of 16, over a lifetime, is at 100% risk of getting lung cancer. In other words, Stanley Watras was living in a home with a virtual death sentence hanging over his head with every breath he took.

The discovery made headlines. Neighbors panicked. One of those neighbors, Kathy Varady, lived across the street from Watras with her husband and four children. They had their house built and had been living in it, happily, since 1977. She thought it was the perfect place to raise a family. "It was close enough to a town," she says, "and at the same time far enough out so that my children could grow up with rural values." Her home is on a knoll overlooking hills and orchards. When her house was tested for radon the following January very high levels were found. State inspectors first did a five-minute grab sample test. (See page 11 for a complete explanation of grab sampling.) They returned several hours later to redo the test results because the levels were so high. A month later the results of a more accurate and sophisticated test showed levels three times what was originally found. It didn't really sink in until she was told that the level of radon in her home was the equivalent of her kids smoking 21 packs of cigarettes a day! She was terrified. She asked the EPA for guidelines. Guidelines didn't exist. The problem was still too new. A state official told her to keep her windows open, it was the middle of February, and to keep her four children out of the basement!

Kathy Varady's house became one of 20 in the EPA demonstration program to determine the best way to treat radon. It was months before the levels in her home were lowered as engineers tried different methods. The levels in her home are now considered safe. She is happy about that. But a lot of anxiety remains. The latency period for radon can be as long as 40 years and she has no way of knowing how her four children will be affected. "We just have to live with what is down the road," she says. "It never leaves you." Kathy Varady never knew that even the possibility of such a problem existed. No one did, then. Since 1984 the EPA has learned a lot about radon but acknowledges it still has only some of the answers.

HOW RADON GETS INTO A HOUSE

Radon comes from the soil. You may think of soil as dense and compact but it's not. Air is always moving in and out. Different factors affect the movement of the air: weather conditions (frozen ground inhibits air movement); soil conditions; and type of soil. Air is drawn into the house when the pressure in your basement or the lowest level of your home is less than the air pressure in the surrounding soil. Radon can enter your home in a variety of ways—through dirt floors, cracks in concrete floors and walls, floor drains, sumps, joints and tiny cracks or pores in hollow block walls.

Because radon is a gas, it is able to move through small spaces in soil. Since air is constantly moving in and out of soil, a wind moving across the soil can push the radon that's in the soil into your basement through minuscule cracks in the walls or floor of your basement. The cracks may even be too small for your eye to see. (Obviously, if your basement has a dirt or partial dirt floor your problems can be much greater.)

Oil burners with condensation drains that drip on the floor can be a source of radon.

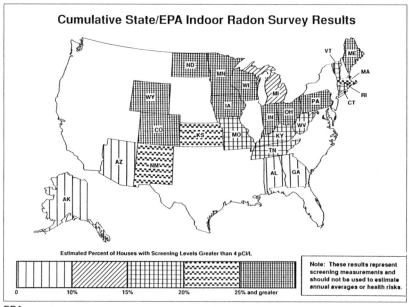

Cumulative State/EPA Indoor Radon Survey Results

Estimated Percent of Houses with Screening Levels Greater than 4 pCi/L

0   10%   15%   20%   25% and greater

Note: These results represent screening measurements and should not be used to estimate annual averages or health risks.

EPA.

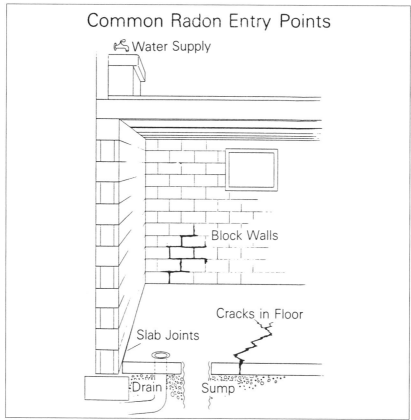

Common Radon Entry Points

EPA.

A woodburning stove can also be a source of radon. The combustion process, which requires a lot of air, results in a drop in air pressure inside the house. When the air pressure goes down *inside* the house and is lower than the air pressure *under* the house, more air with radon is drawn in.

A sump pump in your basement to get rid of water can at the same time enable air/radon to enter.

Radon can also get into your home through your water supply; the EPA estimates that as many as 1,800 lung cancer deaths a year are caused by inhaling radon emitted by household water. Though this happens less frequently, it's more likely to come from well water than community water supplies. (When water is supplied by a municipal system, radon is released while the water is being treated in the system. Also, when water is held in storage, the possibility of radon contamination decreases because the radon is transformed into other substances that are harmless.) Drinking household water that contains radon is not considered a risk because of its low concentration. Radon only becomes a health a health hazard when it is released from the water into the air that you breathe, because the radon progeny can stick to your lungs when inhaled. The radon in the water can be released into the air when you shower, wash dishes—whenever that water is exposed to air.

Usually only a small percentage of the radon found in your home is from the water, between about 2% and 5%. If the radon levels in your home meet the safe guidelines issued by the EPA (see page 14), there is generally no need to test for radon in the water.

FACTORS AFFECTING THE RADON LEVEL

There are several factors that can play a role in the radon levels that are present in your home.

Since natural radon comes from soil and rocks, the land that your house sits on will play a major role. How big a role will depend, in part, on the *amount* of radon gas in the soil, the *pressure* of the radon gas in the soil and the *difference* between the air pressure in your house and the air pressure in the soil.

The ventilation in your house plays a role. You may think that because your house is newer, you'll be less likely to have high levels. In fact, just the opposite is true. Older homes are frequently more drafty, allowing the radon to escape through windows that no longer close snugly. Having a tight, well sealed house can make it very energy efficient, preventing cold air in the winter or hot air in the summer from getting inside. It also means that the air inside the house will be replaced less frequently by outside air. The movement of a volume of air in a given period of time is measured in "air changes per hour" (ACPH). If all the air in a house is replaced in a one-hour period the house has one ACPH. When the ACPH decreases, less radon is being replaced or diluted by fresh, outside air! So while you're cutting down on your heating bill, you may be ending up with dangerous levels of radon.

A third factor is the way your house was built, the materials that were used. The use of slab-on-grade construction (building a house on a flat bed of concrete, generally without a basement or crawl space), may allow more radon gas to enter your home. Radon passes easily through cinder blocks, openings or cracks in the foundation, and openings where water, sewage or gas pipes enter a house.

And finally, as noted earlier, the source of your household water may play a role. It is not common for water to have levels high enough to have a real impact on the amount of radon in the house but there are enough exceptions to make that a possibility.

HOW TO FIND OUT THE RADON LEVEL

The EPA estimates that at least eight million homes nationwide probably need some kind of radon reduction. It recommends that all houses be tested because there is no way to tell which houses have a problem and which do not. (Although Kathy Varady's house tested so high, her neighbors on either side had much lower levels, while someone across the street had levels close to the ones in the Varady home. And if Stanley Watras's home, also across the street, had been four feet to the left, he wouldn't have had a radon problem.) In May of 1988 the National Association of Realtors formally adopted a policy designed to encourage homeowners to test for the presence of radon gas. (You can call your state radiation protection office [see list at the end of this chapter] to find out if they have information on any high levels that have been found in your area.)

The EPA recommends testing during the winter, if possible, when windows are shut and radon levels can build up. Many of the shorter tests require that the house have all the windows closed for the 12 hours before the start of the test and then for its duration.

KINDS OF TESTS

There are a number of different ways to measure radon levels in your home. Some tests require a professional; others you can easily do yourself. Some tests are easier to get; some are a lot more expensive than others; some can be done in a few hours; some take several days; and some involve months.

The biggest concern is getting the most accurate reading possible, since levels can vary from hour to hour and day to day. There will also be different levels in different rooms. Since soil is just about always the source of the radon (the exception being water), the highest levels will most likely be in the basement or lowest level of your house.

Shorter tests are good as a screening device to indicate a possible problem. They are good as a first step (and possibly "last step" if you find insignificant levels!). Generally, the longer the testing the greater the accuracy of the *average* amount of radon over time in your home, which is what you're trying to find out.

Following is a brief description of the different testing methods available—with the advantages, disadvantages and approximate costs:

Charcoal Canister (CC)
The charcoal canister, along with the Alpha Track Detector, is the radon test used most often. The CC is widely available commercially, in

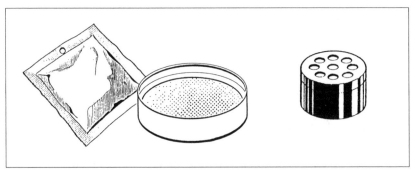

The two most popular commercially-available radon detectors are the charcoal canister (top) and the alpha track detector. Both of these devices are exposed to air in your home for a specified period of time and sent to a laboratory for analysis. EPA.

hardware stores and homecenters, and can be ordered through the mail (see page 261). It is exposed to air in the house, usually in the basement or crawl space where the levels would be highest, and then sent to a lab for analysis. It requires no special skills and can be done by the homeowner. The charcoal canister has a measured amount of activated charcoal that adsorbs the radon gas to be measured. Radon progeny is kept out. You may have to use more than one detector to measure the radon in different areas of your home. The container stays in the house three to seven days and then is resealed and sent for processing and evaluation. A canister is relatively inexpensive, costing up to about $25. Properly analyzed, this method can give very accurate results. (To get as accurate a reading as possible, it is important to follow the instructions precisely. This holds true for any test you do yourself.) Its disadvantages are that some canisters are more sensitive than others to temperature and humidity, the house must be closed for 12 hours prior to and during the test, and the canisters just do short-term testing while radon levels can vary over time.

Alpha Track Detector (AT)
The AT requires no special skills and, like the CC, it can be done by the homeowner. You can get it through the mail. You also may find it in a local hardware or housewares store. It is relatively inexpensive, costing about $20 to $50. The AT container has a small sheet of special plastic material that collects radon progeny. It stays in the house for a minimum of two to four weeks and as long as a year, which means it can measure long-term average concentrations over 12 months. When the testing is finished, it's sent for processing and evaluation. The AT's major disad-

vantage, if you are interested in a quick reading, is that a relatively long measurement period is necessary. In 1989, the consumer advocacy group Public Citizen released the "Citizen's Guide to Radon Home Test Kits," which rated 35 manufacturers. (Public Citizen is listed in Appendix B under radon.)

Grab Sampling

In grab sampling, which must be done by a professional, radon gas is collected in a special flask holding 100 to 2,000 cubic centimeters of air. Radon progeny is collected by drawing air into the flask through a filter. Samples of both gas and progeny can sometimes be obtained during the same procedure, depending on the equipment used. Results are obtained quickly, within hours. It gives an accurate measurement of radon for that "instant" and can indicate a possible emergency situation or the need for additional testing. Grab sampling requires a skilled operator and costs anywhere from $80 to $300, depending on the type of services offered. Its major disadvantage is that it is not a very reliable measure of the "average" radon level to which people in the house will be exposed. Taking grab samples for very short periods may not be representative of the long-term average concentrations. Because radon levels can fluctuate greatly, it's the average level over time that is most accurate and meaningful.

Continuous Radon Monitoring/Continuous Working Level Monitoring

Both methods use an electronic detector to gather and store information in order to get the average amount of radon gas or radon progeny over a period of time (usually an hour). The detector is installed in a house and turned on for a specific period of time. Usually it's a minimum of six hours for screening, 24 hours for follow-up measurements. Because the results must be analyzed by a skilled operator and the equipment used is very expensive, this test really cannot be done by the homeowner. Most of the detectors are very precise. Depending on the type of service required it can cost from about $100 to $300.

Radon Progeny Integrating Sampling Unit (RPISU)

This uses a detector with an air pump that pulls air through constantly. The unit, which runs on AC power is installed by a professional and is on for three days or longer. At the end of the test the operator removes the unit and brings it to the lab for analysis and evaluation. This method directly measures concentrations of radon progeny. It involves a relatively short measurement period. Because this method has been used often, measurement errors are well established. Depending on the type of service provided, the cost ranges from about $40 to $150.

Liquid Scintillation Spectrometer
This is used to measure radon in the water. It uses a liquid which emits light when struck by a nuclear particle. The water sample is mixed with this liquid and the light flashes are then counted on a liquid scintillation counting system to read the radon level. This method must be done by a professional.

ACQUIRING A DETECTION DEVICE

Some states and localities provide detectors to homeowners free of charge or at a nominal cost. Some states have programs to analyze household water. To find out what is available in your state, contact the agency that is dealing with radon, usually under the department of health. (See end of chapter for listing by state.) For example, in New York state the Radiation Protection Agency has a radon testing kit with a charcoal canister, which costs $10.00 (at the time of writing). To get it, people living in New York must call or write the state Bureau of Environmental Protection. The testing device is sent directly to that person, who must send it back when the test is completed. It takes about a month to get the results.

If your state radiation office does not have testing devices available, it should be able to tell you where you can find the devices and how to get them. If your state doesn't have a program to analyze household water it should be able to refer you to a commercial lab. It shouldn't cost more than about $35 per sample. (For more information on testing water see Chapter 4.) You can also check the yellow pages for testing services. Look under "radon" or "environmental." Private companies usually charge more for a radon detector but they generally give results more quickly.

A few states have instituted certification or licensing programs for testing services, but most have not because of how relatively new the radon problem is.

DOING THE TEST YOURSELF

Tests you can do yourself are the Charcoal Canister and the Alpha Track Detector. What you want to do first is use a short-term test to find out the probability of a radon problem in the house. It should be done in the lowest "livable" area in the house—the basement, if you have one—because that is where the level will be highest. Windows and doors should be closed 12 hours before the start of the test and remain closed as much as possible for the test's duration. If you are using more than one detector, be sure to write the location, time you started the test and an identifying number on each testing device you use. That way when you get the results you'll know how the specific areas of your house tested. Once that initial, crude level is obtained, the next appropriate step can be determined. The radon in your home may fall well within the EPA guidelines for safe levels of radon, in which case there may be no need for follow-up testing.

If your house uses well water you may want to test for radon in the water as well. Usually only a small percentage of the radon found in a home comes from household water, though there are some exceptions. In parts of the Northeast and West, high concentrations have been found in groundwater and may be a significant factor in total indoor radon levels. As mentioned earlier, radon in water is only a problem when it gets into the air.

PROFESSIONAL TESTING

To find a person or company to test for radon in your home check first with the EPA. Its Radon/Radon Measurement Proficiency Program (which is voluntary) lets labs and businesses demonstrate their proficiency in testing for radon. The EPA will provide the latest list of those firms that have "demonstrated competence" in measuring indoor radon. The companies on the list are neither endorsed, certified nor recommended by the EPA. But at the time of printing, this list was the best source of places doing radon testing that met EPA quality standards. You can get a copy of the list for your area by calling the regional EPA office. (See listing at the end of this chapter or write to the EPA Office of Radiation Programs, Washington, D.C. 20460.) Again, check with your local state radiation office for any additional help it may be able to provide.

WL and pCi/1: WHAT THOSE LEVELS MEAN

Two measurements are used for radon: the working level (WL) and picocuries per liter of air (pCi/1). The WL is a unit of measure for documenting exposure to radon decay products—radon daughters/radon progeny. The Working Level Month (WLM) is a unit of measure used for cumulative exposure to radon. One WLM equals exposure to 1 WL for 173 hours. The Cumulative Working Level Months

(CWLM) is the total lifetime exposure to radon working levels expressed in total working level months.

While you will see radon measured in WLs, it is more common to see it measured in picocuries per liter of air. That refers to the amount of the radon gas itself. A picocurie is one-trillionth of a curie. Two-hundred pCi/1 is equal to 1 WL. It can get confusing, but the two measurements are just two different ways of looking at the same thing. The average outdoor radon level is about 0.2 pCi/1; the average indoor level is about 1 pCi/1. The EPA has set 4 pCi/1 as the level when action should be taken to reduce radon in the home. The American Society of Heating, Refrigeration and Air Conditioning, which sets standards for indoor air quality, has recommended a 2 pCi/1 guideline. It's all relative. There is no known, safe level of radon, just "safer" levels. The lower the level of exposure the lower the health risk!

RADON RISK EVALUATION CHART

pCi/l	WL	Estimated number of lung cancer deaths due to radon exposure (out of 1000)	Comparable exposure levels		Comparable risk
200	1	440—770	1000 times average outdoor level		More than 60 times non-smoker risk / 4 pack-a-day smoker
100	0.5	270—630	100 times average indoor level		20,000 chest x-rays per year
40	0.2	120—380			
20	0.1	60—210	100 times average outdoor level		2 pack-a-day smoker
10	0.05	30—120	10 times average indoor level		1 pack-a-day smoker / 5 times non-smoker risk
4	0.02	13—50			
2	0.01	7—30	10 times average outdoor level		200 chest x-rays per year
1	0.005	3—13	Average indoor level		Non-smoker risk of dying from lung cancer
0.2	0.001	1—3	Average outdoor level		20 chest x-rays per year

EPA.

LUNG CANCER DEATHS ASSOCIATED WITH EXPOSURE TO VARIOUS RADON LEVELS OVER 70 YEARS

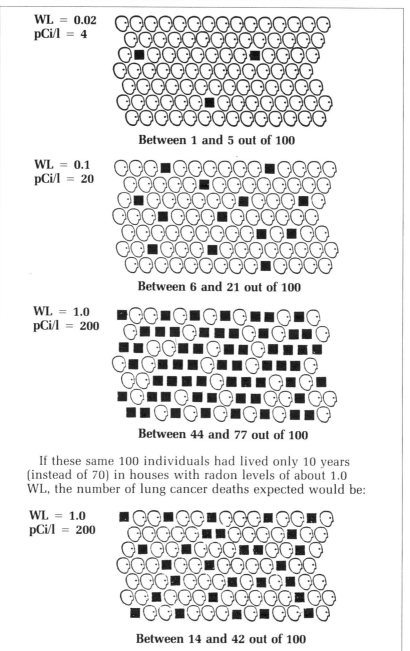

WL = 0.02
pCi/l = 4

Between 1 and 5 out of 100

WL = 0.1
pCi/l = 20

Between 6 and 21 out of 100

WL = 1.0
pCi/l = 200

Between 44 and 77 out of 100

If these same 100 individuals had lived only 10 years (instead of 70) in houses with radon levels of about 1.0 WL, the number of lung cancer deaths expected would be:

WL = 1.0
pCi/l = 200

Between 14 and 42 out of 100

EPA.

EPA GUIDELINE LEVELS

The EPA has set the following guidelines for radon levels in the home:

- **Greater than 1 WL or 200 pCi/1:** Perform follow-up measurements as soon as possible and consider taking immediate action to reduce the level.
- **0.1–1 WL or 20–200 pCi/1:** Perform follow-up measurements for three months or less.
- **0.02–0.1 WL or 4–20 pCi/1:** Perform follow-up measurements for either one year or no more than one week's duration during each of the four seasons.
- **Less than .02 WL or 4 pCi/1:** Follow-up measurements are probably not required. If the measurement was made with the house closed up (windows, doors and any other openings closed for 12 hours prior to testing and during the test), there is very little chance that radon levels in your home will be greater than .02 WL or 4 pCi/1 as an annual average.

RADON REDUCTION: PRELIMINARIES

Since you can't determine what method to use until you know how the radon is getting in, the first step is to discover how the radon is entering your home. This involves an initial visual inspection—looking for any places where radon might be entering. But remember, frequently the radon is entering through cracks that are simply too small for the naked eye to see.

How easily the gas in the soil moves should be evaluated. If ventilation is a possible option, the natural air infiltration rate into the house should be measured. This is done by using a "blower door" (also known as a door fan). The fan is placed in an exterior door and air is blown in (or blown out if you want to measure exfiltration). Pressure gauges measure the air flow. This requires special equipment and a professional.

Radon levels in the water can indicate if the water contributes to the radon levels in the house and to what extent.

There are various remedies for radon reduction. They vary in complexity and cost. In most instances it will fall in the $800 to $1,500 range, though some methods are decidedly higher.

Some remedies are designed to prevent radon from entering the house. Others are designed to get radon out. In most cases, a skilled professional is required to determine the best method to reduce levels and how to implement the methods. The method used should be designed specifically for *your house*. It's not unusual for a combination of methods to be used.

RADON REDUCTION METHODS

Following is a brief description of the ways to reduce radon in your home:

Natural Ventilation

You don't need an expert for this! All you have to do is open your windows. You should ventilate the lowest level of your house, the basement or crawl space, because that is generally where the radon enters. If you do not have a basement or crawl space and your house sits on a concrete slab then your only choice, using this method, is to ventilate your living space. It is a good idea, always, to open as many windows as possible in your home whenever the weather permits it. When you're doing Natural Ventilation it's important to open windows or vents on all sides of the house so that you don't reduce the air pressure inside, thereby allowing MORE radon to enter. When the windows are open fresh air comes in, diluting any radon in the house. The flow of radon from the soil is also slowed.

This is obviously the easiest solution. Unfortunately it is neither practical nor economical in the long run. In addition to the discomfort you might feel, your heating bill could double or triple in the winter and your air conditioning bill in the summer could go up as well. And radon levels can quickly build up to what they were before, once you close the windows. Leaving your windows open could also pose some security problems. So although this method could reduce radon levels by as much as 90%, *most of the time this is just a quick, temporary solution.*

Forced Ventilation

This method operates on the same principles as natural ventilation but uses a fan or fans to draw in outdoor air instead of relying on natural air movement. A fan can be installed to continuously blow fresh air into the house through the existing central forced air heating; fans can blow air into the house through protected intakes in the sides of the house; a fan can be installed to blow outdoor air into a crawl space. As in natural ventilation, you should ventilate the lowest level of your house. It may be advisable to close off your basement and not use it. Air should be blown into the house and exit through windows or vents on the opposite site. *You should never use the fan to pull the air out of the house* because then you can run the risk of decreasing the air pressure inside and drawing in more radon! (For this reason it is usually not a good idea to use a whole-house fan because it usually operates in the exhaust mode.) When ventilating unheated areas be sure to take precautions to prevent pipes from freezing. This is a relatively inexpensive procedure to set up. Depending on the size and sophistication of the fan it can cost as little as $25. However, your heating bill could double or triple. And if you usually use an air conditioner in the summer, your electric bill could increase substantially.

Heat Recovery Ventilation (HRV)

This is a more sophisticated way of ventilating the house, replacing radon-laden air with outside air. The air that is coming in is warmed by the air that it is replacing. A device called a "heat recovery ventilator" or "air to air exchanger" uses the heat in the radon-laden air that is leaving the house to warm the incoming air. The process is reversed in the summer in an air conditioned house. This saves between 50% and 80% of the warmth (or coolness) that would be lost in natural or forced air ventilation. Ducted units are designed, installed and balanced by experienced heating/ventilation/air conditioning contractors. Less complex wall units can sometimes be installed by the homeowner. Ducted units can cost anywhere from $800 to $2,500, including installation.

A wall unit is about $400. HRV is generally cost-effective *only* when there is a big difference between the temperature inside the house and

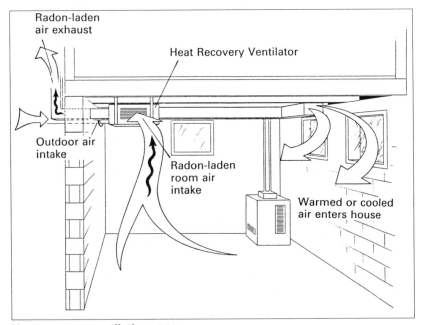

Heat recovery ventilation. EPA.

outside. When you can leave your windows open without using air conditioning or heat, radon is reduced just as effectively. The heat recovery ventilator unit can be put in an inconspicuous part of the house.

Covering Exposed Earth

Covering exposed earth in the basement, storage areas, drain areas, sumps and crawl space will reduce the flow of radon into the house. If you are skilled you can do this yourself; otherwise it should be done by an experienced contractor. The cost, of course, will depend on the size of the area being covered. It is also difficult to tell ahead of time how effective this will be since frequently radon can seep through openings that are too small to see. If you have an earth floor in your basement it should first be excavated, and, before the concrete is poured, four inches of crushed stone should be put down. All joints must be carefully sealed. Once the exposed earth is covered you have to check it regularly since there can be new openings as the house settles and reacts to stresses.

Sealing Cracks and Openings

Even when the soil is covered, cracks in that covering can allow radon to enter. Sealing the cracks and openings reduces the flow of radon. For homes with marginal levels of radon this may do the trick. If your home has a fairly high level this may be the first step when other methods are used. Again, the cost depends on the number of openings to be sealed as well as their location. Some may be in areas difficult to access. For sealing to be effective it requires very careful preparation of the area and controlled application of appropriate substances. Unless you're skilled, it is probably best to have this done by a professional. There is a good possibility that the radon level will not be reduced by as much as you'd hoped, since it is frequently difficult to find all the cracks and openings, settling of the house may create new cracks and openings, and openings in different locations may require different sealing substances. For example, flexible polyurethane membrane sealants should be used for wall and floor joints. Cracks and utility openings should be enlarged enough to allow filling and compatible, gas-proof, non-shrinking sealants, and so forth.

Drain-tile Suction

This method works best with houses that are encircled by drain tiles, the more continuous the loop the better. Drain tiles are perforated pipes that drain water away from the foundation of the house, either to a drainage area or to a sealed sump. With the addition of a fan, they can be used to pull radon from the surrounding soil and vent it away from the house. Generally this method requires an experienced professional, although sometimes, if it is going to be done inside the house and concrete doesn't have to be moved, the homeowner can do it. The cost depends on various factors, including the amount of piping needed and where it and the fan will be put. An exterior drain system can cost anywhere from $700 to $1,500. A system that drains into a sump could go as high as $2,500. In some homes this has reduced radon levels by 99%. The major problems with this method are that some houses do not have complete drain-tile loops, it can be difficult to determine how extensive the drain tile is, and some of the tiles may be damaged or blocked.

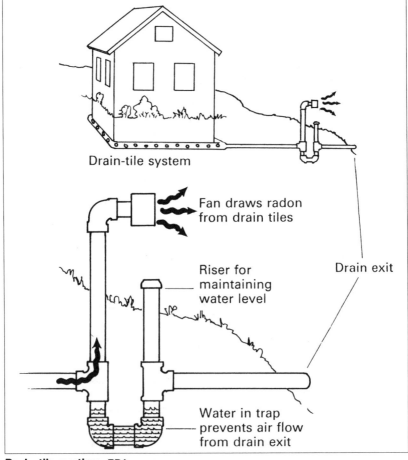

Drain-tile suction. EPA.

Sub-Slab Suction

This has been one of the most widely used and effective methods. Individual pipes are inserted under the concrete slab while a fan blows radon gas away from the foundation through the pipes. Houses with foundations that rest on aggregate soil (a cluster of very small soil granules) or highly permeable soil (soil that can be easily penetrated) are the best candidates for sub-slab suction. When permeability under the slab is not so thorough, the method will still often be applicable. More suction pipes may be needed and the placement of the pipes may be more important. In many cases radon levels are reduced by over 99%. The pipes can be inserted vertically or horizontally. Usually, installation of a sub-slab suction system requires an expert. It can cost from $900 to $2,500.

Block-wall Ventilation

Gas from the soil can get into the concrete block walls through cracks, then travel through the air (empty spaces) in the concrete blocks, eventually entering the basement through holes and cracks in the interior wall blocks. This method is only good for homes that have walls made of hollow concrete blocks and is generally done by an expert. It can be

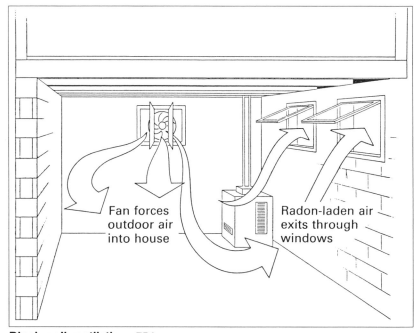

Fan forces outdoor air into house

Radon-laden air exits through windows

Block-wall ventilation. EPA

very effective, reducing radon levels by as much as 99%. It can be done in two ways: wall suction (drawing radon from the spaces within the concrete block walls before it can enter the house) or wall pressurization (blowing air into the blocks so that radon is prevented from entering the walls). The easiest method is putting two pipes in each wall, using fans to push the radon outside; or using fans to pressurize the walls to prevent radon from entering. Another, more complicated approach involves installing a sheet metal baseboard duct around the basement. Holes are drilled behind the duct into the hollow spaces in the blocks. In either method all major holes, especially those on the tops of the blocks, must be sealed. Installation usually requires an expert. It can cost from $1,500 to $2,500 to put in a series of exhaust pipes; $2,500 or more for a baseboard collection system.

Prevention of House Depressurization

The lower the air pressure in your house, compared to that in the soil, the more radon will be drawn in. Depressurization (a lowering of the air

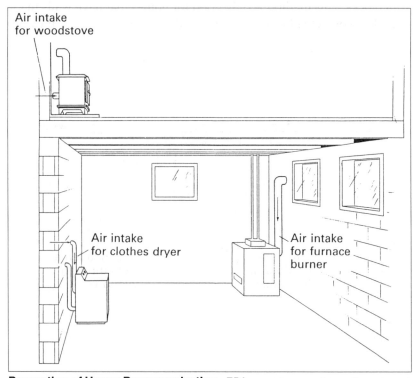

Prevention of House Depressurization. EPA.

pressure in the house) can be caused by an exhaust fan that pushes inside air out or by a combustion unit like a fireplace or woodstove that consumes air. If you have to use an exhaust fan, open a window near it slightly. This will help make-up air from outside to get in. For household combustion units, a permanent system to supply outside air should be installed. Many combustion units are designed to accept outside air. Many others are not, and making a modification can be unsafe as well as illegal. If you have central, forced air heating and cooling, seal off any cold-air return registers (vents) in the basement. That will reduce leakage of basement air into the ducts, and prevent depressurization. Close any openings in the floors to inhibit air movement up through the house. On upper levels, close openings in the shell of the house to reduce the outflow of air. The installation cost for providing supplemental air can vary greatly depending on the type and location of the combustion unit being modified. Therefore it is difficult to give any realistic cost estimate. However, there are some causes of depressurization that can be eliminated easily by the homeowner at very little cost. The effectiveness of this method is difficult to predict because each situation is so different.

House Pressurization
In this method you want to make the air pressure in the basement or crawl space greater than that of the air in the soil under the house. The most common way of doing this is to blow air from upstairs into the basement or crawl space. This can only be done in houses that have a basement or heated crawl space that is tightly sealed from the living area. Installation must be done by an experienced contractor or a careful and skilled homeowner. The cost will vary depending on how much work must be done to tighten the basement shell. Installation costs could be $1,500 to $2,500. It could also increase your heating bill because the increased infiltration upstairs from the fan will bring in more fresh air. This is one of the least-tested techniques, and its reliability at the time of printing was uncertain.

Air Cleaning
There are air cleaning machines that have been available for years and used, for example, to reduce allergy problems. Radon progeny are solid particles and most quickly attach to larger dust particles. When the air is pulled through the device, the dust is removed. An air cleaning device eliminates radon decay products along with the dust. Unfortunately, another problem arises. New radon progeny, which are being generated continuously by the radon gas, have fewer dust particles to cling to. So

while the air cleaner is ridding the air of dust containing radon decay products, the number of unattached radon progeny may increase. There have been indications that unattached decay products may pose a greater health risk but the health data available (as of this printing) are not sufficient to confirm that. High-efficiency air cleaners can remove both attached and unattached progeny, but the air in the house must be moved through very rapidly. For example, to achieve 90% reduction, you could put an efficient air cleaner in the central furnace ducting. However, that would require keeping the furnace fan in continuous operation. This method of radon reduction, at this point, is not recommended by the EPA.

COMPARISON OF RADON REDUCTION METHODS

Method	Cost to Install	Cost to Operate	Maximum Reduction Possible
Natural Ventilation	minimal	high to very high	up to 90-plus%
Forced Ventilation			
basement	low-mod.	very high	up to 90-plus%
crawl space	low-mod.	moderate	up to 90-plus%
Heat Recovery Ventilation			
ducted	mod.-high	low-mod.	50%-75%
wall mounted	low-mod.	low-mod.	no data available
Covering Exposed Earth	moderate to high	low	site specific
Sealing Cracks and Openings	minimal to high	nominal	site specific
Drain-tile Suction	moderate to high	low	up to 99-plus%
Sub-slab Suction	high	low	up to 99-plus%
Block-wall Ventilation	high	low	up to 99-plus%
Prevention of Depressurization	low to moderate	low	site specific
House Pressurization	moderate to high	low	up to 90% (limited data)
Air Cleaning	moderate to high	low to moderate	up to 90% (limited data)
GAC (Water)	moderate	nominal	up to 99-plus%

REDUCING RADON IN WATER

Generally, if there is radon in the water it plays an insignificant role in the overall levels in the house. The homes that can be affected are those with well water and, occasionally, those using a small community well. To contribute significantly to the indoor radon level, the level in the water would be about 40,000 pCi/l, at which point you would probably want to take action. The most common way of reducing the radon in water, at this point, is by installation of a granular activated carbon (GAC) tank. The activated carbon (which also removes other impurities from the water) dissolves radon gas from the water before it gets into the house. The GAC tank should be installed in the incoming water line immediately after the pressure tank. Another way to reduce the radon in the water is by installing an aerator in the water line. (Additional information on these methods is in Chapter 4.)

For more detailed information on radon reduction methods and how to implement them call or write to your regional EPA office and request the booklet "Radon Reduction Techniques for Detached Houses, Technical Guide." (See listing at the end of this chapter.)

FINDING THE CONTRACTOR

Finding the best contractor to do the job can be difficult because this field is so new. You have to be very cautious. Radon has gotten a lot of publicity and there are opportunists who are ready to take the money and run. They have no training or experience in radon mitigation (term for resolving a radon problem) and you could end up paying a sizable sum and being no safer than you were before. Many states now have lists of contractors doing radon mitigation work. Some states have certification programs.

When you do find a contractor, check him or her out with the local better business bureau. Get the proposal (exactly what will be done) in writing. Get the estimate in writing. Ask for references and call the places where the contractor has done work before. Check out those references! If possible, get a second opinion from another contractor or a local government radiological health official. Ask the contractor: How much will the radon in your home be reduced when the job is done; will any follow-up tests be done; what will be done if the levels are still too high; and is any kind of guarantee given?

As you can see in the chart "Comparison of Radon Reduction Methods" there are many choices in radon mitigation. It's important to ask the contractor why the method chosen is the best one for your home.

You also want to know how cost-effective the method is. Sometimes another method that costs slightly more would give you a substantially greater reduction of radon and vice versa.

IT'S FINALLY DONE...OR IS IT? FOLLOW-UP TESTING

After the mitigation is completed, you'll want to do a several-day test of its effectiveness. (Grab sampling is not an appropriate test at this point, because a five-minute sampling period is too brief to provide a meaningful measurement.) Some of the testing methods that are appropriate include charcoal canisters, continuous monitors or RPISU. If the initial, short-term measure shows sufficient reductions, then you should follow that up with an alpha track detector for three months in the winter, when weather conditions can cause the biggest problems with radon. Depending on the radon level and the extent of the original problem, you may want to do additional AT measurements for a year, or longer.

Besides taking those initial and follow-up measurements, there are some other things you'll want to do to make sure that the reduction system has been installed properly and is working properly. First do a visual inspection. For active soil ventilation, one fairly easy and effective tool is a smoke stick, available at your hardware store. It releases a stream of smoke that can reveal air movement. For example, you can hold it up to piping joints and slab/wall closures. If you see smoke, the closings are not adequately sealed.

The following evaluations require special equipment and a professional:

Measurements of the pressure and flow in the piping of active soil ventilation systems and heat recovery ventilators can show various problems in the installation and operation of the system.

Sub-slab pressure field measurements can show whether the sub-slab soil ventilation system is maintaining the desired suction, or pressure, underneath the entire slab.

Measurements in the flues of existing furnaces, water heaters and other combustion appliances can show whether the air that is being sucked out of the house by an active soil suction system is depressurizing the house so that there is back-drafting of the combustion appliances.

In all probability the level of radon in your home does not exceed EPA standards, but the only way to know is by testing the air in your home. Reducing radon to a "safe" level is generally not that difficult or costly. Not doing it, if it's needed, could be very costly, healthwise, to you and your family.

EPA REGIONAL OFFICES FOR RADON

ALABAMA—4
ALASKA—10
ARIZONA—9
ARKANSAS—6
CALIFORNIA—9
COLORADO—8
CONNECTICUT—1
DELAWARE—3
DISTRICT OF
  COLUMBIA—3
FLORIDA—4
GEORGIA—4
HAWAII—9
IDAHO—10
ILLINOIS—5
INDIANA—5
IOWA—7
KANSAS—7

KENTUCKY—4
LOUISIANA—6
MAINE—1
MARYLAND—3
MASSACHUSETTS—1
MICHIGAN—5
MINNESOTA—5
MISSISSIPPI—4
MISSOURI—7
MONTANA—8
NEBRASKA—7
NEVADA—9
NEW HAMPSHIRE—1
NEW JERSEY—2
NEW MEXICO—6
NEW YORK—2
NORTH
  CAROLINA—4

NORTH DAKOTA—8
OHIO—5
OKLAHOMA—6
OREGON—10
PENNSYLVANIA—3
RHODE ISLAND—1
SOUTH
  CAROLINA—4
SOUTH DAKOTA—8
TENNESSEE—4
TEXAS—6
UTAH—8
VERMONT—1
VIRGINIA—3
WASHINGTON—10
WEST VIRGINIA—3
WISCONSIN—5
WYOMING—8

REGION 1
Room 2203
JFK Federal Building
Boston, Massachusetts 02203
(617)565-3234

REGION 2
26 Federal Plaza
New York, New York 10278
(212)264-2515

REGION 3
841 Chestnut Street
Philadelphia, Pennsylvania 19107
(215)597-4084

REGION 4
345 Courtland Street, N.E.
Atlanta, Georgia 30365
(404)347-2904

REGION 5
230 South Dearborn Street
Chicago, Illinois 60604
(312)886-6175

REGION 6
1201 Elm Street
Dallas, Texas 75270
(214)655-7208

REGION 7
726 Minnesota Avenue
Kansas City, Kansas 66101
(913)236-2893

REGION 8
Suite 1300
One Denver Place
999 18th Street
Denver, Colorado 80202
(303)293-1648

REGION 9
215 Fremont Street
San Francisco, California 94105
(415)974-8378

REGION 10
1200 Sixth Avenue
Seattle, Washington 98101
(206)442-7660

STATE AGENCIES FOR RADON

ALABAMA
Radiological Health Branch
Department of Public Health
State Office Building
434 Monroe Street, Room 510
Montgomery, Alabama 36130-1701
(205)261-5313

ALASKA
Department of Health and Social
  Services
P.O. Box H-06F
Juneau, Alaska 99811-0613
(907)465-3019

ARIZONA
Radiation Regulatory Agency
4814 South 40th Street
Phoenix, Arizona 85040
(602)255-4845

ARKANSAS
Department of Health
Division of Radiation Control and
  Emergency Management
4815 West Markham Street
Little Rock, Arkansas 72205-3867
(501)661-2301

CALIFORNIA
Indoor Air Quality Program
Department of Health Services
2151 Berkeley Way
Berkeley, California 94707
(415)540-2469

Environmental Radiation
  Surveillance
Department of Health Services
8455 Jackson Road, Suite 120
Sacramento, California 95826
(916)739-4213 or 322-2073

COLORADO
Radiation Control Division
Department of Health
4210 East 11th Avenue

Denver, Colorado 80220
(303)331-8480

CONNECTICUT
Department of Health Services
Toxic Hazards Section
150 Washington Street
Hartford, Connecticut 06106
(203)566-8167

DELAWARE
Division of Public Health
Bureau of Environmental Health
802 Silver Lake Boulevard
Robbins Building
Dover, Delaware 19903
(302)736-4731

DISTRICT OF COLUMBIA
Department of Consumer &
  Regulatory Affairs
614 H Street, N.W., Room 1014
Washington, District of Columbia
  20001
(202)727-7218

FLORIDA
Office of Radiation Control
Building 18, Pine Hills Service
  Center
7500 Silver Star Road
Orlando, Florida 32818
(407)297-2095

GEORGIA
Department of Natural Resources
Environmental Protection Division
205 Butler Street, S.E.
Floyd Towers East, Suite 1166
Atlanta, Georgia 30334
(404)656-6905

HAWAII
Environmental Protection & Health
  Services
Department of Health
591 Ala Moana Boulevard

Honolulu, Hawaii 96813
(808)548-4383 or 548-3075

IDAHO
Radiation Control Section
Department of Health and Welfare
Statehouse Mall
Boise, Idaho 83720
(208)334-5879

ILLINOIS
Department of Nuclear Safety
Office of Environmental Safety
1035 Outer Park Drive
Springfield, Illinois 62704
(217)785-9956 or
(800)225-1245 (in state)

INDIANA
Division of Industrial Hygiene &
   Radiological Health
State Board of Health
1330 W. Michigan Street
P.O. Box 1964
Indianapolis, Indiana 46206-1964
(317)633-0153

IOWA
Bureau of Environmental Health
Department of Public Health
Lucas State Office Building
Des Moines, Iowa 50319-0075
(515)281-7781

KANSAS
Dept. of Health and Environment
Bureau of Air Quality &
   Radiation Control
Forbes Field, Building 321
Topeka, Kansas 66620-0110
(913)296-1561

KENTUCKY
Radiation Control Branch
Cabinet for Human Resources
275 East Main Street
Frankfort, Kentucky 40621
(502)564-3700

LOUISIANA
Nuclear Energy Division
P.O. Box 14690
Baton Rouge, Louisiana 70898-4690
(504)925-4518

MAINE
Division of Health Engineering
Department of Human Services
Occupational and Residential
   Health Program
State House Station 10
August, Maine 04333
(207)289-3826

MARYLAND
Division of Radiation Control
Dept. of Health & Mental Hygiene
201 West Preston Street
Baltimore, Maryland 21201
(301)333-3130
(800)872-3666

MASSACHUSETTS
Radiation Control Program
Department of Public Health
23 Service Center
Northampton, Massachusetts 01060
(413)586-7525
Boston: (617)727-6214

MICHIGAN
Department of Public Health
Division of Radiological Health
3500 North Logan, P.O. Box 30035
Lansing, Michigan 48909
(517)335-8190 or 335-8200

MINNESOTA
Section of Radiation Control
Department of Health
P.O. Box 9441
717 S.E. Delaware Street
Minneapolis, Minnesota 55440
(612)623-5350
(800)652-9747

MISSISSIPPI
Division of Radiological Health
Department of Health
P.O. Box 1700
Jackson, Mississippi 39215-1700
(601)354-6657

MISSOURI
Bureau of Radiological Health
Department of Health
1730 East Elm, P.O. Box 570
Jefferson City, Missouri 65102-0570
(314)751-6083

MONTANA
Occupational Health Bureau
Dept. of Health & Environmental
   Sciences
Cogswell Building A113
Helena, Montana 59620
(406)444-3671

NEBRASKA
Division of Radiological Health
Department of Health
301 Centennial Mall South
P.O. Box 95007
Lincoln, Nebraska 68509
(402)471-2168

NEVADA
Radiological Health Section
Health Division
Department of Human Resources
505 East King Street, Room 202
Carson City, Nevada 89710
(702)885-5394

NEW HAMPSHIRE
Radiological Health Program
Health and Welfare Building
6 Hazen Drive
Concord, New Hampshire
   03301-6527
(603)271-4674

NEW JERSEY
Department of Environmental

Protection
Bureau of Environmental Radiation
380 Scotch Road, CN-411
Trenton, New Jersey 08625
(609)530-4002
(201)879-2062
(800)648-0394 (in state)

NEW MEXICO
Surveillance Monitoring Section
Radiation Protection Bureau
P.O. Box 968
Santa Fe, New Mexico 87504-0968
(505)827-2957

NEW YORK
Bureau of Environmental Radiation
   Protection
State Health Department
2 University Place, Room 375
Empire State Plaza, Corning Tower
Albany, NY 12203-3313
(518)473-8651 or 458-6461
(800)458-1158 (in state)
(800)342-3722 (in state)

NORTH CAROLINA
Radiation Protection Section
Department of Human Resources
701 Barbour Drive
Raleigh, North Carolina 27603-2008
(919)733-4283

NORTH DAKOTA
Division of Environmental
   Engineering
Department of Health
Missouri Office Building
1200 Missouri Avenue, Room 304
P.O. Box 5520
Bismarck, North Dakota 58502-5520
(701)224-2348

OHIO
Radiological Health Program
Department of Health
1224 Kinnear Road
Columbus, Ohio 43212

(614)644-2727
(800)523-4439 (in state)

OKLAHOMA
Radiation and Special Hazards
  Service
State Department of Health
1000 Northeast Tenth Street
P.O. Box 53551
Oklahoma City, Oklahoma 73152
(405)271-5221

OREGON
State Health Department
1400 S.W. 5th Avenue
Portland, Oregon 97201
(503)229-5797

PENNSYLVANIA
Bureau of Radiation Protection
Department of Environmental
  Resources
P.O. Box 2063
Harrisburg, Pennsylvania 17120
(717)787-2480
(800)23-RADON (in state)

PUERTO RICO
Radiological Health Division
G.P.O. Call Box 70184
Rio Piedras, Puerto Rico 00936
(809)767-3563

RHODE ISLAND
Division of Occupational Health
  and Radiological Control
Department of Health
206 Canon Building
75 Davis Street
Providence, Rhode Island 02908
(401)277-2438

SOUTH CAROLINA
Bureau of Radiological Health
Department of Health and
  Environmental Control
2600 Bull Street
Columbia, South Carolina 29201

(803)734-4700
 or 734-4631

SOUTH DAKOTA
Office of Air Quality and Solid
  Waste
Department of Water and Natural
  Resources
Joe Foss Building, Room 217
523 East Capital Avenue
Pierre, South Dakota 57501-3181
(605)773-3364 or 773-3135

TENNESSEE
Division of Air Pollution Control
Custom House
701 Broadway
Nashville, Tennessee 37219-5403
(615)741-3931

TEXAS
Bureau of Radiation Control
Department of Health
1100 West 49th Street
Austin, Texas 78756-3189
(512)835-7000

UTAH
Bureau of Radiation Control
Department of Health
State Health Department Building
P.O. Box 16690
Salt Lake City, Utah 84116-0690
(801)538-6121

VERMONT
Division of Occupational and
  Radiological   Health
Department of Health
Administration Building
10 Baldwin Street
Montpelier, Vermont 05602
(802)828-2886

VIRGINIA
Bureau of Radiological Health
Department of Health
109 Governor Street

Richmond, Virginia 23219
(804)786-5932
(800)468-0138 (in state)

WASHINGTON
Environmental Protection Section
Office of Radiation Protection
Thurston AirDustrial Center
Building 5, LE-13
Olympia, Washington 98504
(206)586-3311

WEST VIRGINIA
Industrial Hygiene Division
Department of Health
151 11th Avenue
South Charleston, West Virginia
  25303
(304)348-3526 or 348-3427

WISCONSIN
Division of Health
Section of Radiation Protection
Department of Health and Social
  Services
5708 Odana Road
Madison, Wisconsin 53719
(608)273-5181

WYOMING
Radiological Health Services
Department of Health and Social
  Services
Hathway Building, 4th Floor
Cheyenne, Wyoming 82002-0710
(307)777-6015

2

ASBESTOS

WHAT IT IS AND WHAT IT DOES

Asbestos is a group of naturally occurring mineral fibers found in rocks. The six kinds that are generally in products and building materials are: chrysotile, amosite, crocidolite, anthophyllite, tremolite and actinolite. They are all fire resistant and not easily destroyed or degraded by natural processes. Approximately 95% of all asbestos used in commercial products is chrysotile.

You'll find asbestos in a wide variety of products and building materials. It's been used to insulate walls and heating pipes, to soundproof rooms, to fireproof walls and fireplaces, to strengthen vinyl floors and joint compounds and to give many paints their texture. It's been used in such products as patching compounds, oil, coal and wood-burning stoves, radiator covers, siding, roofing shingles and some appliances, including toasters, ovens, broilers, refrigerators and pre-1980 hair-dryers.

Asbestos has many advantages, which is why it was used so extensively. It can strengthen the product material; provide thermal insulation inside a product; provide thermal or acoustical insulation (or decoration) on exposed surfaces; and fireproof a product or material.

But asbestos has at least one disadvantage, and it's a major one. It can kill you. And that was learned as early as 1924!

ITS DISCOVERY/ITS HISTORY

Asbestos had very little use until the early 1900s. At that time it was used as thermal insulation for steam engines. Because of its desirable characteristics—noncombustibility, corrosion resistance, high tensile strength and low electrical conductivity—it caught on quickly. Eventually asbestos, mixed with various kinds of binding materials, was used in some 3,000 different commercial products. It was used in brake linings, floor tile, sealants, plastics, cement pipe, cement sheet, paper products, textile products and insulation. U.S. consumption of asbestos had increased to 800,000 tons per year in the early 1970s. When people became very alarmed and concerned about its health hazards, consumption dropped more than 70%. But there were warning signs of the dangers of asbestos long before the 1970s.

In 1924 it was found that exposure to asbestos could result in fatal illness. The *British Medical Journal* published a report by W.E. Cooke about a young woman who had worked with asbestos and who had died with extensively scarred lungs. He said her death was caused by "pulmonary asbestoses." The name stuck. In the mid- 30s, additional British studies showed that such scarring was very common among workers exposed to asbestos. It was established that asbestos inhalation could be fatal.

Since then, scientific research has resulted in a lot of additional information, but mostly on the different ways asbestos can kill. In 1935, Lynch and Smith in the United States and Gloyne in Great Britain noted the association between lung cancer and working with asbestos. And during the 1940s and '50s, cases of pleural and peritoneal mesothelioma (a cancer) were seen in workers exposed to asbestos. Dr. Irving Selikoff, Director of the Environmental Sciences Laboratory at Mt. Sinai School of Medicine of the City University of New York says the link "was clarified and firmly established in the first half of the '60s by Wagner, Selikoff, Churg, Newhouse and others. Additional neoplasms (malignant growths)—again, further ways of dying—were subsequently found related." (*EPA Journal*, May 1984.)

In the 1970s some uses of asbestos were banned, including the spraying of asbestos-containing materials (ACM), in 1973; certain pipe coverings, in 1975; certain patching compounds and artificial fireplace logs, in 1977; sprayed-on asbestos decorations, in 1978; and asbestos-containing hair-dryers, in 1979. (In 1979 manufacturers voluntarily recalled such hair-dryers.) In July 1989 EPA head William Reilly said asbestos had left a "legacy of dead, dying and crippled" and announced a gradual ban on most of the remaining uses of asbestos, which would affect about 84% of the asbestos products being made in the United States. Among the products affected were brake linings, roofing pipe and insulation. The imposed ban was to be in three stages over six years, with the first part to take effect on August 1990.

DISEASES LINKED TO ASBESTOS

Asbestoses
This is a noncancerous respiratory disease that consists of scarring of lung tissues. It primarily affects people who have worked with asbestos. The disease begins when asbestos fibers accumulate around the lungs' terminal bronchioles. The body responds by surrounding them with tissues called "fibroids" (small benign tumors). When these fibroids increase and start coming together, the symptoms may include a cough, sputum or phlegm, weight loss, increasing shortness of breath and a dry crackling sound in the lungs during inhalation. The prognosis is not good, with a survival rate of about 15 years from the onset of the disease.

Lung Cancer
Of workers heavily exposed to asbestos as many as 25% will die of lung cancer (in the general population the death rate from lung cancer is about 5%). The asbestos worker who smokes is about 90 times more likely to get lung cancer than the smoker who has never worked with asbestos. Symptoms include a cough or a persistent chest pain unrelated to coughing.

Mesothelioma
This is a cancer of the pleura (the membrane lining the chest or lung) or the abdominal cavity. It accounts for 7% to 10% of the deaths among asbestos workers. The symptoms include shortness of breath, pain in the wall of the chest, or abdominal pain. It is inoperable and always fatal. Most cases occur when workers are exposed to crocidolite asbestos fibers. Mesothelioma has been reported in people with little exposure to the fiber—spouses of asbestos workers and people living near plants. The earlier in life one starts inhaling asbestos, the higher the likelihood of developing mesothelioma in later life.

Other cancers
Asbestos workers have a higher than average rate of other cancers, particularly of the esophagus, stomach and intestines. Some medical studies have also suggested a link between asbestos and cancers of the larynx, oral cavity, colon and kidney. The theory is that inhaled asbestos fibers are absorbed into the bloodstream and carried to other parts of the body.

THE TOLL ASBESTOS IS TAKING

In 1984, Dr. Irving Selikoff said we were in the midst of widespread asbestos disease resulting from exposure over the last 60 years. He predicted that more than 200,000 Americans will die before the end of the 20th century because of earlier exposure. Dr. William Nicholson, a professor at the Mount Sinai School of Medicine in New York, has calculated that there have been more than 100,000 deaths from asbestoses-associated disease and that we may look forward to an additional 350,000 due to past exposure. The National Institute for Occupational Safety and Health has reported that people exposed to asbestos may be five times more likely to develop an asbestos-related disease than people who were not exposed to asbestos.

ASBESTOS LEVELS

There are no standards for asbestos levels in indoor air other than industrial standards. The level in your home may be 10 or even 100 times higher than outside levels. The levels in asbestos industry workplaces are 10,000 or even 100,000 times higher than the outside air. Most people exposed to small amounts of asbestos do not develop any health related problems, but the greater the exposure, the greater the risk for developing a serious illness. The people at greatest risk are smokers; children (for two reasons: they inhale more frequently than adults and they have a greater remaining life span, increasing their lifetime risk of developing mesothelioma); and young adults. However, *there is no level of exposure to asbestos that experts consider completely safe.*

EXTENT OF PROBLEM

In EPA's February 1988 report, "EPA Study of Asbestos-Containing Materials in Public Buildings," it was estimated that asbestos-containing materials are in approximately 31,000 schools and 733,000 of the 3.6 million public and commercial buildings in the United States. The EPA said that half a million of those buildings contained potentially dangerous, loose asbestos in deteriorating condition.

About one-quarter of the homes built or remodeled in the United States between 1920 and the mid-70s have asbestos-containing material. One of those houses belonged to Janice and Phillip Murray. (I have changed their names, but their story is true.)

When the Murrays bought their several-hundred-year-old house in Princeton, New Jersey, the last thing they thought about was asbestos. "We'd had an inspection, of course," Janice Murray says. "There was no mention of asbestos." Sometime after they moved in, they were having work done on their floors. The man doing the work told Janice that there was a "bad problem" with asbestos in the basement. With two small children in the house her concern was major. They looked into suing the person who did the inspection but learned he had no insurance. They were advised that even if they won what could be a costly lawsuit, they'd probably never collect.

Janice started asking around and several people in the area recommended the same lab for testing. She was told the flaking asbestos wrapped around the pipes in the basement for insulation posed a real health threat and had to be removed. Several thousand dollars—and many follow-up tests of the air for asbestos—later, the levels were still not low enough. Finally, a sealant was put on the basement floor to keep the fibers from becoming airborne. Janice thought the nightmare was ending. It wasn't. Asbestos had been put in the walls, and any time they tried to do any renovation, they'd have more problems. And there was the constant worry whenever the plumber had to do any repair work in the basement. A few years later they moved to a new home. She says now, "I'd never a buy a house that had any asbestos in it. It's an incredible problem."

WHEN IT'S A HAZARD AND WHEN IT'S NOT

Because asbestos is usually bonded with other substances in home products, most asbestos-containing materials are not harmful, *if intact*. In that condition, they are best left untouched—not disturbed by sanding, scraping or removal. If the asbestos-containing material is not damaged in any way, it poses no threat.

There have been no conclusive studies, to date, determining any health hazards from ingesting food or water containing asbestos and there is no evidence that the fibers can penetrate the skin.

Asbestos becomes dangerous only when it breaks down and fibers are released into the air. The fibers are so small they can pass through the filter of normal vacuum cleaners and get back into the air. You cannot smell them, see them or feel them. But when you breathe you can definitely inhale them! There are no immediate side effects. There will be nothing to indicate you have inhaled the fibers, but once inhaled, the tiny fibers become lodged in tissue for a long time. There is no way they can be removed. After many years diseases like cancer, asbestoses or mesothelioma can develop. The way asbestos is used in the house—how it is applied or installed—is a major factor in whether, and how quickly, it will become a health threat.

Asbestos can be sprayed on or troweled on (applied with a flat- bladed tool). It can be wrapped around hot or cold pipes, ducts, boilers and tanks for insulation. It can also be used as part of a variety of products like ceiling and floor tiles and wall boards. Asbestos is of most concern when it is "applied" to something—rather than being part of a product—because it is likely to be friable (friable material can be crumbled, pulverized or reduced to powder by hand pressure). There is a much greater probability of friable materials releasing fibers when disturbed or damaged. However, this does not mean that non-friable ACM can be ignored. Fibers in non- friable ACM will be released if the material is cut, drilled, sanded or broken during building repairs, renovations or just regular use.

FINDING THE ASBESTOS IN YOUR HOME

If your home was built after the early 1970s there's a pretty good chance that it doesn't contain asbestos. If it was built, or renovated, between 1900 and 1970 it may contain asbestos. Some of the chief indicators are: steam heat—if you have or ever had it; white cotton-like material on any walls or ceilings; false walls with a covering that looks like that white cotton-like material; or a label identifying asbestos as in insulator on your furnace.

If you think you have asbestos in your home, look very carefully throughout the house. There are some spots that can be fairly obvious, like the insulation around pipes in the basement. Other places are much less obvious. Friable materials may be hidden behind dropped ceilings or partitions.

Following is a list of some places where asbestos might be found:

Tile Floors
Asbestos is in some vinyl floor tiles to make them stronger. It can also be in the backing on some vinyl sheet flooring. Asbestos fibers are released when a tile gets damaged, dry-scraped, sanded or just worn out.

Ceilings/Wall Surface
Some homes may have a friable, asbestos-containing material on the ceilings and/or walls. It is either sprayed or troweled on. You may not

Friable, sprayed-on or troweled material. EPA.

be able to tell if the substance contains asbestos. If you don't know the contractor who installed it, or you can't reach him or her, you may have to get help from someone who has worked a lot with asbestos. When it is worn or damaged it can release fibers.

Wood-burning Stoves

Cement sheets, millboard and paper containing asbestos have frequently been used as thermal insulation to protect the floor and walls around the stove. (On cement sheets the label may say whether it contains asbestos.) There's less chance of a problem with cement sheets because they are likely to be coated with a high-temperature paint that will help seal any asbestos into the material. On the other hand, there's a greater chance of fiber release from millboard and paper, especially if they are in a spot where they are subjected to wear.

Furnaces

In older homes it's not uncommon to find oil, coal or wood furnaces with insulation and cement containing asbestos. Check for damage, pieces falling off or wear.

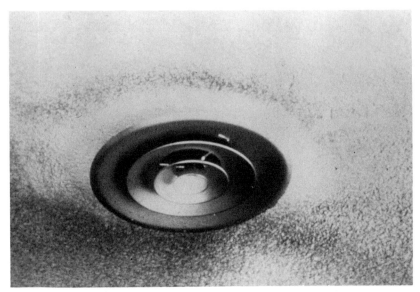

Air stream erosion from a heating vent, which could also be a sign of disturbed asbestos. EPA.

Pipes: Hot Water/Steam
These pipes may be covered with an asbestos-containing material primarily to reduce heat loss and protect nearby surfaces. The pipes may also be wrapped in an asbestos blanket or asbestos tape. Asbestos-containing insulation has also been used on furnace ducts. Most asbestos pipe insulation in homes is made to fit around the diameter of the particular pipe. This type of insulation was manufactured between 1920 and 1972.

Patching Compounds and Textured Paints
Asbestos-containing patching compounds were banned by the Consumer Product Safety Commission in 1979. But in homes built before 1979, some wall and ceiling joints may be patched with ACM. It is only a problem if it is in poor condition, if it is sanded or scraped or if the wall or ceiling needs to be repaired or removed. Some textured paint sold before 1978 contained asbestos. It can become a problem if the paint is sanded or cut.

Wall/Ceiling Insulation
Homes built between 1930 and 1950 may contain insulation made with asbestos. It is usually found inside the walls or ceilings. Generally, this

is pretty difficult to spot. You may see it when you're doing renovations or home improvements.

Door Gaskets

Some door gaskets in furnaces, ovens, wood stoves and coal-burning stoves may contain asbestos. They are subject to wear and can release asbestos fibers under normal use conditions.

Appliances

There are some appliances that have been made with components containing asbestos, among them: toasters, popcorn poppers, broilers, slow cookers, dishwashers, refrigerators, ovens, ranges, clothes dryers and electric blankets. During recent years there has been a general decline in the use of asbestos in these products. The Consumer Product Safety Commission says that when asbestos is used, it is in parts that will probably not result in the release of asbestos fibers. It is unlikely that these appliances present a significant health risk. One exception is hair-dryers. In 1979 manufacturers voluntarily recalled hair-dryers with asbestos- containing heat shields after tests showed that asbestos fibers were released during use. The hair-dryers being sold now do not have asbestos-containing heat shields.

Water damage, which could be a sign of disturbed asbestos. EPA.

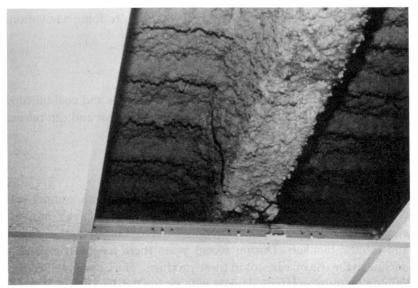

Asbestos-containing material located above a suspended ceiling. EPA.

Roofing, Shingles and Siding

Last, and in this case least, we have asbestos-containing materials not in the house but on the outside of the house. Some roofing shingles, siding shingles and sheets have been made with asbestos using portland cement as a binding agent. Fibers may be released because of wear or damage to the roof or siding. This poses a minimal risk to health because the fibers would be released into the *outside air*.

You may not be able to tell if what you're looking at contains asbestos. For example, the vinyl tile floor in the kitchen was in the house when you bought it. You don't know who the manufacturer was, where it was purchased or who installed it. You've lost touch with the people from whom you bought the house, so you can't ask them. You may want to call someone in for assistance. Frequently, people involved in the construction trades—architects, plumbers, building contractors or heating contractors—who have worked a lot with asbestos materials are able to make a reasonable judgment as to whether something contains asbestos just by looking at it.

TAKING A SAMPLE

Sometimes the only way to be sure that what looks like asbestos is asbestos is to have it analyzed at a lab. A sample should be taken of any material you think might be asbestos. Each sample could cost between $20 and $40 to analyze. If you take more than one sample be sure to label them—where and when they were taken. Your regional asbestos coordinator should be able to supply you with a list of asbestos testing labs.

If you are taking a sample, do not have anyone in the room with you. First, lightly wet the material using a sprayer. That will reduce the release of asbestos fibers. Take a small sample, disturbing the material as little as possible. Penetrate the dampened material with a small container (a 35mm film canister or small glass or plastic vial) to get the sample, then close the container tightly. Use a damp paper towel to wipe around the container and the area around the sample site where fibers may have landed.

If you do find asbestos in your home, it is not necessarily a problem. As noted earlier, because asbestos is rarely used alone, it is generally safe when combined with other materials that have strong bonding agents. It is more likely to be a problem if the asbestos is friable than if it is non-friable. Asbestos that is sprayed or troweled on walls, ceilings and other surfaces can be friable or non-friable. Friable asbestos is very fibrous and fluffy (sometimes like cotton candy). If the material is granular and cement-like in appearance it is usually friable as well. Insulation on pipes, boilers, tanks, ducts and other equipment is frequently friable.

CHECKING THE CONDITION OF THE ASBESTOS

Once you've located ACM, you want to determine if there is a problem or if there is potential for a problem. That requires looking carefully at the condition of the asbestos. The first and most important rule is: DO NOT TOUCH ANYTHING TO SEE IF IT'S FLAKING OR COMING APART. You may dislodge some asbestos. You probably won't see the very small, loose fibers, but not seeing them does not prevent you from inhaling them and that is what is so dangerous. There are no known safe levels of exposure, so you want to be very careful not to dislodge any fibers.

If you suspect that you do have an asbestos problem, that fibers are being released, keep any children out of the area, since they are the most susceptible.

Look for asbestos flaking off the insulation on the pipes in the basement. That is a sure sign of a problem. If there is debris on horizontal surfaces, hanging material, dislodged chunks, scrapings, indentations or cracks there is a good possibility that the ACM is in poor condition.

Look at how the asbestos was installed. If it was done poorly, it will be more prone to deterioration or damage.

Check for water damage to the ACM. That is usually caused by roof leaks, plumbing leaks, or a leak in a skylight. Water can dislodge, disturb, or separate into layers, friable ACM that was otherwise in good condition. It can dissolve or wash out the binder in the ACM, thereby increasing the possibility of fibers being released. Materials that haven't been considered friable may become friable when the binder is gone. Water can also carry fibers to other parts of the house. When the water evaporates you're left with fibers floating in the air.

Check for any signs of water damage. You might find discoloration or stains on the ACM or on adjacent walls, floors or the ceiling. The water damage may extend beyond the water stain. Buckling in the floors or walls is also a warning sign. There is always the possibility that water damage has occurred since the original inspection and has caused more areas to become friable. Any of those conditions is an indication that fibers have been released, are being released or are likely to be released. Even in well bonded materials like floor tiles and painted surfaces, asbestos can become loose and airborne, especially when the materials are cut, scraped, filed, sanded or removed.

Someone who has had a lot of experience with asbestos can give you an opinion or assessment of the problem or potential problem. It would be wise to ask the person you're calling in, how often he or she checks for asbestos, and what kind of training, if any, he or she has had.

OTHER CONSIDERATIONS

If all the asbestos you've found is intact and presents no problem, there are several considerations that could eventually cause it to become damaged and release fibers. Following are three factors to be aware of:

Exposure

If you can see the ACM, it is considered to be exposed. If it is exposed, chances are it's in areas of the home used frequently or where there is periodic maintenance. Under those conditions, it is more likely to get damaged. For example, if it's in the walls or floor and you have several children, their constant activity could wear down or cause cracks in the ACM. It is also considered exposed if the ACM is located behind a suspended ceiling made of movable tiles, which has a plenum (a space filled with air that is at a pressure *greater* than the atmospheric pressure) above it; or if the suspended ceiling has many openings. A careful inspection of the condition of the ceiling will determine whether the ACM is exposed.

Accessibility

This means that friable ACM is in a place where it can be reached by maintenance or repair people or where objects can damage it. The closer the ACM is to heating, ventilation, lighting and plumbing systems the more accessible it is. The greater the accessibility, the greater the possibility of damage, especially during maintenance or repair of those systems.

Location

If the ACM is located in a place where it will be subject to vibrations, there is a greater possibility of damage to it. For example, if it is in a place where there are vibrations from mechanical equipment (the refrigerator, a fan, the basement workshop) there is a greater likelihood of the ACM being damaged. Besides driving you crazy, your teenager's stereo may be setting airwaves in motion at a frequency that damages ACM. As the soundwaves impact on ACM, they can vibrate the material, contributing to the release of asbestos fibers. ACM in an air plenum or near a forced airstream (air from a heating vent) is likely to suffer surface erosion and release fibers. Fibers released into an airstream may be transported to other parts of the home, resulting in greater exposure to the occupants.

MONITORING THE AIR FOR ASBESTOS

The definitive way to assess an asbestos problem that is present is to monitor the air for the level of fibers. To get an air sample, fibers are collected by drawing air through a filter at a measured rate. The sampling equipment is usually placed at a specific location for a fixed period of time. However, if the sampling is done for a short period of time and there is little air movement, many fibers will settle on the floor and other surfaces and may not be captured on the filter. One way to deal with this is "aggressive sampling." Air is blown around to dislodge fibers, then a slow-speed fan keeps the fibers airborne during the sampling. Anyone doing sampling should wear a respirator for protection.

It is important to remember that air monitoring measures only current conditions and gives no information about the potential release of fibers or air levels in the future. Another drawback is that there are few measuring devices that are sufficiently sophisticated to distinguish between asbestos fibers in the air and other fibers that are present. And not many devices can pick up the very, very small fibers that may be present and hazardous.

The National Institute for Occupational Safety and Health (NIOSH) developed a way to measure airborne asbestos in buildings. The method it uses, called phase contrast microscopy (PCM), may be effective in industrial settings where most airborne fibers are asbestos. But it's much less sensitive to very small fibers, with diameters under 0.2 micrometers and lengths shorter than 5 micrometers (a micrometer is one-millionth of a meter). In homes, the fibers are likely to be even thinner and shorter than that, so you stand a good chance of not getting an accurate reading. To get a better idea of how small those fibers can be, think of a human strand of hair. An average strand of hair is approximately 1,200 times thicker than an asbestos fiber.

There are some methods that measure smaller fibers and can distinguish between asbestos and non-asbestos. Scanning electron microscopy (SEM) is somewhat more specific for asbestos and more sensitive to thin fibers than PCM. Fibers are counted by electron microscopy. The major drawback of SEM is that there is no standard measurement protocol presently available for it.

In 1988, the analytical transmission electron microscope (TEM) was the most sensitive and asbestos-specific instrument. However, it is expensive, costing from $200 to $600 per sample. Frequently, more than one sample is needed. There are few labs qualified to perform it. And, again, it gives no information on future conditions.

With the growing public concern over asbestos it is likely that more sensitive, more accessible and less costly measurement tools will be devised.

EVALUATING THE PROBLEM/DECIDING WHAT TO DO

Now is the time to evaluate the information you have accumulated. If the ACM is in good condition, with no water damage, physical damage or deterioration, the most appropriate thing to do is nothing, other than regular, periodic inspections of the condition of the asbestos. However, if there is a problem, a plan for abatement is needed. What you do about the asbestos, and how quickly, depends on a number of factors: where the asbestos is, what kind it is and how badly damaged it is.

Some conditions are so serious, immediate abatement is needed, while in some cases, even if there is a potential for a problem in the future, you do not have to take immediate action. You may just look into the alternatives you have and be prepared. One thing you'll certainly want to do is to watch for any changes so that you don't suddenly find yourself in the middle of a crisis.

There might be asbestos in one room that needs immediate attention while there are no problems with the asbestos in another part of the house. Any work with asbestos should be done by a professional.

IT'S OK...FOR NOW

If the asbestos problem does not require immediate action, some other factors may come into play when making decisions about abatement.

If you've been thinking about doing some renovation work in the basement, or upgrading the electrical system, or repairing vents or ducts, this may be the perfect time to do your asbestos abatement, killing two birds with one stone. It does call for careful planning and will increase the amount of the bill, but it may be more cost-effective in the long run.

While the abatement is being done, you will want to stay as far from the site as possible, especially if children are at home. It might be a good time for that weeklong vacation or visit to the relatives the family was planning.

YOU'RE READY TO BEGIN—FINDING A CONTRACTOR

What you are ready to do is find the most knowledgeable, competent and affordable contractor to do the job. That could be the most important thing you do. (The EPA strongly recommends that you always use a professional. If you want do it on your own, first make sure that your state does not require asbestos abatement work to be done by a licensed professional!)

Because of all the publicity and concern over asbestos there are some (perhaps many) fly-by-nighters. What you don't want is some opportunist running off with your money and, even worse, leaving behind an asbestos problem that is worse than what you originally had. When asbestos abatement is done, it is crucial that certain safety measures be observed and that the work be done thoroughly. A small hole left in the ceiling, a small part of the pipe insulation not sealed, and you have those fibers floating around in the air you breathe. *The abatement process itself, if not done correctly, can increase the level of fibers.*

The best way to start your search for a contractor to do the job, is to call your Regional Asbestos Coordinator or state asbestos office. (See listing at the end of this chapter.) Find out if there is a list of approved or certified contractors. (The EPA is currently encouraging all states to establish certification programs. At the time of publication, over a dozen states had certification programs.) Find out from the regional coordinator or state office who else you might speak to and what kind of regulations your state has.

It's a good idea to speak with more than one contractor if you can. When you do, you should get answers, with which you can be comfortable, to the following:

- evidence of the contractor's experience and/or training in asbestos abatement;
- references from other home owners, or building owners, where the contractor has done work (check them out!);
- a detailed, written description of how the abatement will be done;
- information on the contractor's worker protection and site containment plans;
- a written estimate (since prices among contractors can vary, sometimes substantially, it's a good idea to get several estimates);
- specifics as to what constitutes successful job completion;
- follow-up plans for thorough cleaning of the abatement area (absolutely essential) and air monitoring.

FINAL PRE-ABATEMENT INSPECTION

A thorough, final inspection of the ACM, as well as the underlying surface, is needed before the work is started. For example, the height of the ceiling may mean that enclosing the ACM will not be practical. The type of wall (smooth or rough concrete, block or brick, plasterboard) may indicate that an encapsulant will be needed if material is removed. The thickness of the ACM must be considered, since encapsulants should not be applied to thick material.

WORKER PROTECTION

It is mandatory that safety precautions be observed. Anyone working with asbestos must wear a respirator. Protective gloves, hats and other protective clothing should also be worn. Whenever there is a possibility of exposure to fibers, a respirator should be used.

CONTAINMENT DURING ABATEMENT

The area where the asbestos is to be removed must be properly contained. Typical containment includes putting up barriers of polyethylene plastic sheets joined with folded seams, using sealing tape at the seams and boundaries. (If the ACM is likely to be disturbed while the containment is being put up, a respirator should be worn.) All return air vents should be sealed to prevent asbestos contamination of other parts of the home. During abatement, any tear in the containment should be repaired immediately to prevent fibers from getting into the house.

ABATEMENT METHODS

There are three ways of dealing with your asbestos problems: removal, enclosure and encapsulation. Which you choose, will, again, depend mainly on the severity of the problem. The type of asbestos and its location are also factors and you may use a combination of methods.

Following is a brief description of each abatement method:

Removal

The more serious the problem, the greater the need for removal. (You may have to remove only the asbestos-containing material that is causing the problem at the time, in which case you'd have to periodically check the remaining asbestos.) Although it is the most expensive way to go, removing the asbestos does have several advantages. It can be done in just about any situation. It is a *permanent* solution. You don't have to do any maintenance or make periodic checks for any change in the ACM material. However, you may have to replace the asbestos that's been removed with a new material.

If the ACM is not removed properly, you could end up with an increased level of fibers. This is not something you want to do yourself! A properly trained (and if possible certified or licensed) professional is needed. (More on that later.) There times when special removal techniques may be required, for example if there are complex surfaces, or utilities are present. Once removed, disposal of the asbestos may be a problem, depending on where you live and what facilities are available for waste disposal. (For information on where you can dispose of asbestos, check with the EPA Solid and Hazardous Waste Agency in your state; you'll find a list at the end of Chapter 8.)

An asbestos enclosure project.

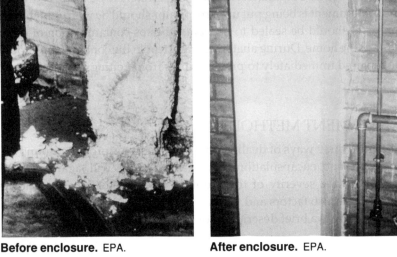

Before enclosure. EPA.   **After enclosure.** EPA.

Enclosure
Enclosure involves putting up airtight walls and ceilings around the asbestos-containing material to prevent asbestos fibers from getting into the air outside the enclosure. This method can only be used if the underlying structure can support new walls and ceilings. Enclosure is more of a stopgap measure. Generally, it is cheaper than removal; however, it could become quite costly if utilities have to be moved or major changes are required. Because you are enclosing the ACM, replacement is usually not needed. There is a downside. The source of the asbestos remains and, in all probability, will eventually have to be removed. Asbestos will continue to be released behind the enclosure. If the enclosure is damaged, in any way, it requires immediate repair. That means you have to regularly check the enclosure, closely, for any problems. During construction of the enclosure fibers can be released. In the long run this solution, because it is not permanent, could end up costing more than removal.

Encapsulation

Instead of trapping the fibers behind the air-tight barrier to keep them from getting into the air your family breathes, this method prevents the fibers from being released from the ACM by applying a sealant. Sealants should be used only on granular, cement-like material (commonly known as acoustical plaster). It should not be used on ACM that is deteriorated or extensively damaged. The sealant should bind together the asbestos fibers and other components of the material. It should also offer as much resistance to damage from impact as possible. This is less costly, initially, and does not require any replacement. It does require regular inspections, though, to make sure the sealant is intact. If it isn't, immediate repair work is required. As with enclosure, this is a stopgap measure. Eventually the ACM will have to be removed, and in the long run encapsulation may be more costly than removal.

HOW IT'S DONE

The contractor's been hired, the containment is up and the abatement is about to begin. This is, very briefly, what your contractor will be doing.

An asbestos removal project. EPA.

Protective clothing for asbestos abatement work. EPA.

Removal
First the ACM must be treated with a solution of water and wetting agent to reduce fiber release. When the ACM is removed, the asbestos waste as well as the containment plastic and sealing tape must be put in a sealed container for disposal. When that's done, a check should be made to see if a sealant is needed on the exposed surface. Sealants are necessary when the underlying surfaces are porous, like in concrete blocks or slabs, since some fibers remain after removal.

Enclosure
New construction material should be impact resistant and assembled to be as airtight as possible. Some of the materials answering that description are gypsum panels taped at the seams, tongue-and-groove boards (boards cut so that they fit into each other like Lincoln logs), and boards with spline joints (boards with grooved edges, so they can be joined by a narrow strip of wood or other material). Not acceptable are suspended ceilings with lay-in-panels (ceilings where panels are inserted into a frame that is suspended from the ceiling). Joints between wall and ceilings should be caulked. If lights are recessed in the ACM they must be taken out very carefully to prevent fiber release. *Lights should be installed beneath the new ceiling* and not recessed, to keep the ceiling as airtight as possible. Plumbing lines and computer cables may have to be relocated. If any drilling is going to be done the drill should be equipped with a HEPA (high efficiency particulate air) filtered vacuum to reduce the release of any fibers. It is a special kind of filter that can trap the asbestos fibers. It is very important to have a HEPA-vacuum when cleaning up after asbestos work, as a regular vacuum cannot pick up the smallest fibers. (HEPA-vacuums are used commercially and cost about $700 or $800, which is another reason why trained professionals do this potentially harmful work.) You should keep a record of the work done, for yourself as well as for the new owner, if you sell your home.

Encapsulation with Sealants
This is the one method that it may be feasible for you to do yourself. The sealant should be able to form a tough skin over the ACM, withstand moderate impact, be flexible and flame-retardant, resist deterioration over time and be *non-toxic*. (The EPA has evaluated many sealants. For more information on the findings you can call the EPA's Office of Toxic Substances, TSCA Assistance Office, at (202)554-1404.) Latex paint has

been used as a sealant for granular, cement-like materials. At the paint store, explain that the paint is being used as a sealant. To encapsulate or cover ACM, apply paint much more thickly than recommended for painting. You should have a continuous, unbroken covering. Apply sealants with airless spray equipment or a roller. It's a good idea to first apply a light (mist) coat, and then apply a full coat at a 90 degree angle to the direction of the first. (It's also a good idea to use a respirator when applying a sealant. The paint store should have the appropriate respirator.) As with enclosure, keep a record of what has been done—the sealant used and the type of ACM—to avoid unintentional release of fibers during any later remodeling.

CLEANUP/FOLLOW-UP

When the abatement is finished you will need at least two cleanups. This should include wet-mopping (when the fibers are wet they're less likely

Using a HEPA vacuum to clean up. EPA

to become airborne) or HEPA-vacuuming of all horizontal and vertical surfaces in the work area. NEVER DRY MOP OR SWEEP. You could send asbestos fibers flying. It's a good idea for surfaces outside the work areas to be cleaned as well. There should be a second cleaning of the work area the next day. By then, suspended fibers should have settled and a second cleaning will provide greater fiber reduction. Any debris should be put in 6-millimeter-thick plastic trash bags. The clothing worn should be disposed of in the same trash bags. Clothing that isn't thrown away should be washed well and separately from other clothing.

The EPA recommends testing the air after abatement has been done to make sure there are no fibers still airborne. You should take several samples. (See "monitoring the air," earlier in this section.)

If you used the enclosure or encapsulation method, the location of the remaining ACM and its condition will determine how often you have to check for deterioration or damage of the ACM, the sealant or the enclosure.

EPA REGIONAL OFFICES FOR ASBESTOS
(For information on asbestos identification, health effects, abatement options, analytic techniques and certification.)

ALABAMA—4	KENTUCKY—4	OHIO—5
ALASKA—10	LOUISIANA—6	OKLAHOMA—6
ARIZONA—9	MAINE—1	OREGON—10
ARKANSAS—6	MARYLAND—3	PENNSYLVANIA—3
CALIFORNIA—9	MASSACHUSETTS—1	PUERTO RICO—2
COLORADO—8	MICHIGAN—5	RHODE ISLAND—1
CONNECTICUT—1	MINNESOTA—5	SOUTH
DELAWARE—3	MISSISSIPPI—4	CAROLINA—4
DISTRICT OF	MISSOURI—7	SOUTH DAKOTA—8
COLUMBIA—3	MONTANA—8	TENNESSEE—4
FLORIDA—4	NEBRASKA—7	TEXAS—6
GEORGIA—4	NEVADA—9	UTAH—8
GUAM—9	NEW HAMPSHIRE—1	VERMONT—1
HAWAII—9	NEW JERSEY—2	VIRGINIA—3
IDAHO—10	NEW MEXICO—6	VIRGIN ISLANDS—2
ILLINOIS—5	NEW YORK—2	WASHINGTON—10
INDIANA—5	NORTH	WEST VIRGINIA—3
IOWA—7	CAROLINA—4	WISCONSIN—5
KANSAS—7	NORTH DAKOTA—8	WYOMING—8

REGION 1
Room 2203
JFK Federal Building
Boston, Massachusetts 02203
(617)223-0585

REGION 2
Woodbridge Avenue
Edison Avenue
Edison, New Jersey 08837
(201)321-6668

REGION 3
841 Chestnut Street
Philadelphia, Pennsylvania 19107
(215)597-9859

REGION 4
345 Courtland Street, N.E.
Atlanta, Georgia 30365
(404)881- 3864

REGION 5
230 South Dearborn Street
Chicago, Illinois 60604
(312)886-6006

REGION 6
Interfirst Two Building
Dallas, Texas 75270
(214)767-2734

REGION 7
726 Minnesota Avenue
Kansas City, Kansas 66101
(913)236-2835

REGION 8
1860 Lincoln Street
Denver, Colorado 80202
(303)293-1742

REGION 9
215 Fremont Street
San Francisco, California 94105
(415)974-8588

REGION 10
1200 Sixth Avenue
Seattle, Washington 98101
(206)442-2870

STATE AGENCIES FOR ASBESTOS

ALABAMA
Department of Public Health
Division of Environmental
  Health/Indoor
  Air Quality Section
434 Monroe Street, Room 254
Montgomery, Alabama 36130-1701
(205)261-5007

ALASKA
Department of Health & Social
  Services
Division of Public Health
Section of Epidemiology
P.O. Box 240249

Anchorage, Alaska 99524-0249
(907)561-4406

Department of Labor
Occupational Safety & Health
Mechanical Inspection Division
Pouch 107022
Anchorage, Alaska 99510-7022
(907)465-4856

ARIZONA
Department of Health Services
Office of Risk Assessment &
  Investigation
3008 North Third Street

Phoenix, Arizona 85012
(602)230-5858

Department of Environmental
    Quality
Office of Air Quality
2005 North Central Avenue
Phoenix, Arizona 85004
(602)257-2300

ARKANSAS
Department of Health
Bureau of Environmental Health
    Services
4815 West Markham Street
Little Rock, Arkansas 72205
(501)661-2574

Department of Pollution Control &
    Ecology
Air Division
8001 National Drive
P.O. Box 9583
Little Rock, Arkansas 72209
(501)562-7444

CALIFORNIA
Department of Health Services
Indoor Air Quality Program
Air & Industrial Hygiene
Laboratory
2151 Berkeley Way
Berkeley, California 94704
(415)540-2469

Department of Industrial Relations
Division of Occupational Safety &
    Health
525 Golden Gate Avenue
San Francisco, California 94102
(415)557-2037

State Legislature
Assembly Office of Research
1100 J Street, Room 535
Sacramento, California 95814
(916)445-1638

COLORADO
Department of Health
Air Pollution Control Division
4210 East 11th Avenue
Denver, Colorado 80220
(303)331-8587

Disease Control & Environmental
    Epidemiology Division
(same address as above)
(303)331-8330

CONNECTICUT
Department of Health Services
Division of Preventable Diseases
150 Washington Street
Hartford, Connecticut 06106
(203)566-3186

DELAWARE
Department of Health & Social
    Services
Division of Public Health
Bureau of Environmental Health
802 Silver Lake Boulevard
Robbins Building
Dover, Delaware 19901
(302)736-4731

Department of Administrative
    Services
Division of Facilities Management
Occupational Safety and Health
P.O. Box 1401
Dover, Delaware 19903
(302)736-5261

DISTRICT OF COLUMBIA
Dept. of Consumer Affairs and
    Regulatory Affairs
Environmental Control Division
Air Branch
5010 Overlook Avenue, S.W.
Washington, D.C. 20032
(202)767-7370

Department of Employment
    Services
Occupational Safety & Health

950 Upshur Street, N.W.
Washington, D.C. 20011
(202)576-6339

FLORIDA
Department of Health &
  Rehabilitative Services
Occupational Health Program
Laboratory Services
1217 Pearl Street
Jacksonville, Florida 32202
(904)359-6125

Department of Environmental
  Regulation
Bureau of Air Quality Management
2600 Blair Stone Road
Tallahassee, Florida 32399
(904)488-1344

GEORGIA
Department of Human Resources
Division of Public Health
47 Trinity Avenue, S.W.
Atlanta, Georgia 30334
(404)894-6644

GUAM
Guam Environmental Protection
  Agency Services
Government of Guam
P.O. Box 2999
Agana, Guam 96910
(671)646-8865

Department of Public Health and
  Social Services
Division of Environmental Health
P.O. Box 2816
Agana, Guam 96910
(671)734-2671

HAWAII
Department of Health
Environmental Protection/Health
  Services Branch
Pollution Investigation &
  Enforcement Branch

1250 Punchbowl Street
Honolulu, Hawaii 96813
(808)548-8484 or 548-6455

IDAHO
Department of Health and Welfare
Division of Environmental Quality
Air Quality Bureau
450 State Street
Boise, Idaho 83720
(208)334-5898

Department of Labor & Industrial
  Services
Building Division
277 North Sixth Street
Statehouse Mall
Boise, Idaho 83720
(208)334-3896

ILLINOIS
Department of Public Health
Division of Environmental Health
Environmental Toxicology
525 West Jefferson Street
Springfield, Illinois 62761
(217)782-5830

INDIANA
State Board of Health
Division of Industrial Hygiene
1330 West Michigan Street
P.O. Box 1964
Indianapolis, Indiana 46206
(317)633-0692

Department of Environmental
  Management
Office of Air Management
105 South Meridian Street
Indianapolis, Indiana 46225
(317)633-8232

IOWA
State Department of Public Health
Bureau of Compliance/Health Care
  Services
Lucas State Office Building

Des Moines, Iowa 50319
(515)281-5719

Division of Labor Services
1000 East Grand Avenue
Des Moines, Iowa 50319
(515)281-3606

KANSAS
Department of Health and
  Environment
Bureau of Air Quality and
  Radiation Control
Environmental Toxicology Section
Forbes Field
Topeka, Kansas 66620
(913)296-1543 or 296-1544

KENTUCKY
Natural Resources/Environmental
  Protection Cabinet
Department of Environmental
  Protection
Division of Air Quality
18 Reilly Road
Frankfort, Kentucky 40601
(502)564-3382

Department of Education
Division of Buildings and Grounds
1532 Capitol Plaza Tower
Frankfort, Kentucky 40601
(502)564-4326

LOUISIANA
Department of Health and
  Hospitals
Office of Preventive & Public Health
  Services
Environmental Epidemiology
P.O. Box 60630
New Orleans, Louisiana 70160
(504)568-5053

Department of Environmental
  Quality
Air Quality Division
P.O. Box 44096

Baton Rouge, Louisiana 70804
(504)342-1201

MAINE
Department of Administration
Bureau of Public Improvements
Division of Asbestos Management
Statehouse Station 77
Augusta, Maine 04333
(207)289-4509

Division of Health Engineering
Occupational & Residential Health
  Program
Consumer Product Safety
Statehouse Station 10
Augusta, Maine 04333
(207)289-5679

MARYLAND
Department of the Environment
Toxics, Environmental Science &
  Health
Center for Environmental Health
201 W. Preston Street
Baltimore, Maryland 21201
(301)225-5753 or 225-5755

Air Management Administration
(same address as above)
(301)225-5252

MASSACHUSETTS
Dept. of Environmental Quality
  Engineering
Division of Air Quality Control
One Winter Street
Boston, Massachusetts 02108
(617)292-5593

Department of Public Health
Division of Community Sanitation
Environmental Hygiene
150 Tremont Street
Boston, Massachusetts 02111
(617)727-2660

MICHIGAN
Department of Labor

Building Construction Codes
P.O. Box 30015
Lansing, Michigan 48909
(517)322-1801

Department of Public Health
Bureau of Environmental &
  Occupational Health
3500 North Logan Street
P.O. Box 30035
Lansing, Michigan 48909
(517)335-9218

MINNESOTA
Department of Health
Asbestos Abatement Unit
P.O. Box 9441
Minneapolis, Minnesota 55440
(612)623-5380

Pollution Control Agency
Division of Air Quality
520 Lafayette Road North
St. Paul, Minnesota 55155
(612)296-7802

MISSISSIPPI
Department of Natural Resources
Bureau of Pollution Control
Air Quality Branch
P.O. Box 10385
Jackson, Mississippi 39209
(601)961-5171

MISSOURI
Department of Health
Division of Environmental Health &
  Epidemiology
1730 Elm Street
P.O. Box 570
Jefferson City, Missouri 65102-0570
(314)751-6102

Department of Natural Resources
Air Pollution Control Program
P.O. Box 176
Jefferson City, Missouri 65102
(314)751-4817

MONTANA
Department of Health &
  Environmental Sciences
Occupational Health Bureau
Cogswell Building, Room A-113
Helena, Montana 59620
(406)444-3671

NEBRASKA
Department of Health
Department of Environmental
  Health & Housing
  Surveillance
301 Centennial Mall South
P.O. Box 95007
Lincoln, Nebraska 68509
(402)471-2541

NEVADA
Department of Industrial Relations
Occupational Health & Safety
  Division
1390 South Curry Street
Carson City, Nevada 89710
(702)885-3032

NEW HAMPSHIRE
Department of Health and Human
  Services
Division of Public Health
Bureau of Environmental Health
Consumer Product Safety
6 Hazen Drive
Concord, New Hampshire
  03301-6527
(603)271-4664

Air Resources Division
64 North Main Street
Caller Box 2033
Concord, New Hampshire 03302
(603)271-1370

NEW JERSEY
Department of Health
Division of Occupational &
  Environmental Health
CN-360

Trenton, New Jersey 08625
(609)984-1863
or 984-2193

NEW MEXICO
General Services
Property Control Division
Joseph Montoya Building
Room 2022
1100 Saint Francis Drive
Santa Fe, New Mexico 87501
(505)827-2141

NEW YORK
Department of Health
Division of Occupational Health &
  Environmental Epidemiology
2 University Place, Room 375
Albany, New York 12203-3313
(518)458-6433
(800)458-1158 (in state)

Division of Housing & Community
  Renewal
Hampton Plaza
38-40 State Street
Albany, New York 12207
(518)473-9845

Department of Labor
Asbestos Control Program
Harriman State Office Building
Albany, New York 12240
(518)457-7054

Department of Labor
Asbestos Control Program
One Main Street
Brooklyn, New York 11201
(718)797-7674

NORTH CAROLINA
Department of Human Resources
Division of Health Services
Environmental Epidemiology
  Branch
225 North McDowell Street
Raleigh, North Carolina 27602
(919)733-3410

Department of Natural Resources &
  Community Development
Division of Environmental
  Management
Air Quality Section
512 North Salisbury Street
P.O. Box 27687
Raleigh, North Carolina 27611
(919)733-3340

Department of Labor
Division of Occupational Safety &
  Health
4 West Edenton Street
Raleigh, North Carolina 27603
(919)733-4880

Department of Human Resources
Division of Health Services
Occupational Health Branch
P.O. Box 2091
Raleigh, North Carolina 27602
(919)733-3680

NORTH DAKOTA
Department of Health &
  Consolidated Laboratories
Division of Environmental
  Engineering
1200 Missouri Avenue, Room 304
P.O. Box 5520
Bismarck, North Dakota 58502-5520
(701)224-2348

OHIO
Department of Health
Bureau of Environmental Health
246 North High Street
Columbus, Ohio 43266-0588
(614)466-1450

Ohio Environmental Protection
  Agency
Division of Air Pollution Control
P.O. Box 1049
1800 WaterMark Drive
Columbus, Ohio 43266-0149
(614)644-2270

OKLAHOMA
State Department of Health
Radiation & Special Hazards
  Service
P.O. Box 53551
1000 Northeast 10th Street
Oklahoma City, Oklahoma 73152
(405)271-5221

Department of Labor
Asbestos Division
1315 Broadway Place
Oklahoma City, Oklahoma 05350
(405)235-0530

OREGON
Department of Environmental
  Quality
811 Southwest Sixth Avenue
Portland, Oregon 97204
(503)229-5713 or 229-6414

Office of Health Status Monitoring
State Health Division
(same address as above)
(503)229-5792

Department of Insurance & Finance
Accident Prevention Division
Resource Center
Labor & Industries Building
Salem, Oregon 97310
(503)229-3872

PENNSYLVANIA
Department of Health
Division of Environmental Health
P.O. Box 90
Harrisburg, Pennsylvania 17108
(717)787-1708

Department of Environmental
  Resources
Bureau of Air Quality Control
Third & Locust Street
Fulton Bank Building
P.O. Box 2063
Harrisburg, Pennsylvania 17120
(717)787-4310

PUERTO RICO
Environmental Quality Board
204 Ramaiada Street
P.O. Box 11488
Santurce, Puerto Rico 00910
(809)725-8898 or 722-0077

RHODE ISLAND
Department of Health
Asbestos Control Program
206 Cannon Building
75 Davis Street
Providence, Rhode Island 02908
(401)277-3601

Department of Health
Division of Occupational Health
206 Cannon Building
75 Davis Street
Providence, Rhode Island 02908
(401)277-2438

SOUTH CAROLINA
Dept. of Health and Environmental
  Control
Air Compliance & Management
  Division
Bureau of Air Quality Control
2600 Bull Street
Columbia, South Carolina 29201
(803)734-4750

Department of Labor
Occupational Safety & Health
  Division
3600 Forest Drive
P.O. Box 11329
Columbia, South Carolina
29211-1329
(803)737-9644

SOUTH DAKOTA
Office of Air Quality and Solid
  Waste
Department of Water and Natural
  Resources
Joe Foss Building, Room 217
523 East Capitol Avenue

Pierre, South Dakota 57501-3181
(605)773-3153

Department of Health
Division of Public Health
(same address as above)
(605)773-3364

TENNESSEE
Department of Health &
   Environment
Bureau of Environment
Division of Air Pollution Control
Customs House
701 Broadway
Nashville, Tennessee 37219-5403
(615)741-3931

Department of Education
Facilities Division
126 Cordell Hull Building
Nashville, Tennessee 37219
(615)741-2731

TEXAS
Department of Health
Occupational & Health Division
1100 West 49th Street
Austin, Texas 78756
(512)458-7255

UTAH
Department of Health
Bureau of Air Quality
P.O. Box 16690
288 North 1460 West
Salt Lake City, Utah 84116
(801)538-6108

VERMONT
Department of Health
Division of Environmental Health
60 Main Street
P.O. Box 70
Burlington, Vermont 05402
(802)863-7220

VIRGINIA
Department of Health

Division of Health Hazards Control
James Madison Building
109 Governor Street
Richmond, Virginia 23219
(804)786-1763

Air Pollution Control Board
Ninth Street Office Building
8th Floor
202-205 North Ninth Street
Richmond, Virginia 23219
(804)786-5783

Department of General Services
Division of Engineering & Buildings
805 East Broad Street, 8th Floor
Richmond, Virginia 23219
(804)225-4446

Department of Education
Division of Energy & Facility
   Services
P.O. Box 6Q
Richmond, Virginia 23216
(804)225-2035

WASHINGTON
Department of Social & Health
   Services
Health Services Division
Environmental Health Programs
Toxic Substances Section
Mail Stop LD-11
Olympia, Washington 98504
(206)753-2556

Superintendent of Public
   Instruction
Old Capitol Building, FG-11
Olympia, Washington 98504
(206)753-6703

Department of Labor & Industries
Division of Industrial Safety &
   Health
Mail Stop HC-412
P.O. Box 207
Olympia, Washington 98504
(206)281-5325

WEST VIRGINIA
Department of Health
Office of Environmental Health
  Services
Indoor Air Quality Program
4873 Brenda Lane
Charleston, West Virginia 25312
(304)348-0696

Department of Labor
Safety & Boiler Division
1800 Washington Street East
Charleston, West Virginia 25305
(304)348-7890

WISCONSIN
Department of Health & Social
  Services
Bureau of Community Health &
  Prevention
Environmental & Chronic Disease
  Epidemiology

P.O. Box 309
Madison, Wisconsin 53701-0309
(608)266-9337 or 266-7897

Department of Natural Resources
Bureau of Air Management
P.O. Box 7921
Madison, Wisconsin 53707
(608)266-0171

Division of Health
Section of Occupational Health
1414 East Washington Avenue
Room 112
Madison, Wisconsin 53703
(608)266-7168

WYOMING
Department of Education
Hathaway Building
Cheyenne, Wyoming 82002
(307)777-6198

3

LEAD

There is no known safe level of lead in the blood. The American Academy of Pediatrics calls lead poisoning one of the most severe toxicological hazards threatening children. Dr. John Rosen, professor of pediatrics at the Albert Einstein College of Medicine in New York, says lead poisoning is the most common and most preventable childhood disease, affecting as many as 3.5 million children in the United States. Its effects are wide-ranging and so are its symptoms, which can easily go undiagnosed or even unnoticed.

Lead from many different sources can accumulate in the body. Lead poisoning can result from ingesting large amounts in a short period of time or small amounts taken in over a long period of time. *Lead has no beneficial function in the human body.* It can only do harm.

Lead is a heavy, comparatively soft, malleable, bluish-grey metal. It cannot be broken down or destroyed. As a result of industrialization, lead, in greater or lesser degree, can be found everywhere in the environment. As some of its "advantages" became known, in the 19th and 20th centuries, its use increased greatly. For example, it was found that paint containing high levels of lead was more durable. Leaded paint could continuously caulk the inside of the home and weather the outside. It also looked fresher for a greater length of time, which meant fewer repaintings.

A BRIEF HISTORY

The adverse effects of lead on people have been known for a long time, as early as the Greco-Roman era. In the 18th and 19th centuries, sterility, abortion, stillbirth, and premature delivery were observed in women who worked with lead and in the wives of lead workers. Their children died at a higher than average rate and the incidence of low birth weight, convulsions, failure to thrive and mental retardation was greater than in the general population.

The prevalence of direct lead poisoning in children was first examined, in Australia, in the 1890s. It was found that children in contact with lead-based paint on exterior railings and walls had lead poisoning.

In the United States in 1917, lead was reported as a cause of encephalopathy (inflammation of the brain) in a number of children. Starting in the 1930s, there was more and more data on lead poisoning in children.

Dr. Herbert Needleman, M.D., now professor of psychiatry at the University of Pittsburgh Medical School, was at Harvard when his study on the effects of low levels of lead in the blood was published in 1979. Testing first and second graders he found that the children with the lowest IQs, academic achievement, language skills and attention spans were the children with the highest levels of lead. However, none of the children tested had blood levels higher than the Centers for Disease Control's (CDC) toxicity threshold.

The small amount of research done so far on lead's long-term effects suggest that intellectual impairment may be irreversible. When the first graders in Dr. Needleman's study were retested five years later, the children who had shown higher lead levels still had significant IQ deficits and required more special education classes.

There is evidence that lead can be a hazard to fetuses. Unborn children who absorb small amounts of lead from their mothers (who were exposed to small amounts) may be affected. A study done by Dr. Needleman in 1987 found that children who had absorbed the most lead while in the womb performed significantly worse on developmental tests in their first two years of life than did children with low exposures.

As the increasing number of studies showed the toxic effects of lead in the human body, the federal government started taking some action. In 1970 Congress passed the Clean Air Act, which led to creation of the Environmental Protection Agency (EPA). In 1971 it passed the Lead-Based Paint Poisoning Prevention Act. In 1975, under court order the EPA evaluated atmospheric lead as a "criteria pollutant" as it was referred to in the Clean Air Act. That, in turn, led to an examination of the lead problem everywhere in the environment. At the same time the National Institutes of Health (NIH) and other public agencies started funding significant research on lead poisoning.

WHO'S AT RISK AND WHY

Young children up to six years of age are at the greatest risk from exposure to lead, followed by pregnant women, middle-aged men and adults.

Children's higher rates of respiration and metabolism result in greater lead levels. They absorb and retain more lead than adults, at a time when their young, still developing bodies are most susceptible to harm. Their bodies also handle lead differently; they are not as efficient at keeping the lead in the bones, which means that a higher percentage of the lead that's in the body is circulating in the blood stream.

Lead impairs the production of hemoglobin and vitamin D, both of which occur naturally in the body and are building blocks for normal functioning of virtually every organ in the child's body. Therefore, the higher the level of lead, the greater the potential for damage to developing body organs.

Young children are also likely to ingest lead. The younger they are, the greater the number of things that end up in their mouths—toys, dirt, paint chips from the floor, walls, windowsills or woodwork, inside. Outside, hands covered with soil frequently end up inside the mouth, as does the dirt that the inquisitive, hungry or just playful child eats intentionally.

Lead blood levels are measured in micrograms per deciliter. (A microgram [ug] is one millionth of a gram; a deciliter [di] is one tenth of a liter.) An estimated 17% of preschool children have blood levels exceeding 15 micrograms per deciliter (ug/di). At any level they are susceptible to a wide range of psychological and neurological problems, including:

- kidneys and blood abnormalities;
- partial hearing loss;
- slower neural transmission;
- hyperactivity;
- learning disabilities;
- lowered IQ scores;
- impaired ability to metabolize vitamin D, absorb iron and use calcium in any bodily processes;
- disturbances in the formation and maintenance of red blood cells;
- decreased muscle tone; and
- interference with the creation and function of certain enzymes and amino acids.

It used to be thought that only inner-city kids were in danger since they were the ones living in deteriorating housing where there was a greater likelihood of exposure to lead. Today, lead poisoning is recognized as being widespread, affecting children in all socioeconomic groups in every part of the United States.

In pregnant women exposed to lead, it's really the fetus that is at risk. The pregnant woman is more likely to have a miscarriage, premature delivery or stillbirth. The weight of the baby at birth may be lower and there may be minor congenital abnormalities.

Because lead is readily transferred across the placenta, the fetus's developing organs and organ systems, such as the central nervous system, can be irreversibly damaged. That can result in later impairment of physical and intellectual development.

Middle-aged men are at risk because lead can affect blood pressure. As blood pressure levels rise in a middle-aged man, so does his risk of hypertension and high blood pressure. According to a CDC study in 1985, lead levels as low as five micrograms per deciliter can increase blood pressure.

Lead poisoning can present another problem for adults. James Keck, deputy commissioner for the Department of Housing and Community Development in Baltimore, Maryland, says physicians often attribute

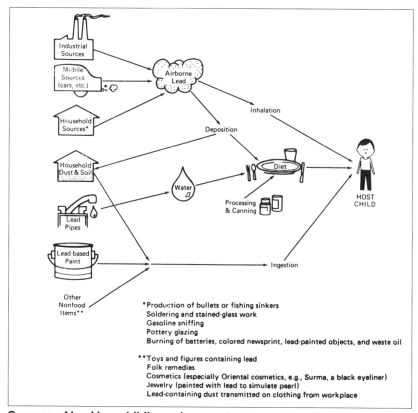

Sources of lead in a child's environment. EPA

muscle pain, joint aches and memory loss in the elderly, to the process of aging. But Keck says those symptoms could be a result of lead poisoning.

SOURCES OF LEAD

The major sources of lead in the environment and the home are paint (the leading source), gasoline, water, dust/oil, food and chemicals from industrial sites.

Leaded Paint

Paint with lead remains the major source of high exposure and lead poisoning. If you live in a house built before 1950, you should assume that the indoor painted surfaces contain lead. Even houses built after 1950 and through the late '70s may contain leaded paint.

In the late 1950s, some paint manufacturers voluntarily restricted lead content to 1%. In 1977, the Consumer Product Safety Commission (CPSC) mandated that the amount of lead allowed in paint not exceed .06% However, leaded paint already manufactured did not have to be recalled. Before the CPSC mandate, paints contained as much as 50% lead.

About 27 million households in the United States are contaminated by approximately five million tons of leaded paint. Approximately 12 million American children under the age of seven live in housing with some lead paint at potentially toxic levels. The number of children exposed to enough lead paint to raise their blood levels to above 15 ug/dl is about 1.2 million.

Leaded Gasoline

Government regulations, since the early 1970s, have required the phasing down of lead in gasoline. This has substantially reduced lead emissions into the air from vehicles, which in turn has decreased the rate at which lead from the atmosphere is deposited in the soil. The positive impact that this has had so far is expected to increase so that by 1992 the gasoline lead "phasedown" will result in lowered lead blood levels (under 15 ug/dl) in millions of children.

Water

Lead in drinking water is primarily the result of lead pipes in old homes and/or joints that are soldered with lead. Lead is a dull gray metal that is soft enough to be easily scratched by a key. It is not usually found in the water from your local treatment plant or your well. Lead leaches into the water when the pipes corrode—the metal dissolves or wears away. Corrosion is caused by soft water (that's the water that makes soap, soapy).

Up until the early 1900s lead pipe was commonly used for plumbing as well as for connections that linked homes to public water supplies. (It was still being used in some areas until the mid-80s.) After 1930, the pipes were more likely to be copper. The new pipes weren't a problem, but they are often soldered with lead, which experts consider the major cause of lead contamination of household water today.

In 1986, under the Safe Drinking Water Act, the use of lead solder and other lead-containing material was banned in plumbing connected to public water supplies. In June 1988, an amendment to the Safe Drinking Water Act mandated that all new homes use only lead-free solder on drinking water pipes.

But there is also evidence that *the newer the house, the greater the risk of lead contamination.* That's because lead levels decrease over time. Mineral deposits form a coating on the inside of the pipes, protecting the water from the solder with one exception. Soft, corrosive water will corrode that protective lining.

Soil/Dust

The lead in soil and dust is usually from cars, industrial sites, flaking paint and similar sources. In soil the lead tends to remain in the top centimeter. Most soil is contaminated to a greater depth when the topsoil is disturbed and turned under. Studies in New Jersey and California have shown that *children living within 100 feet of major roadways have higher blood lead levels* than those living further away. Those at greater risk are toddlers and very young children who may intentionally, or unintentionally ingest the soil.

Food

There are several ways lead can get into food. Fruits and vegetables that contain lead may have been sprayed with pesticide that contains lead, grown on land near heavily traveled roads or grown on land near stationary sources of lead. Lead may be inadvertently added to food during processing and solder in the seams of the cans containing food can also contaminate the contents.

The U.S. Food and Drug Administration began regulating lead contamination in food several decades ago when residues, with lead-containing pesticides, were found on sprayed fruits.

The percentage of food cans that are lead-soldered continues to decline. In 1979 the percentage was over 90%; in the late '80s, the figure was around 20%. However, imported food may still come in lead-soldered cans.

Stationary Sources

Stationary sources include industrial sites such as lead smelters, refineries and acid-lead battery plants, as well as municipal incinerators which can produce concentrated zones of exposure. Climatic conditions also play a role in concentrations of airborne lead. Aridity, low wind velocity and frequent thermal inversions minimize dispersal of airborne lead.

TESTING FOR LEAD

There are basically two different types of lead level tests: those that measure external levels in the environment and those that test for internal lead blood levels. In the environment you can test for lead concentrations in painted surfaces inside and outside the home, and in water, air and soil.

Blood Lead Levels

Since lead poisoning is caused by high levels of lead in the blood, testing for the lead blood level of those at greatest risk seems an obvious thing to do. It is.

Before you test for lead in the paint or water, you may want to test any children in your home who are seven or under. If there are no problems with their blood levels, any other testing may very well be unnecessary.

Dr. John Rosen, professor of pediatrics at the Albert Einstein College of Medicine says every child from nine months to six years of age should be screened for lead poisoning at least once a year. "Screening", he says "is critical. It should be part of all routine pediatric health exams." The American Academy of Pediatrics recommends regular testing for young children and pregnant women. The blood test at a screening clinic or doctor's office, for the initial screen, is just a finger prick. The physician can get an immediate reading and, depending on the level, determine what further testing and, eventually, treatment may be needed.

While blood screening tests for lead will now show the source of the lead, if the blood test is positive (since there is no known safe level, any level is positive) it means that somewhere in the environment lead is being released.

A high lead blood level can be the result of high exposure to one source, low-level exposure to several different sources or continual exposure to low levels over a period of time.

When a child tests positive it is imperative to find the source or sources of lead and take steps to eliminate the hazard immediately. It may be necessary to remove children and pregnant women from the premises until the problem is resolved. (Medical treatment may also be required.)

Lead in Paint
The U.S. Center for Disease Control recommends testing all painted surfaces, interior and exterior, that may contain lead. Any damaged surface should be considered a hazard requiring immediate abatement. That includes all painted wood trim, inside and out, that is blistering, scaling, peeling or powdering; walls, ceilings, floors with unsound paint; or painted, peeling wallpaper. Lead-based paint is not considered to be an immediate hazard when it is smooth and intact, undamaged, and not in an area that toddlers can reach. However, it is important to note that lead-based paints can become very hazardous if the surface becomes damaged. Therefore, all leaded paint surfaces should be monitored regularly.

There are two ways to test for the presence of lead in paint. One is the portable X-ray fluorescence test (XRF). The XRF analyzer is a probability sampling device, which means that its reliability depends on repeated readings. This must be done by a testing firm that has this equipment.

If XRF isn't available, wet, chemical methods of analysis must be used. You would bring in a chip or flake of the paint to a lab for analysis.

To find a lab, check with your local Health Department. If labs are not certified in your state and they can make no recommendation find one in the yellow pages. Ask if they employ any certified industrial hygienists. Ask for their lab number and then check the lab out with the American Board of Hygiene in Ohio (at 517-321-2638).

If there are surfaces that test positive for lead, the next step is to determine how much of a hazard each surface presents—both inside and outside the home. To pose an immediate hazard, the leaded paint with a positive XRF reading over 0.7 mg/cm^2 must be on surfaces that are reachable and chewable by young children (windowsills, woodwork) or damaged (cracked, chipped or loosened).

Lead in Water—When to Test
Since there are no known safe levels of lead, *everyone should have their drinking water tested*. It is especially important if you have lead pipes or

if your home is less than five years old. If you're not sure whether the pipes in your home are lead, call in a plumber. If it was built before 1930, they probably are.

Testing for lead is also important if you live in an apartment. In November of 1988, a study by the Plumbing Foundation of New York City found that as many as 12% of the city's buildings may have tap water with levels exceeding federal standards. Twenty-eight percent had levels exceeding more stringent EPA standards that take effect early in 1990.

Old buildings have old, frequently corroded lead plumbing. Lead builds up in water that sits in the pipes, so you could be ingesting high levels of lead every time you drink the water, use it in cooking or wash off food. Flushing the water (running the cold water for several minutes to clear out all of the water that was sitting for a long time in the pipes and becoming lead-contaminated) may not work.

It's especially hazardous to use lead-contaminated water when making baby formula. Small amounts of lead might not harm you but may do irreparable harm to an infant.

Some of the other warning signs that your water may be lead contaminated are:

- frequent leaks;
- rust-colored water;
- stained dishes;
- stained laundry;
- non-plastic plumbing less than five years old.

How to Test Your Water

The first thing you should to is contact your local water utility or local health department. Sometimes they will test your tap water for you free of charge, or for a nominal fee. (See phone numbers at the end of Chapter 4.) If they do not provide that service, they should be able to refer you to a qualified lab.

You may also find a qualified testing company under "laboratories" in the yellow pages. When you do find a lab, make sure it has been approved by your state or the EPA to test for lead contamination. (See listing at the end of this chapter.)

Whoever is doing the test (the health department, the water utility or the lab) may send someone over to get water samples, or they may supply you with containers to hold the samples, along with instructions. It's important to follow those instructions exactly. If you don't, the results may not be reliable.

The first sample should be of water taken after the tap has not been used for at least six hours. The sample must be the very first water taken from the tap, as soon as you open the spigot. Have that bottle ready! This will show the lead level at its highest.

The second sample should be taken after the water has been fully flushed. This will show how effective flushing is.

LEVELS

Blood

Before the mid 1960s, a level of below 60 micrograms of lead per deciliter of whole blood was not considered dangerous enough to warrant intervention. By 1975, the Centers for Disease Control had cut the level for intervention in half, to 30 ug/dl. In 1985 the CDC identified a blood lead level of 25 ug/dl as evidence of toxicity. In 1986, the World Health Organization identified a level of 20 ug/dl as the unacceptable level. Since 1987 the EPA has said that 15 ug/dl is the appropriate level; the CDC is expected to cut the level for intervention to 10-15 ug/dl, in the early 1990s. And even more recently, in July of 1988, the Agency for Toxic Substances and Disease Registry issued a report to Congress called "The Nature and Extent of Lead Poisoning in Children in the United States." It contained evidence that levels as low as 10 ug/dl in children and fetuses could be harmful.

In the meantime, new evidence has indicated that lead can be toxic at even lower levels—levels that previously had been thought to be safe. There is still controversy over what level, if any, may be safe.

Paint

The level of lead in paint on any surface in your home or outside should not exceed .7 milligrams per square centimeter.

Water

Under the authority of the Safe Drinking Water Act, the EPA limited the acceptable amount of lead in drinking water to 50 parts per billion (ppb). This amount is expected to be reduced to between 10 and 20 ppb in 1991. One ppb is equal to 1.0 microgram per liter [ug/1] or 0.001 milligram per liter [mg/1]. Utilities must assure that their tap water meets the EPA standard and notify residents of all violations of the standard. Although that more stringent level may not yet be in effect, you may very well want to act as if it is!

LEAD ABATEMENT METHODS FOR PAINT

How you get rid of the leaded paint in your environment will be determined by a number of different things: its location, the immediacy of the problem and the condition of the paint. As noted earlier, if the paint is intact, it may require nothing more than regular monitoring. However, anytime a child in the house tests positive for lead and if paint is the source of the lead, immediate action is required, regardless of how the surfaces look.

At one time it was thought that limiting the paint to an area unreachable by children was sufficient precaution. It is now known that dust or paint chips that fall from above are also a major hazard for children. The CDC recommends removal of all leaded paint that is unsound.

You cannot consider a leaded paint problem in an old house "permanently abated" unless the house is gutted and completely restored. But there are "long term" methods that are far less extensive and commonly used. The effectiveness and tenacity of those methods will depend on how well the procedure is done, the soundness of the underlying structure, and the condition of the plumbing. Leaky pipes behind walls can cause paint to blister and scale.

There are three long-term ways to treat the paint—removal, replacement, and encapsulation—all of which can be costly, time-consuming and hazardous.

Removal

Removal involves just that, removing the paint. If there are children in the house who have tested positive for lead you want to take immediate short-term action by removing all visible scaling paint from window sills, door frames, doors and porch railings that are accessible to children. This should be followed by a long-term abatement procedure as quickly as possible. Removal can be an extremely difficult, big, time-consuming and costly job—one that you will probably not want to do yourself.

There are several ways it can be done. You can do on-site removal—stripping the paint from the walls, floors, ceilings, doors and woodwork with paint remover, a special paste, a gas torch or heat gun, sanding or scraping. The other alternative is off-site removal—actually removing the woodwork, doors or windowsills and bringing them to a place to be stripped. This is generally more expensive and time-consuming than just replacing a door or windowsill, but it may be the only solution for saving old woodwork that is irreplaceable.

Replacement

This involves removing windows, doors, woodwork, railings, etc. and replacing them with new ones. This can be quite costly. If you are in an old house, which you bought because of architectural details like the doors and woodwork, much of which is no longer available, this may very well not be a solution you'd want to consider. However, if the wood under the paint is deteriorating, or has rotted, you may have no choice but to replace it.

Encapsulation

This involves covering or sealing the surfaces that contain leaded paint. New moldings can be put over old ones, new windowsills can cover old windowsills and so on. Plywood paneling, wallboard, hardboard, fiberglass and sheetrock can be put up to cover the walls, floors or ceilings. Encapsulation is often the most practical solution for walls, floors, or ceilings. Any encapsulation must be completely sealed to prevent any lead dust from getting out.

BEFORE STARTING THE ABATEMENT

Because a potentially very hazardous material is going to be handled, it is essential to take some precautions. Deleading can result in a substantial increase in circulating, airborne lead, especially if not properly done.

Children and pregnant women should be kept out of the room or area being worked in, and should not return until the job and cleanup are completed. (Ideally, anyone who can stay in a different location, should do so.)

Before starting any procedure, furniture, rugs and any other items that can be removed from the house and professionally cleaned, should be. Carpets, rugs, upholstered furniture, bedding, clothing, and eating and cooking utensils that remain must be protected. They should be wrapped in 6mm plastic as tightly as possible. Openings should be sealed with heavy industrial tape. This is to prevent, as much as possible, any of the additional lead-bearing dust released during the procedure from taking up (permanent) residence in rugs or elsewhere. Once minute particles of lead dust get into rugs or upholstery it is virtually impossible to remove them.

In addition, a layer of loose plastic that can be removed each day with the day's debris should be spread over the area. That debris, which is a toxic waste, must be well wrapped in heavy plastic and disposed of in an approved dumpsite. Any adjacent area not being abated should be sealed off.

A respirator should be used by anyone doing the work. If using a liquid paint remover, you should use an organic vapor high efficiency respirator. They run about $30. If you are scraping or sanding paint off use a high efficiency respirator. A disposable one costs about $10. The respirator should be approved by the National Institute for Occupational Safety and Health (NIOSH). Look for the "T.C.," which stands for testing and certified. You should be able to find respirators at stores selling safety supplies. Look in the yellow pages. If you have any questions about which respirator to use call NIOSH at (304) 291-4331. Other protective gear includes goggles, rubber or plastic gloves, and coveralls. Disposable items are best. Any article of clothing that was exposed to lead and that is not being thrown out *should be washed away from the home.*

If any kind of liquid paint remover is used, the area must be well ventilated.

REMOVAL

Scraping and Sanding

All lead-based paint that is chipping, flaking or peeling should be scraped or sanded immediately. This can be a stopgap emergency measure—or it may be all that is needed at the particular time. It is not as time-consuming, expensive or difficult as removing all the paint. The scraped or sanded surface should be patched, sealed and repainted. Be sure no children or pregnant women come into the room before *both the removal and cleanup* are finished.

Liquid Paint Removers

Most paint removers contain metholine chloride, which is a carcinogen. In some places, it is illegal for anything but small jobs. Paint-removing paste is also hazardous and must also be used very carefully. Liquid paint removers should be used only as a last resort in small areas such as windowsills, doors and woodwork. If possible the surface being treated should be taken outside. If that is not possible, and you must do the stripping inside, remember it is very important to *ventilate, ventilate, ventilate.* Have windows open and plenty of fresh air coming in. The same goes for using a paste to remove the paint. The paste must be left on the surface for 24 to 48 hours. The paste is good for woodwork or uneven surfaces.

Electric Sanders
Sanding devices are the biggest offenders in terms of generating lead dust. As with heat removal, sanders are not good for ornate surfaces.

Off-site Removal
This requires removing the woodwork, doors or fixtures from the house and bringing them to a professional stripper. Each piece must be wrapped well in plastic and should be labeled as well so that you'll know exactly where each piece belongs when it is returned. This is especially important if there are many similar pieces of woodwork, windowsills, doors and the like.

Heat Removal
A heat gun, gas-fired torch, or infrared lamp can be used to remove the paint. These are quite dangerous and increase greatly air lead levels in the work place. *They should be used only by a professional!!* The heating device should be used just long enough to soften the paint, so that it can be scraped off. Removing lead-based paint with a heating device is not good for ornate surfaces.

REPLACEMENT

Replacement, obviously, can really only be done with items that can be removed—woodwork, banisters, windows, windowsills, doors and staircases. Dislodging parts of the interior of the house will release lead into the air. Ready-made or customized pieces are used as replacements for what was removed.

ENCAPSULATION

You can encapsulate virtually any surface. If you are handy, you can frequently do this yourself. One of the most practical materials to use in covering the walls is an impermeable fiberglass mat that will not crack or chip. It comes in a 58-inch roll, and you should be able to find it at a hardware store or store selling building supplies. The fiberglass is glued onto the wall and should last for 20 years. Other coverings that can be cemented, glued or nailed onto surfaces are: sheetrock, wallboard, hardboard, plywood paneling or a similar durable, fire resistant material. They must be caulked to prevent any lead dust from being emitted. It is very important that the material be tightly sealed. Any material you use should be vermin proof. If it is next to a furnace, fireplace, stove or hallway, it is especially important that it be fire retardant.

POST-ABATEMENT: THE CLEANUP

A thorough cleanup of the entire area (walls, floors and ceilings) is a must, regardless of which method you use. There will obviously be more lead dust after scraping or sanding; but there can be quite a bit as well after pulling off woodwork or nailing up new paneling. When the dust has settled, the room should be vacuumed (with an industrial model vacuum, if possible) to make sure you get as much of the leaded dust as possible. All surfaces—walls, floors, ceilings and woodwork—should be wet-scrubbed with a high-phosphate detergent like Spic and Span. To be on the safe side, it's a good idea to wet-scrub twice. All the stripped surfaces should then be immediately repainted with lead-free paint. Any debris should be sealed in a plastic bag and placed in a toxic waste dump approved by the Environmental Protection Agency. (See end of chapter 9 on where to call for information on approved dump sites.)

RIDDING YOUR WATER OF LEAD

If you've tested your water and it has unacceptable lead levels, there are a few immediate measures you can take. First of all, *never use hot water from your tap for cooking.* Hot water dissolves more lead, more quickly than cold water.

If you have not turned on your tap for six hours, let the cold water run until it gets as cold as possible (about two or three minutes). That should flush out any lead that's accumulated while sitting in the pipes. (This may not be effective in apartment buildings because of the amount of piping. The longer the water is exposed to lead pipes or lead solder, the greater the possible lead contamination.) You must do this for every faucet from which you drink. Taking a 10-minute shower will have no effect on your kitchen sink tap.

Once you've flushed out the pipes you might want to fill some containers with water and refrigerate them so that you'll have drinking water available when you want it.

You can also buy bottled water for drinking, cooking, ice cubes and any other consumption.

Long Term
There are more permanent things you and your water supplier can do, to reduce the amount of lead in your water.

Since corrosion can cause the lead in pipes and solder to leach into the water, if you get your water from a well, or another private water source, you can treat it to make it less corrosive.

Filters can be installed in the line between the water source and any lead service connections or lead-soldered pipes. The filter will raise the Ph level, making the water less acidic and therefore less corrosive. You might ask your local health or water department for help in finding a filter. (See end of Chapter 4 on where to call.)

You can also reduce the lead in the water as it comes out of the tap in your home. "Point-of-use"(POU) treatment devices are installed at the point of use such as the kitchen tap. Reverse osmosis devices and distillation units are available commercially. They may be either purchased or leased. They can be pretty pricy, their effectiveness varies, and they must be maintained. You should check how well the device is working, i.e., how much the lead level is being reduced, and set up and follow a practical maintenance system in line with the manufacturer's recommendations. Since these devices soften water, and soft water is corrosive, they should be installed only at the faucet. Provided it's doing its job, only the water from the tap that has the device will have the lowered lead level. (See Chapter 4 for more information on these devices.)

If you are having repairs done, instruct your plumber, in writing, that you want only lead-free materials used.

If you get your water from a public water system, ask the supplier whether the supply system contains lead piping and if the water is corrosive. If the answer to either question is "yes," ask what is being done to deal with the problem of lead contamination. Drinking water can be treated at the plant to make it less corrosive. Water mains containing lead pipes, as well as those portions of lead service connections between the water supply and your home that are under the jurisdiction of the supplier, should be replaced.

As this is a problem affecting the entire community, and not just you, a call to the local paper, television or radio station on your findings may prompt an investigation and story on this potentially hazardous condition. It also can't hurt to call a few neighbors, explain the dangers and urge them to call the water supplier, the local health department and local lawmakers.

REMOVING THE LEAD THREAT FROM DUST/SOIL

Of course, the first choice is preventing lead from getting into the soil. Measures have been taken, somewhat successfully, to do that. Requiring the use of unleaded gasoline has had a big impact on lead levels in soil. But it will take some time before air lead levels (the source of lead in soil) are reduced to near zero.

If there is a hazardous level of lead in the soil where your children play, whether it's from vehicles or from leaded paint flaking off the side of your house, you'll want to do something about it.

You can render the area inaccessible by putting up a fence or impenetrable thorn bushes or by covering the area with cement. However, if one of the reasons you bought the house was so that your children could play in the wonderful yard, you might, instead: cover the contaminated area with low-lead topsoil; remove the surface soil and replace it with low-lead soil; or rototill the soil. After each of these methods you can plant new grass or vegetation.

If the lead content of dust in the house is high, it is most likely because of leaded paint. Until you have solved that problem there are interim measures you can take to reduce the level of lead in the household dust. Wet-mopping regularly, even every day, will do a lot to lower the amount of lead in the dust.

ELIMINATING OTHER SOURCES: FOOD/POTTERY

Do not cook with or drink water that contains lead. Be sure to wash fruits and vegetables thoroughly before eating them since lead dust can contaminate them.

Don't store leftover food in the tin can it came in; if the can does have some lead, the longer the food remains in it, the more lead will leach into the food. For years lead solder was used in the seams of tin cans. In the mid-1970s the Food and Drug Administration pressured the food industry into stopping the use of lead solder in cans containing baby food. In the United States the percentage of canned foods in lead-soldered cans has been substantially reduced. However, that is not necessarily the case with imported foods.

Never cook, eat or store food in glazed pottery without first making sure it contains no leachable lead. There are simple and inexpensive test kits that you should be able to find at a hardware or housewares store, if you want to test some dishes you have. In the United States ceramic-ware must be fired at a temperature that will prevent any lead in the glaze from getting into food. Many countries do not have similar regulations. If you're not sure about that lovely bowl from Aunt Bertha, it's better to use it for display purposes only.

EPA REGIONAL OFFICES FOR LEAD

ALABAMA—4
ALASKA—10
ARIZONA—9
ARKANSAS—6
CALIFORNIA—9
COLORADO—8
CONNECTICUT—1
DELAWARE—3
DISTRICT OF
  COLUMBIA—3
FLORIDA—4
GEORGIA—4
GUAM—9
HAWAII—9
IDAHO—10
ILLINOIS—5
INDIANA—5
IOWA—7
KANSAS—7

KENTUCKY—4
LOUISIANA—6
MAINE—1
MARYLAND—3
MASSACHUSETTS—1
MICHIGAN—5
MINNESOTA—5
MISSISSIPPI—4
MISSOURI—7
MONTANA—8
NEBRASKA—7
NEVADA—9
NEW HAMPSHIRE—1
NEW JERSEY—2
NEW MEXICO—6
NEW YORK—2
NORTH
  CAROLINA—4
NORTH DAKOTA—8

OHIO—5
OKLAHOMA—6
OREGON—10
PENNSYLVANIA—3
PUERTO RICO—2
RHODE ISLAND—1
SOUTH
  CAROLINA—4
SOUTH DAKOTA—8
TENNESSEE—4
TEXAS—6
UTAH—8
VERMONT—1
VIRGINIA—3
VIRGIN ISLANDS—2
WASHINGTON—10
WEST VIRGINIA—3
WISCONSIN—5
WYOMING—8

REGION 1
JFK Federal Building
Boston, Massachusetts 02203
(617)223-7210

REGION 2
26 Federal Plaza
New York, New York 10007
(212)264-2525

REGION 3
6th & Walnut Streets
Philadelphia, Pennsylvania 19106
(215)597-9814

REGION 4
245 Courtland Street, N.E.
Atlanta, Georgia 30308
(404)881-4727

REGION 5
230 South Dearborn Street
Chicago, Illinois 60604
(312)353-2000

REGION 6
1201 Elm Street
Dallas, Texas 75270
(214)767-2600

REGION 7
1735 Baltimore Avenue
Kansas City, Missouri 64108
(816)374-5493

REGION 8
1860 Lincoln Street
Denver, Colorado 80203
(303)837-3895

REGION 9
215 Fremont Street
San Francisco, California 94105
(415)556-2320

REGION 10
1200 Sixth Avenue
Seattle, Washington 98101
(206)442-1220

STATE AGENCIES FOR LEAD

If there is no specific lead agency for your state, call your EPA regional office or your local health department.

ARIZONA
Energy Office
1700 West Washington Street
Phoenix, Arizona 85007
(602)255-4945

CALIFORNIA
Department of Health Services
Indoor Air Quality Program
Air & Industrial Hygiene
Laboratory
2151 Berkeley Way
Berkeley, California 94704
(415)540-2469

CONNECTICUT
Department of Health Services
Division of Preventable Diseases
150 Washington Street
Hartford, Connecticut 06106
(203)566-3122

ILLINOIS
Department of Public Health
Division of Environmental Health
Environmental Technology
525 West Jefferson Street
Springfield, Illinois 62761
(217)782-5830

KANSAS
Department of Health and
  Environment
Bureau of Air Quality and
  Radiation Control
Environmental Toxicology Section
Forbes Field
Topeka, Kansas 66620
(913)296-1543

MAINE
Department of Agriculture
Division of Food & Rural Resources
Board of Pesticides Control

Statehouse Station 28
Augusta, Maine 04333
(207)289-2731

OKLAHOMA
Department of Health
Radiation & Special Hazards
  Service
P.O. Box 53551
1000 Northeast 10th Street
Oklahoma City, Oklahoma 73152
(405)271-5221

Department of Agriculture
Plant Industry Division
Plant Management Section
Pest Management Section
2800 North Lincoln Boulevard
Oklahoma City, Oklahoma 73105-4298
(405)521-3864

RHODE ISLAND
Department of Health
Asbestos Control Program
206 Cannon Building
75 Davis Street
Providence, Rhode Island 02908
(401)277-3601

SOUTH CAROLINA
Department of Health and
  Environmental Control
Air Compliance & Management
  Division
Bureau of Air Quality Control
2600 Bull Street
Columbia, South Carolina 29201
(803)734-4750

SOUTH DAKOTA
Office of Air Quality and Solid
  Waste
Department of Water and Natural
  Resources

Joe Foss Building, Room 217
523 East Capitol Avenue
Pierre, South Dakota 57501-3181
(605)773-3153

Department of Agriculture
Division of Regulatory Services
Anderson Building
445 East Capitol Avenue
Pierre, South Dakota 57501
(605)773-3724

TENNESSEE
Department of Agriculture
Plant Industries Division
P.O. Box 40627, Melrose Station
Nashville, Tennessee 37204
(615)360-0130

TEXAS
Department of Health
Occupational & Health Division
1100 West 49th Street
Austin, Texas 78756
(512)458-7254

WASHINGTON
Department of Social & Health
  Services
Health Services Division
Environmental Health Programs
Toxic Substances Section
Mail Stop LD-11
Olympia, Washington 98504
(206)753-2556

WISCONSIN
Department of Health & Social
  Services
Bureau of Community Health &
  Prevention
Environmental & Chronic Disease
  Epidemiology
P.O. Box 309
Madison, Wisconsin 53701-0309
(608)266-2895

Division of Health
Section of Radiation Protection
5708 Odana Road
Madison, Wisconsin 53719
(608)273-5181

4

WATER

A FEW WATER FACTS

In 1970, a study concluded that about 360,000 Americans were drinking "dangerous" water. According to the EPA, the study also found that 41% of Americans were drinking "inferior" water. Water is a necessary part of life. The average person could survive for two months or longer without food. No one can survive without water for more than a few days.

There is no such thing as "pure" water. All water picks up harmful toxins as it travels though the environment; water also picks up contaminants when toxic materials are put into the earth or dropped into water.

Concern over contaminated drinking water is not new. A Sanskrit manuscript from 2000 B.C. states: "It is good to keep water in copper vessels, to expose it to sunlight, and filter it through charcoal." And around 400 B.C. Hippocrates stressed the importance of water quality to health. He recommended boiling and straining rainwater.

By the mid-1800s, contaminated water in the United States had caused two cholera epidemics, and typhoid fever was one of the 10 leading causes of death. In 1908, chlorination was added to water systems in the U.S.—killing the typhoid and cholera germs as well as improving the taste and smell of the water. It was only later that it was discovered that Chlorine can interact with other elements in water to form carcinogenic compounds!

A BRIEF SURVEY OF FEDERAL ACTION

Since the early 20th century the United States has taken steps to monitor, regulate and control the quality of water. In 1912, Congress passed the Public Health Service Act, which authorized surveys and studies of water pollution. Two years later the first drinking water standards were put into effect, listing safe levels for contaminants. However, they were only for water supplies serving people using interstate means of transportation.

In 1948, Congress approved the Water Pollution Control Act. The Clean Water Act, a major amendment to the Water Pollution Act, was passed in 1972. It contained comprehensive provisions for restoring and maintaining all bodies of surface water in the United States. It also set limits on the amount of industrial effluents that can be discharged into surface water.

In the early 1970s the Safe Drinking Water Act (SDA) was passed. It expanded the scope of federal responsibility for the safety of drinking water—to all community water systems with 15 or more outlets or 25 or more customers.

The Safe Drinking Water Act was amended in 1977 to provide technical assistance, information, training and grants to states in maintaining clean water supplies. Nearly a decade later, it was further amended. In 1986 mandatory deadlines were set for the regulation of key contaminants; also, monitoring of unregulated contaminants was required; benchmarks for treatment technologies were established; enforcement powers were bolstered; and major new authorities were provided to promote protection of groundwater resources.

In spite of those efforts, a survey done by the United States Geological Survey in October of 1988, found contamination of groundwater increasing in every state. In June of 1989, the EPA adopted rules aimed at eliminating microbes from public drinking water. Under the rules, many water systems relying on surface water will have to operate and maintain pollution control equipment that destroys disease-causing bacteria, viruses, protozoa and other waterborne organisms. The EPA said some 90,000 annual cases of illness caused by polluted water will be eliminated once all the systems are operating.

If you are concerned about the water you and your family are drinking every day, you have good reason to be. To find out if that water contains any of the 26 pollutants regulated by the EPA you can have it tested.

THE SOURCE OF DRINKING WATER

The world contains 326 trillion gallons of water. The amount doesn't change—only the form of it changes. About half of the drinking water in the United States is surface water—water from rivers and streams. The other half, groundwater, comes from reserves of water under the surface of the earth in areas known as aquifers. Water wells tap into aquifers.

HOW WATER BECOMES CONTAMINATED

There are all kinds of opportunities for water to become contaminated, and many sources of contamination—both natural and man-made. Today, industry and agriculture use over 70,000 toxic chemicals and about 1,000 more are introduced each year. But not all contamination is man-made. Some is a result of naturally occurring substances. Water moving through rock, soil and other substances can pick up undissolved material known as suspended matter. It can also pick up materials and salts, such as sulfates. Among the naturally occurring substances that can contaminate water are minerals and salts, decay products of uranium, radium and radon; human and animal organic waste; and salt water when it intrudes into depleted aquifers near the seashore.

Contamination of water by man occurs when: a water storage tank is defective; hazardous waste landfills leak; fertilizers and pesticides run off farmland and into surface water or groundwater; rainwater causes surface run-off from overflowing storm sewers, oil-slicked and salt-treated highways and chemical spills; and when septic tanks leak.

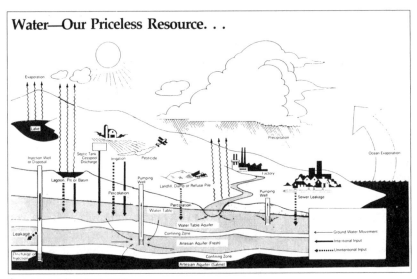

Water—Our Priceless Resource. . .

Sources of water. EPA

THE CONTAMINANTS: WHAT THEY ARE AND WHAT THEY DO

There are four major categories of contaminants: microbiological contaminants; inorganic chemicals; organic chemicals (including natural and synthetic organics); and radionuclides.

Generally, the more highly concentrated the contaminant is in the water, the greater the prospect of its being a health hazard. Different people are susceptible to different concentrations of contaminants. There are people who have vacationed in Mexico, drunk the water and had a wonderful time. Their companions, drinking the same water, end up with a case of dysentery that leaves them weak and miserable (and sometimes hospitalized).

Different factors will affect the impact of a particular contaminant. Age is one of the most significant factors. Children, up to the age of five consume twice as much water per body weight as adults, which means they will be much more susceptible to any hazardous contaminants in the water they drink. People in warmer climates drink more water. People who spend more time at home (women, children, the elderly) will naturally drink more water at home.

Some of the contaminants listed below are of benefit to the body, some are even essential, and some, like lead, play no useful role in the human body. Any of the contaminants, whether they are needed by the body or not, can become harmful in large doses.

The EPA has two sets of standards for water. The first and more important are the "primary drinking water standards." These consist of enforceable, maximum contaminant levels (MCL) set by the EPA for all the contaminants considered harmful. Secondary drinking water standards are not enforceable and are more for aesthetic reasons—such as the color, smell or taste of water. We'll take a look at those later.

PRIMARY DRINKING WATER STANDARDS: HOW MCLS ARE MEASURED

Contaminants can be measured in several different ways. Bacteria is measured by total coliforms in parts per milliliters. Coliforms are bacteria that live in the intestines of humans and animals. By themselves, they are not harmful. However, when they are found in the water, it is an indication that human or animal wastes are polluting the water. The coliform count acts as a gauge for other forms of bacterial contamination.

Organics and inorganics are measured in parts per million (ppm), parts per billion (ppb), milligrams per liter (mg/l) or micrograms per liter (ug/l). To make it a little less confusing, ppm is roughly equivalent to mg/l; ppb is roughly equivalent to ug/l.

Radionuclides (radioactive atoms) are measured in picocuries per liter (pCi/l). A picocurie is one-trillionth of a curie. The exception is gross beta particle activity, which is measured in "MREMS." An MREM (or millirem) is 1/1000 of a rem.

MICROBIOLOGICAL CONTAMINANTS

Microbes, living organisms that are much too small to see, were the first contaminants in water to raise concern. Microbes come in three forms: bacteria, protozoa and virus. They are still the most dangerous threat in drinking water. In 1989 the EPA adopted rules that will eventually require many water systems to eliminate all microbes.

Bacteria
Bacteria are responsible for the deaths of more people than any other contaminant in the water. They are single-celled organisms that can live on their own. Most bacteria are not harmful. The ones that are harmful are called pathogens.

Bacteria is measured in terms of total coliforms. The MCL is one per 100 milliliters. However, scientists presume that water containing any coliform bacteria is unfit to drink. Coliforms do not necessarily cause disease; however, they can be indicators of human or animal waste containing organisms that can cause assorted gastroenteric infections, dysentery, hepatitis, typhoid fever, cholera and others. Coliforms also interfere with the disinfection process.

The bacteria you definitely do not want to have in your water include:

- **Salmonella:** Causes typhoid fever, enteric fever and gastroenteritis; the salmonella that causes typhoid fever is no longer a real health threat in the United States.
- **Vibrio Cholerae:** Causes cholera; as is the case with salmonella, this bacteria is no longer a real health threat in the United States.
- **Shigella:** Causes three diseases: dysentery, gastroenteritis and bloody diarrhea.
- **Pathogenic E. Coli:** Causes traveler's diarrhea.
- **Yersinia and Edwardsiella:** Cause gastroenteritis.

Protozoa Parasites
Protozoa are made up of one cell, like bacteria, but they are bigger and more complex. Giardia lamblia is the one that is best known. It causes watery diarrhea, nausea, flatulence, bloating, weight loss, weakness and chronic fatigue. It can be difficult to diagnose and is, therefore, frequently misdiagnosed. The symptoms may go away after two to six weeks, or last for months. In some people who have not been treated, the

symptoms will recur periodically. Giardia is the most common, disease-causing protozoan. It is responsible for the greatest number of water-borne epidemics in the United States.

Giardia is just one of the reasons you should not drink from that pristine creek or lake you come across on your camping trip or hike. (Other contaminants can be present as well, but giardia is the one found most frequently.) The cool, inviting water may shimmer and sparkle and taste just fine. But that can de deceptive because you can neither see nor taste giardia in the water. A very small amount, 10 cells or fewer, can cause giardiasis.

The giardia parasite can get into the water system in a number of ways. Animals that live in the water, like beavers, are a common source. (Giardiasis is sometimes called beaver fever.) Animal feces can contaminate the most isolated streams, creeks and lakes. A defect in the normal operations of the water treatment plant can lead to an outbreak of the disease. Leakage from sewer lines into water lines is another way water can become contaminated.

Between 1971 and 1977 there were 20 recorded outbreaks of giardiasis in the United States, affecting thousands of people.

There are no EPA standards for giardia, or other protozoa, in the water. Water in treatment plants can not be routinely checked for protozoa because they are difficult to detect. Giardia can be especially hard to detect because they are usually not found in large numbers.

Viruses
Like protozoa, viruses can generally survive in the environment longer than bacteria and are more resistant to chlorination. While it could take one million bacteria cells to make some people ill, a single virus cell can cause disease in some people.

The most well known diseases caused by viruses in the water are polio and hepatitis A, but viruses can cause many other less well known and less severe illnesses that can be extremely unpleasant.

Most of the viruses in drinking water cause gastrointestinal disorders. Because these diseases frequently go undiagnosed, untreated and unreported, it is hard to know how widespread they are.

Some of the lesser known viruses, which can cause quite a bit of discomfort, include:

- **Norwalk:** causes gastroenteritis and headaches
- **Rotavirus:** causes gastroenteritis with significant dehydration
- **Echo:** causes meningitis, respiratory problems and muscular paralysis

- **Coxsackie:** causes respiratory problems, meningitis, pharyngitis and muscular paralysis

As with protozoa, there are no national standards for viruses in water, and it is very difficult and expensive to test for them. In general, treatment plants are not designed to eliminate viruses.

Turbidity
Turbidity (dissolved solids, particles and other types of sediment, which make the water cloudy and dense) is a result of erosion, runoff and discharges. While not harmful itself, it interferes with disinfection.

INORGANIC CHEMICALS

Inorganics are minerals (such as mercury, silver, zinc) that do not have the structure or characteristics of living organisms.

Among the common inorganic chemicals in water are:

- arsenic
- barium
- calcium
- cadmium
- chromium
- copper
- fluorides
- iron
- lead
- mercury
- silver
- sodium
- beryllium
- cobalt
- magnesium
- manganese
- molybdenum
- nickel
- potassium
- tin
- vanadium
- zinc

Some of the inorganics are beneficial, and some are even essential, in small amounts. Most are present, to some extent, in water.

As the amount of a particular substance increases, the possibility that the substance can cause harm increases as well. If there is an insignificant amount of a particular inorganic chemical in the water, it can become significant, and harmful, when that same chemical is also present in the air or food or both. A small amount of an inorganic chemical can also be harmful if it is ingested and builds up in the body, over time. Data on the health hazards of some of these inorganic chemicals are in preliminary stages, frequently based on animal studies. (The same goes for the organic chemicals discussed in the next section.) The EPA has, nevertheless, set MCLs for many of the questionable substances (along with the substances definitively known to be a health hazard), believing that eventually there will be evidence of their potential harmful effects and, as the old adage goes, better safe than sorry.

Usually inorganic substances get into water naturally, as the water travels through the earth. They can also end up in water as a result of

EPA PRIMARY DRINKING WATER STANDARDS

CONTAMINANT	HEALTH EFFECTS	MCL*	SOURCES
Microbiological total coliforms (coliform bacteria, fecal coliform, streptococcal)	Not necessarily disease producing themselves, but can indicate organisms that cause assorted illnesses; also interferes with disinfection process	1/100 millileters	human and animal fecal matter
Turbidity	Interferes with disinfection of water	1-5tu	erosion, runoff, discharge
Inorganic Chemicals			
Arsenic	Dermal and nervous system toxicity effects	50	geological, pesticide residues, industrial wastes, smelter operations
Barium	Circulatory system effects	1,000	metal plating/industrial waste
Cadmium	Kidney	10	geological, mining, smelting
Chromium	Liver/kidney	50	metal plating, industrial waste
Fluoride	Skeletal damage	4,000	geological, added to water systems
Lead	Nervous system, kidney; highly toxic to infants and pregnant women	50	leaches from lead pipes and solder
Mercury	Central nervous system/kidney	2	used in manufacture of paint, paper, vinyl chloride; used in fungicides; geological
Nitrate	Methemoglobinemia ("blue baby syndrome")	10,000	fertilizer, sewage, feedlots, geological
Selenium	Gastrointestinal	10	geological, mining
Silver	Skin discoloration (argyria)	50	geological, mining
Fluoride	Skeletal	4,000	geological, added to water, toothpaste, foods processed with fluoridated water
Organic Chemicals			
Benzene	Cancer	5	fuel, solvent used in making industrial chemicals, pharmaceuticals, pesticides, paints and plastics
Endrin	Nervous system	0.2	insecticide in cotton, small grains, orchards (banned in 1979)

CONTAMINANT	HEALTH EFFECTS	MCL*	SOURCES
Lindane	Nervous system/liver	4	soil/seed insecticide, foliage application, wood protection
Methoxychlor	Nervous system/kidney	100	fruit tree, vegetable insecticide
2,4-D	Liver/kidney	100	herbicide for broadleaf weeds, forests, range, pastures and water environments
2,4,5-TP Silvex	Liver/kidney	10	herbicide (canceled in 1984)
Toxaphene	Cancer risk	5	cotton, corn, grain insecticide
Carbon tetrachloride (CTC)	Possible cancer	5	cleaning agents, industrial wastes from manufacture of coolants
p-Dichlorobenzene	Possible cancer	75	insecticides, moth balls, air deodorizers
1,2-Dichloroethane	Possible cancer	5	used in making gasoline, insecticides
1,1-Dichloroethylene	Liver/kidney	7	used in making plastics, dyes, perfumes, paints
1,1,1-Trichloroethane	Nervous system	200	used in making food wrappings, synthetic fibers
Trichloroethylene (TCE)	Possible cancer	5	dry cleaning material waste; used in making pesticides, paints, waxes, varnishes, paint stripper, metal degreaser
Total trihalomethanes (TTHM)	Cancer risk	100	formed when surface water is treated with chlorine
Vinyl chloride	Cancer risk	2	polyvinylchloride (PVC) pipes and solvents used to join them, industrial waste from making plastics and synthetic rubber
Radionuclides			
Gross alpha particle activity	Cancer	15 pCi/l	radioactive waste, uranium deposits
Gross beta particle activity	Cancer	4mrem/year	radioactive waste, uranium deposits
Radium 226 & 228 (total)	Bone cancer	5 pCi/l	radioactive waste, geological

* MCLS are in parts per billion (ppb).

human activity. For example, lead can leach into water from lead pipe or lead solder. Nitrates in fertilizers can run off into surface or ground water.

Following is a brief look at some of the inorganics found in water, their MCL set by the EPA and the possible health threat they pose:

Arsenic

Arsenic gets into the water from rocks, pesticide runoff, shellfish decay, industrial waste and smelter operations. It is found widely in natural water in the United States, generally in amounts of 10 ppb or less. In small amounts, arsenic may be an essential nutrient in the body. However, in greater amounts it can affect the nervous system and skin. It can cross the placenta. Arsenic can accumulate in the body, especially in the liver, kidney, intestinal walls, spleen and lungs.

The MCL set by the Environmental Protection Agency is 50 ppb.

Barium

Barium can leach from metal plating into the water. It can also be a by-product of industrial waste.

It can affect the circulatory system.

The current MCL is 1,000 ppb.

Cadmium

Cadmium can leach from pipes into water so it is more likely to be a problem in areas with soft water, which is more corrosive to pipes.

It's found in low concentrations in surface water. Because cadmium is also used in fertilizer, it can get into water by runoff from farm land into surface or groundwater. It also comes from rock formations and smelting operations.

Large amounts of cadmium can cause symptoms similar to food poisoning and affect the kidneys. Preliminary studies with animals indicate that cadmium can increase hypertension.

The current MCL for cadmium is 10 ppb.

Chromium

Chromium does not appear to be too widespread in waters in the United States, and generally, when it is present, the levels are not high. However, relatively low levels can be harmful, affecting the liver and kidneys.

Chromium can come from rocks, mining and smelting.

The current MCL is 50 ppb.

Fluoride

Fluoride is present in most soils and in groundwater. It is also in most toothpastes. And it is added to many water systems.

In the 1930s researchers discovered that people who grew up drinking water containing fluoride had fewer cavities. At the same time it was discovered that people who had mottled or discolored teeth were drinking water containing fluoride. The more fluoride, the more discoloration. So a downside of fluoridating water is discolored teeth, or dental fluorosis as it came to be called.

While that is not a health hazard, it's not so pretty to look at. What is a health hazard is high levels of fluoride, which can lead to skeletal fluorosis, a condition in which the bones get thicker and denser, eventually crippling the victim. Though this is not common, it is something to be aware of. Those at greatest risk are people with kidney disease.

The MCL for fluoride is 4,000 ppb.

Lead

Lead is one of the major (and most dangerous) contaminants of water.

Its MCL is 50 ppb. The proposed MCL is 5 ppb. The proposed MCL goal (MGLC) is zero. This hazard is covered in detail in Chapter 3.

Mercury

Mercury is used in the manufacture of paint, paper and vinyl chloride. It is used in fungicides and it can also be found in the earth.

Mercury can affect the central nervous system and kidneys.

The current MCL is 2 ppb.

Nitrates

The main sources of nitrates are nitrogen fertilizers and manured fields, improper sewage disposals, sanitary landfills, industrial waste waters and animal wastes.

Nitrates themselves are harmless. They become a problem when they change to nitrites inside the body. This can be especially harmful to infants, six months and younger, causing the disease methemoglobinemia. In methemoglobinemia blood cannot circulate enough oxygen through the body.

If you have a well, the deeper it is and the farther it is from your septic system, the lower the level of nitrates should be.

While nitrates are found in water, they are actually more common in food.

Currently, the MCL for nitrates in water is 10,000 ppb.

Selenium

Selenium is a natural chemical found in soil. Mining activity also adds selenium to the water. It is found more often in groundwater than in surface water.

Selenium is an essential nutrient at low levels. At high levels it is toxic and can cause gastrointestinal problems, depression, nervousness and liver damage.

The current MCL is 10 ppb.

Silver

Silver is found naturally in the earth. Mining increases its concentration in the water.

The MCL is 50 ppb.

ORGANIC CHEMICALS

Organic compounds are natural or synthetic (man-made) substances based on carbon. They are generally categorized by being large or small. Small organics are usually more volatile, evaporating more quickly than the nonvolatile organics (which are in the larger organics group). Because volatile organics do evaporate quickly there is the risk of inhaling these chemicals while taking a shower, bath, washing dishes, and so on.

There is very little data on the amount of volatiles released from drinking water. Some researchers believe you could risk just as significant an exposure from inhalation of some of the volatiles as you could from drinking the water.

In the early 1980s, the EPA sponsored the Groundwater Supply Survey (GWSS). The study was done to determine the dimensions of the problem of groundwater contamination in the United States. Groundwater supplies serving some 1,000 communities, in all 50 states, were tested for 34 volatile organics. The study concluded that *if you live near a dumpsite, in a community of more than 10,000 people, your chances of having organic contaminated water are higher than if you live in the country.*

Relatively speaking, little is known about the health hazards of organics—or at what level, if any, they are entirely safe. There have not been enough conclusive studies to date, though there is a lot of preliminary data.

Following are the organics believed to pose a threat, for which MCLs have been set by the EPA:

Benzene

Benzene is an additive in gasoline and is also a by-product of oil refining. It can get into groundwater from leaking tanks.

Studies of people working with benzene have shown abnormally high rates of cancer. The EPA has estimated that over 200,000 people in the United States are exposed to dangerous concentrations of 5 ppb or higher.

The current MCL for benzene is 5 ppb.

Endrin

An insecticide that was used on cotton, small grains and orchards. It was banned in 1979.

It can affect the nervous system and kidneys.

The current MCL is 0.2 ppb.

Lindane

An insecticide used in seed and soil treatments, foliage applications and wood protection.

It can affect the nervous system and liver.

Currently, the MCL is 4 ppb.

Methoxychlor

An insecticide used on fruit trees and vegetables.

It affects the nervous system and kidneys.

The current MCL is 100 ppb.

2,4-D

A herbicide used to control broadleaf weeds in agriculture, in forests, ranges, pastures and water environments.

It has been linked with liver and kidney damage.

The current MCL is 100 ppb.

2,4,5-TP Silvex

A herbicide that was banned in 1984.

It can affect the liver and kidneys.

The current MCL is 10 ppb.

Toxaphene

An insecticide used on cotton, corn and grain.

It can affect the liver and kidneys.

The current MCL is 5 ppb.

Carbon Tetrachloride (CTC)

Used in cleaning agents and solvents and found in industrial wastes from the manufacture of coolants, and in grain fumigants.

CTC is considered a possible carcinogen. (The National Cancer Institute [NCI] classifies it as a liver carcinogen in mice and rats.) It can cause liver damage and has been implicated in heart attacks.

The current MCL is 5 ppb. The recommended level in drinking water is zero!

p-Dichlorobenzene

Used in insecticides, moth balls and air deodorizers.

It is a possible carcinogen. High doses in humans have produced nausea, loss of appetite and liver damage.

The current MCL is 75 ppb.

1,2-Dichloroethane

A solvent used in the manufacture of vinyl chloride, gasoline, insecticides, paint, varnish and finish remover.

It is considered a possible carcinogen. (NCI studies have found that it is carcinogenic in rats.)

The current MCL is 5 ppb. The recommended level is zero!

1,1-Dichloroethylene

Used in the manufacture of plastics, dyes, perfumes and paints.

It can affect the liver and kidneys.

The current MCL is 7 ppb.

1,1,1-Trichloroethane

Used in food wrappings, synthetic fibers, cleaners, as a degreaser of metals, and as a solvent. It can affect the nervous system. It is replacing TCE in many industrial and household products.

The current MCL is 200 ppb.

Trichloroethylene (TCE)

Found in the waste from the disposal of dry cleaning materials. It's used to clean cesspools and in the manufacture of pesticides, paints, waxes, varnishes, paint strippers and metal degreasers. In household products it is in many spot removers, rug cleaners and air fresheners. Because it is used so widely it is the synthetic organic found most often in groundwater.

TCE is a possible carcinogen.

The current MCL is 5 ppb. The recommended level is zero.

Total Trihalomethanes (TTHM): chloroform, bromoform, bromodichloromethane, dibromochloromethane

TTHMs are primarily formed when surface water containing organic matter is treated with chlorine. (As noted earlier, this is one of the bad effects of chlorine, which otherwise has had such a positive impact on diseases, virtually wiping out cholera and typhoid.)

TTHMs pose a cancer risk.

The current MCL is 100 ppb.

Vinyl Chloride

Used to make polyvinyl chloride—a plastic in rubber, paper, glass, electrical wiring, piping, medical supplies, food packaging and building materials.

It is a known carcinogen that can cause cancer of the liver, brain, lungs and hemolymphopoietic system, which produces blood and lymph cells. It causes other illnesses as well, including edema of the lungs, hyperemia of the kidneys and liver, cardiovascular manifestations, and disturbances of the central nervous system.

The current MCL is 2 ppb.

RADIONUCLIDES

The three major radionuclides (radioactive atoms) with MCLs set by the EPA are gross alpha particle activity, gross beta particle activity, and radium 226 and 228. It is these three that are primarily responsible for radioactivity in the water.

- **Gross Alpha Particle Activity:** from radioactive waste and uranium deposits. It can cause cancer. The MCL is 15 picocuries per liter (pCi/l).
- **Gross Beta Particle Activity:** from radioactive waste and uranium deposits. It can cause cancer. The MCL is 4 mrem/yr (annual dose equivalent).
- **Radium 226 and 228:** from radioactive waste as well as the land. The MCL is 5 pCi/l.

(Radon is a decay product of radium 226, which is a decay product of uranium. For more information on radon in water refer to Chapter 1.)

SECONDARY DRINKING WATER STANDARDS

These are standards for non-hazardous contamination of water, set by the EPA. They are recommendations and not enforceable. For the most part they have to do with the aesthetics of the water. Following is a list of the contaminants:

pH
pH represents the degree of acidity or alkalinity. Water should not be too acidic or too alkalinic. It should fall between 6.5 and 8.5 on the pH scale of 1 to 14.

Hardness
The hardness or total dissolved solids (mainly magnesium and calcium), in the water can affect the taste. There is also some evidence that hardness may play a role in reducing cardiovascular disease. Hard water has been correlated with a lower incidence of hypertension, heart attack and stroke. Hard water can damage plumbing and limit the effectiveness of soaps and detergents.

Hardness is measured in units called grains per gallon. This measure shows the total amount of inorganics present (mostly magnesium and calcium). There are no official standards, but generally water with less than one grain per gallon (or about 17 ppm total dissolved solids or 17 milligrams per liter) is considered soft; one to three grains per gallon is considered slightly hard; three to six grains per gallon is considered moderately hard; six to 12 is considered hard; and over 12 is considered very hard.

There are no official standards to distinguish hard water from soft water. The National Research Council considers water with less than 4.4 grains per gallon soft, and above 4.4 grains, hard.

Chloride
Chloride which is put into water supplies to kill bacteria, can affect the taste of the water and also lead to corrosion of the pipes.

The standard for chloride is 250 mg/l.

Copper
The main sources of copper are copper pipes, industrial wastes and by-products of sewage treatment plants.

Ingestion of large amounts of copper can cause irritation of the gastrointestinal tract. Copper can give the water a metallic taste and can stain porcelain.

The current level of 1 ppm is a guideline set for the taste and smell of the water.

Sulfates
The major sources of sulfates are rainwater, leaching from rocks, waste discharges, manufacturing and septic systems.

Sulfate can affect the taste of the water and make it smell like rotten eggs. It also can have a laxative effect, with levels of 750 ppm and higher sometimes causing diarrhea in a person not used to the water.

The EPA recommended guideline for sulfates in the water is 250 ppm.

Zinc
Zinc occurs naturally or can be the result of industrial activity. It can affect the taste of the water. The EPA recommended guideline is 5 ppm.

Iron
Iron in water is very common. It occurs naturally or can be the result of industrial activity. It doesn't take much to stain porcelain sinks, dishes and kitchen utensils, and give the water a metallic taste.

The EPA recommended guideline is 0.3 ppm.

Manganese
Manganese occurs naturally, or can be the result of industrial activity. It can make the water have a metallic taste.

The recommended guideline is 0.05 ppm.

Foaming Agents
Foaming agents are on this list solely for aesthetic reasons. These contaminants cause water to foam or froth (like detergent would) and may give the water a foul taste.

The EPA recommended guideline is 0.5 ppm.

HOW SAFE IS YOUR WATER?

The steps you take to determine how healthy your drinking water is depend on whether you are getting your water from a public water system (community water or a private supplier) or from a well that is on your property.

If you are one of the approximately 40 million people with a private well, your water is not regulated and you, for the most part, must be responsible for it.

Most people in the United States, about 85%, get their water from a public or community system. Generally speaking, the larger the city and the bigger the water supplier, the more likely it is that the water will be healthy, complying with all the MCLs set by the EPA.

If you are concerned about your water and it comes from an outside source, the first thing to do is contact your water supplier. Water suppliers are required by federal law to report to the state at least once a month on the status of the water. Water suppliers must notify consumers when water standards are not met. Call your water supplier and ask for that month's printout of the condition of the water, which it has sent to the state authority. If you're not sure who your supplier is, check your bill. If you are not paying for the water call your local health department or state water agency. (See listing at the end of this chapter.) However, the water supplier does not have to send you a copy of the report. Some water suppliers simply don't have the means to make it available.

If you can't get the printout from your supplier, call your state water office. Your state *must* supply it under the Freedom of Information Act. You may have to submit your request in writing and be prepared to wait!

Another thing you want to find out from your state is its own standards for MCLs or contaminants. The state's MCLs must at least match those set by the EPA; some states have more stringent levels!

If your water supplier is not meeting these standards, you will want to find out what the supplier is doing about it. First ask the supplier. If you have additional questions, call the local health department or state office.

Once you know where you stand on the water you are getting from your supplier, you want to find out how the water has fared on its journey to your tap. The water may start out being just fine, but as it travels to you—through connecting pipes from the original water supply, then through the plumbing in your home—it can undergo significant changes, for the worse.

WHEN TO TEST YOUR WATER

When should you test your water? *When you have any reason to suspect* that there may be a problem.

If you are getting your water from a public utility or private supplier, and are satisfied that the water is leaving the facility in good condition, you want to make sure the water is not becoming contaminated in the connecting pipe carrying the water to your home, or by your own plumbing. You may want to test for lead, copper, vinyl chloride (if you have plastic pipes in your home) or bacteria that get in through leaks in old connecting pipes.

If you use well water, you may want to do more tests. First you'll want to get as much information as possible from your local health department on what it knows about local groundwater conditions. You'll also want to find out about soil conditions and the likelihood of harmful substances leaching from the soil.

The tests you choose to perform will depend on a number of factors related primarily to location and the condition of your house. There are many different situations that indicate a potential problem. Following are some of the circumstances that could mean problems with your water:

- living near a landfill, chemical dump or farmland where pesticides and herbicides are being used;
- living near an industrial park, chemical manufacturing plant or military base where large amounts of fuel are stored, or an area where there is a high concentration of cesspools or septic systems;
- using water drawn from a river where upstream cities or towns dump waste;
- water that looks bad, smells bad or tastes bad; or has changed in the way it looks, tastes or smells;
- if your house was built before the '50s, is less than five years old, has lead plumbing or lead-soldered pipes;
- if your house has tested positive for very high levels of radon or you live in an area where the underground rock strata contains uranium.

HOW TO TEST YOUR WATER

Testing your water is relatively easy and, depending on what you are testing for, can also be relatively inexpensive. The more substances you test for, the steeper the price.

Most people will want to start out by testing for bacteria (especially if your water is from your own well), since that is the most common problem.

Check first with your local health department. Find out if they test and what they can test for. Some will do a basic test, for bacteria, for free or for a nominal charge. Some health departments will also test for pH, hardness and nitrates (in agricultural areas where it is suspected nitrates have contaminated the water).

If your local health department does not do as extensive a test as you'd like, ask for a recommendation for a laboratory, or check in your yellow pages. (See also the listings at the end of this chapter.) Make sure the lab is certified. Labs are required to have state certification. Sometimes you can have an analysis done by the chemistry or microbiology department of a local university.

If you are using a commercial lab, and want an extensive analysis done, it is a good idea to shop around if possible. Some labs have special rates for certain groups of chemicals. There are also labs that specialize in analyzing samples that are sent in and they may have a better price as well. If you are testing for just one or two things it probably is not worth shopping around.

Getting the samples of water for analysis is simple, but it is extremely important to follow the instructions and take the samples correctly! If the place where you are having the analysis done does not give you instructions, ask for them.

The basic instructions are the same. The sample should go in a sterile bottle, which you get from your health department or the lab you are using. Be careful not to touch the cap or mouth of the bottle with anything. Don't open the bottle until you're ready to use it and don't rinse it. Before taking the sample, check the cold water tap handle for any leaks, remove any attachments like a hose or aerator, clean the outside of the faucet, and let the water run at full force for about two minutes to clear the pipes and storage unit. (If you are testing for lead in your water, be sure to consult Chapter 3.) Reduce the flow and run for another two minutes, then open the bottle and fill to within one inch of the top. Put the cab back on immediately. Get the sample to the lab as soon as possible.

When you receive the analysis, compare the levels of contaminants in your water with the MCLs set by the EPA (see table on pages 91-92).

STOPGAP MEASURES TO MAKE YOUR WATER POTABLE

If your water has unacceptable levels of contaminants, there are a number of stopgap measures you can take until you decide on a permanent solution. (You may decide that you will simply keep using the stopgap measure you've chosen, making it the permanent solution rather than investing in a water treatment device.) Here are the things you can do, immediately, on your own:

- Buy bottled water for drinking and cooking.
- Boil any water you'll be drinking or cooking with for 20 minutes. Boiling will kill off bacteria in the water.

- If you have not used the water for six hours or more, let it run, full force, for two or three minutes. That will reduce the levels of lead, cadmium and cobalt that have built up. (This may not work in an apartment building; there are just too many pipes to flush out!)
- To remove volatile organics from the water you can: boil it; mix it with an electric mixer for 10 minutes; or let it stand in the open air for at least two days (which is probably the least practical). Volatile organics evaporate rapidly into the air—and doing any of the above allows that to happen.

WATER TREATMENT—PRELIMINARY STEPS

When a more thorough treatment is needed to reduce levels of contaminants in your water, make sure the method you choose *won't create another problem while eliminating the original one*. If you are not sure what would be the most effective treatment consult with an expert. A "water quality improvement equipment dealer" (look in the yellow pages) can help you. Ask the dealer for references and if you have any doubts, check with the Better Business Bureau. The next step is to purchase the equipment. The Water Quality Association (WQA) awards a "gold seal" to water treatment devices that meet industry standards for performance, capacity and longevity. Their directory is updated every six months and includes water softeners, filtration systems, reverse osmosis systems and distillation systems. The nonprofit WQA can also steer you to sources of water treatment devices. Its number is (312)369-1600.

Check on whether the company from whom you're buying the water treatment device has a maintenance contract. If you have to do the maintenance yourself, find out what is required in advance and make sure you can do it. Many water treatment devices must be monitored as well as maintained to ensure that they are operating at maximum effectiveness—doing the job! Before you start, make sure you understand the instructions for the device or procedure and follow them, exactly. The importance of following directions accurately cannot be stressed enough.

WHERE TO TREAT THE WATER

There are basically to places where you can treat your water: as it enters the house, at its "point of entry" (POE); or at its "point of use" (POU), the specific tap you use for drinking and cooking water. In most households, only .5% of the water in the home is used for drinking and cooking. Therefore it makes sense to treat it at the point of use, and that is generally what is done. POE devices are usually larger, costlier and often not really necessary.

PURIFICATION VERSUS FILTRATION

To make your drinking water healthy you can kill off the contaminants or you can keep them from getting into the water, or you can do a combination of both. Here, briefly, are how the two methods work:

Purification
Purifying the water involves treating it in order to kill or deactivate all types of disease-causing microorganisms that are in the water, including bacteria, viruses and protozoan cysts. You can purify chemically or physically. Chemically, the most common purifier is chlorine, which is very effective in eliminating bacteria and viruses. Water can also be disinfected with ozone, iodine, bromine and silver.

Filtration
Filters are designed to keep contaminants from getting into the water you drink by trapping them. The contaminants the filter traps are the organics and inorganics. They generally are not useful in removing disease-causing microbes from the water. In fact, the filter that is collecting chemicals may also be trapping bacteria. The "living" bacteria may multiply, with the end result being greater amounts of bacteria getting into the water!

WATER TREATMENT—PURIFICATION

Distillation
Distillation can reduce just about every type of contaminant, and it is also a very slow process. The cost of energy to heat the water can run quite high.

Distillers, which come in many sizes and shapes, vaporize water and then condense it. During this process dissolved solids, metals, minerals, asbestos fibers, particles and some organics are eliminated. However, some organics are vaporized and condensed along with the water. The heat in distillers kills bacteria, although some bacterial spores sometimes survive.

Distilled water should be kept in the refrigerator.

A portable or tabletop distiller is around $200. Full-size units, depending on the capacity can range from $300 to $1500.

Ultraviolet Disinfection (UV)

UV is most effective in eliminating bacteria. It is an especially good treatment for well water with only microbiological problems.

The UV device is quite simple. Its main part is the UV light source, enclosed in a protective transparent sleeve. It is mounted so that the water can pass by and be exposed to the light, which destroys bacteria and inactivates many viruses. It is not as effective against viruses and parasites as against bacteria. The ultraviolet light disinfects water without adding any chemicals. It leaves no taste or odor.

The UV must be maintained and cleaned regularly. Dirt buildup on the transparent parts of the unit can make it ineffective. Both dissolved and suspended solids can also decrease the effectiveness of the unit.

UV devices cost between about $400 and $700.

Water Softening

Water softening is probably the most common water treatment in the United States today. The Water Quality Association estimates that about six million American homes have water softening devices.

Hard Water is not a health hazard. It may even have some health advantages (reducing the risk of hypertension). But it can be very annoying.

Hard water leaves a dingy film on clothes, dishes, food, hair, and skin. It makes it very difficult for soaps to form suds, so more soap is used. Its most damaging aspect is what it can do to your pipes. It leaves deposits, called scales, inside the pipes, which decreases the inner diameter and eventually clogs the plumbing.

Water softeners work by exchanging positively charged molecules or ions with sodium. Regular coarse salt is normally used, but potassium salts are also available.

There are many different water softeners on the market. A manual one is the cheapest to purchase, but requires a lot of maintenance. Semi- or fully automatic softeners are just that. They come with a timing device and your work is minimal.

When you are buying a softener make sure you're getting a *certified unit*. Ask if it meets the standards of the Water Quality Association. (You can call the WQA at [312]369-1600.)

It isn't necessary to soften all the water going into our home. You'll save money by just softening your hot water, which is what you use for washing.

You can rent softeners for about $20 a month. Buying a unit can cost from $500 to $1500 depending on its features.

WATER TREATMENT—FILTRATION

There are many ways to eliminate the contaminants in your water and make it healthy. You may use one method or a combination of methods. Following is a brief list of the different approaches and where they are most effective;

Filtration

Filtration is primarily used for keeping the particles and bacteria in the water from reaching you. There are two basic filters, depth and screen. They can be used singly or together.

Depending on your needs, filters can be quite economical, with some carbon filters available for as little as $20. On the other hand, a carbon filter system for the whole house can cost $800.

A depth or sediment filter is made of layers that trap particles as the water flows though. The denser the filter, the smaller the size of the particles and the greater the number it can trap.

Depth filters have several advantages. They are inexpensive, they can retain relatively large amounts of dirt and debris without clogging and they are easier to replace, when clogged, than a screen filter.

A major disadvantage of a depth filter is that bacteria can grow inside it and get pushed farther and farther down. The bacteria can eventually exit at the other end of the filter, *into the water you are and your family are drinking*. The greater the pressure of the water going through the filter, the more contaminants will be pushed through and end up in the water coming out of the faucet.

A screen filter is flat, like the screen on a screened-in porch, and comes in a wide range of sizes. Anything bigger than the openings will not get through.

Membrane screen filters have very small openings and have been used by hospitals to sterilize liquids that cannot be heat-sterilized. With a pore size of 0.2 microns membrane filters will keep out all bacteria. However, if eliminating all bacteria is your goal, you may want to consider an Ultraviolet Disinfection device. Besides being quite expensive, screen filters can clog quickly.

You may have a hard time finding a membrane filter. It is far easier to find a depth or sediment filter, which many companies sell. If your local hardware store doesn't have it, your water supplier should be able to steer you to a source; or call the WQA.

Activated Carbon Filtration

Activated carbon filters come in several forms: granular activated carbon (GAC), powdered activated carbon (PAC), PAC-coated paper filters and pressed carbon block filters. Given enough time, activated carbon can remove many organic substances, which results in the elimination of most odors, colors and tastes from the water. Less soluble organics are removed more easily than organics that dissolve in the water. Though some inorganics, like chlorine, can be removed, these filters are not effective at removing most inorganics.

Carbon is also not really effective in the removal of microorganisms. Carbon can get overloaded with contaminants, or bacteria can collect on a filter's surface, resulting in a greater concentration of contaminants.

You can put an activated carbon filter right on the faucet so that the water is filtered as it flows through; you can connect a filter to the pipe carrying water to the faucet from which you get your drinking water; or you can get a filter that is not hooked up to your plumbing, but sits on the counter where you can pour through any water you will be using for drinking or cooking.

The price range for the device is from less than $100 to as much as $800 for top of the line models.

Reverse Osmosis (RO)

RO can reduce virtually all the contaminants found in water: bacteria, most giardia lamblia, some viruses, organics, inorganics and particulates.

RO uses an extremely dense filter that acts like the natural membrane that surrounds living cells. The membrane filter is semi-permeable, allowing about 25% of the water, but not the contaminants, to pass through. The remaining 75% of the water, along with the contaminants it contains, is washed away, into a waste stream. Therefore, the filter remains relatively free of contaminants. It has a lifetime of about a year.

The treated water comes out much more slowly than water from a regular tap, necessitating storage of treated water in a tank so that it is available when you need it. It can take about four gallons of water to get one potable gallon.

A RO system consists of a module, a storage tank and a separate faucet. An RO device that you put on your kitchen counter should cost about $100. An under-the-sink device could run $500 or more.

If you are buying an RO device, ask what its salt rejection value is. The efficiency of the device is indicated by the amount of salt on the filter. The higher the percentage the more contaminants will be eliminated. It should be at least 90%.

Maintenance is very important. Be sure to get specific instructions on when and how to sanitize the unit.

In a survey done by the WQA, more than 90% of the people questioned nationwide said they would like more control over their water. This chapter will enable you to greatly affect your own household water.

EPA REGIONAL OFFICES FOR WATER

ALABAMA—4	KENTUCKY—4	OHIO—5
ALASKA—10	LOUISIANA—6	OKLAHOMA—6
ARIZONA—9	MAINE—1	OREGON—10
ARKANSAS—6	MARYLAND—3	PENNSYLVANIA—3
CALIFORNIA—9	MASSACHUSETTS—1	PUERTO RICO—2
COLORADO—8	MICHIGAN—5	RHODE ISLAND—1
CONNECTICUT—1	MINNESOTA—5	SOUTH
DELAWARE—3	MISSISSIPPI—4	CAROLINA—4
DISTRICT OF	MISSOURI—7	SOUTH DAKOTA—8
COLUMBIA—3	MONTANA—8	TENNESSEE—4
FLORIDA—4	NEBRASKA—7	TEXAS—6
GEORGIA—4	NEVADA—9	UTAH—8
GUAM—9	NEW HAMPSHIRE—1	VERMONT—1
HAWAII—9	NEW JERSEY—2	VIRGINIA—3
IDAHO—10	NEW MEXICO—6	VIRGIN ISLANDS—2
ILLINOIS—5	NEW YORK—2	WASHINGTON—10
INDIANA—5	NORTH	WEST VIRGINIA—3
IOWA—7	CAROLINA—4	WISCONSIN—5
KANSAS—7	NORTH DAKOTA—8	WYOMING—8

REGION 1
JFK Federal Building
Boston, Massachusetts 02203
(617)853-0361

REGION 2
26 Federal Plaza
New York, New York 10278
(212)264-1800

REGION 3
841 Chestnut Street
Philadelphia, Pennsylvania 19107
(215)587-8227

REGION 4
245 Courtland Street, N.E.
Atlanta, Georgia 30308
(404)881-8731

REGION 5
230 South Dearborn Street

Chicago, Illinois 60604
(312)353-2650

REGION 6
1201 Elm Street
Dallas, Texas 75270
(214)767-2618

REGION 7
726 Minnesota Avenue
Kansas City, Missouri 66101
(913)236-2815

REGION 8
999 18th Street, Suite 1300
Denver, Colorado 80202-2413
(303)293-1413

REGION 9
215 Fremont Street
San Francisco, California 94105
(415)974-0912

REGION 10
1200 Sixth Avenue

Seattle, Washington 98101
(206)442-4092

STATE AGENCIES FOR WATER

ALABAMA
Water Supply Branch
Department of Environmental
  Management
1751 Federal Drive
Montgomery, Alabama 36130
(205)271-7773

ALASKA
Drinking Water Program
Water Quality Management
Department of Environmental
  Conservation
P.O. Box O
Juneau, Alaska 99811
(907)465-2653

ARIZONA
Waste and Water Quality
  Management
2005 North Central Avenue
Room 202
Phoenix, Arizona 85004
(602)257-2235

ARKANSAS
Division of Engineering
Department of Health
4815 West Markham Street
Little Rock, Arkansas 72201-3867
(501)661-2000

CALIFORNIA
Sanitary Engineering Branch
Department of Health
714 P Street, Room 600
Sacramento, California 95814
(916)323-6111

COLORADO
Drinking Water Section
Department of Health

4210 East 11th Avenue
Denver, Colorado 80220
(303)320-8333

CONNECTICUT
Department of Health
Water Supply Section
79 Elm Street
Hartford, Connecticut 06115
(203)566-1251

DELAWARE
Office of Sanitary Engineering
Division of Public Health
Jesse Cooper Memorial Building
Capital Square
Dover, Delaware 19901
(302)736-4731

DISTRICT OF COLUMBIA
Dept. of Consumer &
  Regulatory Affairs
Water Hygiene Branch
5010 Overlook Avenue, S.W.
Washington, D.C. 20032
(202)767-7370

FLORIDA
Department of Environmental
  Regulation
Twin Towers Office Building
2600 Blair Stone Road
Tallahassee, Florida 32301-8241
(904)487-1779

GEORGIA
Water Protection Branch
Environmental Protection Division
Department of Natural Resources
270 Washington Street S.W.
Atlanta, Georgia 30334
(404)656-3530

GUAM
Environmental Protection Agency
Government of Guam
P.O. Box 2999
Agana, Guam 96910
(671)646-8863

HAWAII
Drinking Water Program
Sanitation Branch
Environmental Protection & Health
  Services Division
P.O. Box 3378
Honolulu, Hawaii 96801
(808)548-4682

IDAHO
Water Quality Bureau
Division of Environment
Department of Health & Welfare
Statehouse
Boise, Idaho 83720
(208)334-5867

ILLINOIS
Division of Public Water Supplies
Environmental Protection Agency
2200 Churchill Road
Springfield, Illinois 62706
(217)785-8653

INDIANA
Division of Public Water Supply
State Board of Health
1330 West Michigan Street
Indianapolis, Indiana 46206-1964
(317)633-0174

IOWA
Water Supply Section
Surface & Ground Water Protection
  Bureau
Department of Natural Resources
Henry A. Wallace Building
900 East Grand
Des Moines, Iowa 50319
(515)281-8998

KANSAS
Permits and Compliance Section
Bureau of Water Protection
State Dept. of Health and
  Environment
Forbes Field, Building #740
Topeka, Kansas 66620
(913)862-9360

KENTUCKY
Division of Water
Department of Environmental
  Protection
18 Reilly Road, Fort Boone Plaza
Frankfort, Kentucky 40601
(502)564-3410, ext. 543

LOUISIANA
Office of Preventative & Public
  Health Services
Dept. of Health & Human
  Resources
P.O. Box 60630
New Orleans, Louisiana 70160
(504)568-5105

MAINE
Department of Human Services
Bureau of Health
Division of Health Engineering
State House
Augusta, Maine 04333
(207)289-3826

MARYLAND
Division of Water Supplies
Inspection & Compliance Program
Department of Health & Mental
  Hygiene
201 W. Preston Street
Baltimore, Maryland 21201
(301)225-6360

MASSACHUSETTS
Dept. of Environmental Quality
  Engineering
Division of Water Supply
One Winter Street

Boston, Massachusetts 02108
(617)292-5770

MICHIGAN
Water Supplies Services Division
Environmental & Occupational
  Health Services Administration
3500 North Logan Street
P.O. Box 30035
Lansing, Michigan 48909
(517)335-8318

MINNESOTA
Department of Health
Section of Public Water Supplies
717 Delaware Street
Minneapolis, Minnesota 55440
(612)623-5330

MISSISSIPPI
Division of Water Supply
Board of Health
P.O. Box 1700
Jackson, Mississippi 39205
(601)354-6616
or 490-4221

MISSOURI
Public Drinking Water Program
Dept. of Natural Resources
P.O. Box 176
Jefferson City, Missouri 65102
(314)751-3241

MONTANA
Drinking Water Section
Water Quality Bureau
Health & Environmental Services
Cogswell Building, Room A-206
Helena, Montana 59620
(406)444-2406

NEBRASKA
Division of Environmental Health
  & Housing
Department of Health
P.O. Box 95007

Lincoln, Nebraska 68509
(402)471-2541

NEVADA
Public Health Engineering
Department of Human Resources
505 East King Street, Room 103
Carson City, Nevada 89710
(702)885-4750

NEW HAMPSHIRE
Water Supply Division
Water Supply & Pollution Control
  Division
P.O. Box 95, Hazen Drive
Concord, New Hampshire 03301
(603)271-3503

NEW JERSEY
Bureau of Potable Water
Division of Water Resources
Department of Environmental
  Protection
P.O. CN-029
Trenton, New Jersey 06825
(609)984-7945

NEW MEXICO
Water Supply Section
Environmental Improvement
  Division
P.O. Box 968
Santa Fe, New Mexico 87504-0968
(505)827-2778

NEW YORK
Department of Health
Bureau of Public Water Supply
  Protection
Office of Public Health
Corning Tower Building, Room 478
Albany, New York 12237
(518)474-5577

NORTH CAROLINA
Water Supply Branch
Division of Health Services
Department of Human Resources

Bath Building
P.O. Box 2091
Raleigh, North Carolina 27602-2091
(919)733-2321

NORTH DAKOTA
Division of Water Supply &
   Pollution Control
Department of Health
1200 Missouri Avenue
Bismarck, North Dakota 58501
(701)224-2370

OHIO
Office of Public Water Supply
Environmental Protection Agency
361 Broad Street, P.O. Box 1049
Columbus, Ohio 43216
(614)466-8307

OKLAHOMA
Water Facility Engineering Service
Department of Health
P.O. Box 53551
Oklahoma City, Oklahoma 73152
(405)271-5204

OREGON
Drinking Water Systems Section
Department of Human Resources
Health Division
1400 Southwest Fifth Avenue
Portland, Oregon 97201
(503)229-6310

PENNSYLVANIA
Bureau of Water Supply
Department of Environmental
   Resources
P.O. Box 2063
Harrisburg, Pennsylvania 17120
(717)787-9035

PUERTO RICO
Drinking Water Supply
   Supervision Program
Department of Health
P.O. Box 70184

San Juan, Puerto Rico 00936
(809)766-1616

RHODE ISLAND
Department of Health
Division of Water Supply
75 Davis Street, Health Building
Providence, Rhode Island 02908
(401)277-6867

SOUTH CAROLINA
Division of Water Supply
Dept. of Health & Environmental
   Control
2600 Bull Street
Columbia, South Carolina 29201
(803)734-5310

SOUTH DAKOTA
Bureau of Drinking Water
Water & Natural Resources
Joe Foss Building
523 Capitol Avenue East
Pierre, South Dakota 57501
(605)773-3151

TENNESSEE
Department of Health &
   Environment
Division of Water Supply
150 Ninth Avenue North
Nashville, Tennessee 37219-5405
(615)741-6636

TEXAS
Division of Water Hygiene
Department of Health
1100 West 49th Street
Austin, Texas 78756
(512)458-7533

UTAH
Bureau of Public Water Supplies
Department of Health
288 North 1460 West Street
Room 2207
Salt Lake City, Utah 84111
(801)538-6159

VERMONT
Department of Health
Division of Environmental Health
Sanitary Engineering
60 Main Street
P.O. Box 70
Burlington, Vermont 05401
(802)863-7220

VIRGIN ISLANDS
Natural Resources Management
Department of Conservation &
  Cultural Affairs
Government of Virgin Islands
P.O. Box 4340
Charlotte Amalie
St. Thomas, Virgin Islands 00801
(809)774-6420

VIRGINIA
Department of Health
Bureau of Water Supply
Engineering
James Madison Building
109 Governor Street
Richmond, Virginia 23219
(804)786-1766

WASHINGTON
Drinking Water Operations
Mail Stop LD-11
Olympia, Washington 98504
(206)753-5954

WEST VIRGINIA
Drinking Water Division
Office of Environmental Health
  Services
Department of Health
1800 Washington Street, East
Charleston, West Virginia 25305
(304)348-2981

WISCONSIN
Bureau of Water Supply
Department of Natural Resources
P.O. Box 7921
Madison, Wisconsin 53707
(608)267-7651

WYOMING
Water Quality Division
Department of Environmental
  Quality
401 West 19th Street
Cheyenne, Wyoming 82002
(307)777-7781

STATE CERTIFICATION OFFICES FOR DRINKING WATER LABORATORIES

ALABAMA
Department of Public Health
Birmingham Branch Laboratory
P.O. Box 2646
Birmingham, Alabama 35202
(205)933-1388

Department of Public Health
Clinical Laboratory
University Drive
Montgomery, Alabama 36130-0001
(205)277-8660

Water Supply Branch
Dept. of Environmental
  Management
1751 Federal Drive
Montgomery, Alabama 36109
(205)271-7773

ALASKA
Department of Environmental
  Conservation
Douglas Laboratory Facility
750 St. Ann's Avenue

Douglas, Alaska 99824
(907)364-2165

ARIZONA
Department of Health Services
Laboratory Licensure Office
1520 West Adams Street
Phoenix, Arizona 85007
(602)255-1188

ARKANSAS
Microbiological Branch
Division of Public Health
  Laboratories
4815 West Markham
Little Rock, Arkansas 72205-3867
(501)661-2217

CALIFORNIA
Department of Health Services
Southern California Laboratory
  Section
1449 Temple Street
Suite 101
Los Angeles, California 90026
(213)620-3376

COLORADO
Department of Health
4210 East 11th Avenue
Denver, Colorado 80220
(303)331-4545

CONNECTICUT
Laboratory Division
Department of Health
Hartford, Connecticut 06115
(203)566-3896

DELAWARE
Public Health Administrator/
  Director of Laboratories
Division of Public Health
P.O. Box 618
Dover, Delaware 19903
(302)736-4714

FLORIDA
Office of Laboratory Services
Dept. of Health & Rehabilitative
  Services
P.O. Box 210
Jacksonville, Florida 32231
(407)359-6457

Radiological Health Laboratory
P.O. Box 15490
Orlando, Florida 32858
(407)299-0581

GEORGIA
Environmental Protection Division
Department of Natural Resources
Floyd Towers East
205 Butler Street S.E.
Atlanta, Georgia 30334
(404)656-4807

GUAM
Monitoring Services Division
Environmental Protection Agency
Government of Guam
P.O. Box 2999
Agana, Guam 96910
(671)646-7916

HAWAII
Department of Health
P.O. Box 3378
Honolulu, Hawaii 96801
(808)548-6345
or 548-6325

IDAHO
Bureau of Laboratories
2220 Old Penitentiary Road
Boise, Idaho 83702
(208)334-2235

ILLINOIS
Department of Public Health
825 North Rutlidge
Springfield, Illinois 62702
(217)782-6562, ext. 29

Division of Laboratories
Environmental Protection Agency
2200 Churchill Road
Springfield, Illinois 62706
(217)782-6455

INDIANA
Safe Drinking Water Branch
US-EPA—Region V
230 South Dearborn Street
Chicago, Illinois 60604
(312)886-5251

Quality Assurance Office
US-EPA—Region V
(same address as above)
(312)353-3114

IOWA
Surface and Ground Water
   Protection Bureau
Department of Natural Resources
Henry A. Wallace Building
900 East Grand
Des Moines, Iowa 50319
(515)281-8869

KANSAS
Environmental Laboratory
   Certification Officer
Division of Laboratories and
   Research
Department of Health &
   Environment
Forbes Field, Building 740
Topeka, Kansas 66620
(913)296-1639

KENTUCKY
Division of Water
Department of Environmental
   Protection
18 Reilly Road, Fort Boone Plaza
Frankfort, Kentucky 40601
(502)564-3410

Division of Environmental Services
(same address as above)
(502)564-2150

LOUISIANA
Division of Laboratory Services
Department of Health & Human
   Services
325 Loyola Avenue
New Orleans, Louisiana 70112
(504)568-5375

MAINE
Public Health Laboratory
State House
Augusta, Maine 04333
(207)289-2727

MARYLAND
Food, Water & Shellfish Micro
   Section
Department of Health & Hygiene
201 W. Preston Street
Baltimore, Maryland 21201
(301)225-6150

MASSACHUSETTS
Lawrence Experiment Station
Department of Environmental
   Quality Engineering
37 Shattuck Street
Lawrence Massachusetts 01843
(617)682-5237

MICHIGAN
Division of Public Water Supply
Department of Public Health
3500 North Logan Street
Lansing, Michigan 48909
(517)335-8279

MINNESOTA
Department of Health
Section of Analytical Services
717 Delaware Street, S.E.
Minneapolis, Minnesota 55440
(612)623-5304

MISSISSIPPI
Department of Health
Public Health Laboratory
P.O. Box 1700

Jackson, Mississippi 39216
(601)960-7582

MISSOURI
Public Drinking Water Program
Department of Natural Resources
P.O. Box 176
Jefferson City, Missouri 65102
(314)751-5331

MONTANA
Department of Health &
  Environmental Sciences
Cogswell Building
Helena, Montana 59601
(406)444-2642

NEBRASKA
Division of Laboratories
Department of Health
P.O. Box 2755
Lincoln, Nebraska 68509
(402)471-2122

NEVADA
Bureau of Laboratories & Research
State Health Department
1660 North Virginia Street
Reno, Nevada 89503
(702)789-0335

NEW HAMPSHIRE
Department of Environmental
  Services Laboratory
6 Hazen Drive
Concord, New Hampshire 03301
(603)271-3445

NEW JERSEY
Office of Quality Assurance
Department of Environmental
  Protection
P.O. Box CN-402
Trenton, New Jersey 08625
(609)292-3950

NEW MEXICO
Community Services Bureau

Environmental Improvement
  Division
Health & Environmental
  Department
P.O. Box 968
Santa Fe, New Mexico 87504-0968
(505)827-2793

NEW YORK
Environmental Lab Approval
  Program
Center for Laboratories and
  Research
Department of Health
Empire State Plaza, Tower Building
Albany, New York 12201
(518)474-8519

NORTH CAROLINA
Division of Health Services
Department of Human Resources
P.O. Box 28047
Raleigh, North Carolina 27611
(919)733-7308

NORTH DAKOTA
Laboratory Services Section
Division of Chemistry
P.O. Box 937
Bismarck, North Dakota 58502
(701)224-6174

OHIO
Public Water Supply Office
State Environmental Agency
P.O. Box 1049
361 East Broad Street
Columbus, Ohio 43215
(614)481-7025

OKLAHOMA
State Environmental Laboratory
  Service
State Dept. of Health
P.O. Box 24106
Oklahoma City, Oklahoma 73124
(405)271-5240

OREGON
Certification Coordinator
Public Health Laboratory
1717 S.W. Tenth Avenue
Portland, Oregon 97201
(503)229-5882

PENNSYLVANIA
Department of Environmental
  Resources
P.O. Box 1467
Harrisburg, Pennsylvania 17120
(717)787-4669

PUERTO RICO
Quality Assurance Office
Department of Health
Call Box 70184
San Juan, Puerto Rico 00936
(809)767-1616

RHODE ISLAND
Department of Health
50 Orms Street
Providence, Rhode Island 02904
(401)274-1011

SOUTH CAROLINA
Dept. of Health and Environmental
  Control
Laboratory Certification
P.O. Box 72
State Park, South Carolina 29147
(803)737-7025

SOUTH DAKOTA
Office of Drinking Water
Dept. of Water and Natural
  Resources
Joe Foss Building
523 East Capitol Avenue
Pierre, South Dakota 57501
(605)773-3754

Department of Health Laboratory
Laboratory Building
(same address as above)
(605)773-3368

TENNESSEE
Department of Health &
  Environment
630 Ben Allan Road
Nashville, Tennessee 37219-5402
(615)262-6354
or 6356 or 6358

TEXAS
Environmental Microbiology
  Section
Department of Health
1100 West 49th Street
Austin, Texas 78756-3194
(512)458-7580
or 7585

UTAH
State Health Laboratory
44 Medical Drive
Salt Lake City, Utah 84113
(801)522-6131

VERMONT
Department of Health
Public Health Laboratory
115 Colchester Street
Burlington, Vermont 05401
(802)863-7335

VIRGINIA
Division of Consolidated
  Laboratory Services
One North 14th Street
Richmond, Virginia 23219
(804)786-7905

VIRGIN ISLANDS
Quality Assurance Office
Dept. of Planning & Natural
  Resources
P.O. Box 4399
Charlotte Amalie
St. Thomas, Virgin Islands 00801
(809)774-3320

WASHINGTON
Office of Licensing and Certification

1610 N.E. 150th Street
Seattle, Washington 98155
(206)361-2812

WEST VIRGINIA
Clinical Laboratory Services
  Division
State Health Department
167 11th Avenue
South Charleston, West Virginia
  25303
(304)348-3530

Environmental Laboratory
  Services Division
Office of Laboratory Services
State Health Department
1511 11th Avenue
South Charleston, West Virginia
  25303
(304)348-0197

Industrial Hygiene & Radiological
  Health Division
State Health Department

(same address as above)
(304)348-3526

WISCONSIN
Department of Health &
  Social Services
Laboratory Certification Section
P.O. Box 309
Madison, Wisconsin 53701
(608)266-5753

Public Water Supply Section
Department of Natural Resources
101 South Webster
P.O. Box 7921
Madison, Wisconsin 53707
(608)267-7633

WYOMING
Environmental Services Division
US EPA-Region VIII
P.O. Box 25366
Denver, Colorado 80225
(303)236-5073

5

CHLORDANE AND THE PESTICIDES

In September 1986, an elderly couple in Virginia died within several days of each other. They had had their home fumigated with sulfuryl fluoride (a fumigant commonly used commercially) to get rid of termites. They went home when the exterminator said it was safe to return. Both became ill within 24 hours. The husband died the next day. His wife died several days after that. Cause of death: exposure to a highly toxic chemical.

This tragedy was highly unusual. However, it dramatically points out the dangers of pesticides. *They can be deadly*, especially if the directions for their use are not followed precisely.

A BRIEF HISTORY OF PESTICIDE USE

Most of the pesticides in use today were developed after the Second World War, during which many new chemicals were introduced for military purposes. Before then, pesticides were rarely used. Their use has increased steadily since. In 1985, over one billion pounds of pesticides were used in the United States. Today, around 600 chemicals are used in over 45,000 pesticide products. Research has resulted in pesticides that are both more efficient and more effective.

Pesticides have been regulated by the federal government since the late '40s. In 1947 the Federal Insecticide, Fungicide, and Rodenticide Act (FIFRA) was passed. It provided a legislative framework for regulation. It governs the registration, or licensing, of pesticide products. Until 1970 the Department of Agriculture was responsible for regulating pesticides. In 1970, the Environmental Protection Agency (EPA) was created and took over that responsibility. A set of amendments known collectively as the Federal Environmental Pesticide Control Act of 1972 extended the authority of FIFRA.

Under the current regulations, all pesticides sold in the United States must be EPA approved. That approval must appear on the label of the container along with, among other things, an EPA registration number and the purpose for which the pesticide may be used.

The Federal, Food, Drug and Cosmetic Act (FFDCA) also plays a regulatory role. It governs pesticide residue levels in food or feed crops sold in the United States.

WHAT PESTICIDES ARE USED FOR

Pesticides are used to eliminate or, to put it more realistically, control pests that can damage the structure of your home, lawn or garden, or crops that are being farmed.

A pest is any plant, animal or microorganism that can cause an economic loss, an illness or is just plain bothersome. Some of the more common and well known pests are termites, cockroaches, fleas, rodents, algae. Some may be more of a nuisance than anything else while others can be quite hazardous. "Cide" comes from Latin and means "killer." Thus a pesticide is a killer of pests.

Pesticides include insecticides, herbicides, fungicides, rodenticides, disinfectants, termiticides and plant-growth regulators. Many pesticides are considered harmless, especially if directions for their use are followed precisely. (Following directions precisely cannot be stressed enough.) The Virginia couple who died after exposure to sulfuryl fluoride (SF) is an example of what can happen if all the directions for the application of a pesticide are not followed exactly. Although the workers did ventilate the home after using the pesticide, they failed to test for residual levels of the SF in the air. If they had, they would have found that the levels were still too high, and the couple would have been told not to return.

THE PROBLEM

When pesticides were first developed they were viewed as miraculous. Pesticides could control pests; prevent disease; increase crop yields on farms. It was believed that groundwater was protected from pesticide contamination by layers of soil and rock; that pesticides would be absorbed by, and bound to, soil until they degraded. Only later did some of the problems of the wonder solution come to light.

In 1979, two pesticide chemicals were found in groundwater in several states. As of 1987, at least 17 pesticides had been detected in groundwater in 23 states.

It has been established that some of the early pesticides, like DDT, can remain in the environment almost indefinitely. They move up through the food chain, from plant to animal to, eventually, humans. DDT has been banned since 1971.

In November of 1987, FIFRA issued a formal notice of intent to cancel and deny all registrations of pesticides containing the highly toxic chemical dinoseb. Its reasons were that dinoseb could cause birth defects in children whose mothers were exposed during pregnancy. It could cause sterility or decreased fertility in men, acute toxic poisoning or other potential adverse health effects.

There is still a lot that is not known about the health hazards of pesticides. However, more data is coming in regularly. In 1986, the National Caner Institute issued a report on a study of farmers in Kansas exposed to the chemical 2,4-D, a popular herbicide in agriculture and home lawn care products. The study showed that the exposed farmers were more likely to develop a certain type of cancer than those who were not exposed.

PRACTICING PREVENTION—AVOIDING THE NEED FOR PESTICIDES

It is said that "an ounce of prevention is worth a pound of cure." Maybe that ounce of prevention is worth two or three pounds of pesticide. If you do not already have termites, or another pest problem, it is possible to avoid using messy, and possibly hazardous, pesticides by taking steps to increase the likelihood of staying pest-free.

First of all, you want to be a very inhospitable host and make your home as uninviting to household pests as possible. Most of these measures are just common sense, but a little reminder never hurts, so here they are:

Water
All pests, vertebrate or invertebrate, need water to survive. Eliminate as many of their sources as possible. Fix plumbing that leaks and do not let water accumulate anywhere in your home, for example, in dishes sitting in a sink or plants sitting in wet trays.

Food
As with water, pests find food essential to their good health and overall survival. Make it inaccessible! Store food in sealed glass or plastic

containers. If you have a pet, don't leave the food out for an extended period of time. Put any garbage, especially food scraps, in a tightly covered, heavy-gauge garbage can.

Pest Shelters

Make a pest homeless; send him out to find other shelter. Caulk those cracks and crevices that only the smallest, and most annoying, critters can get through. Remove piles of wood from under or around your home to avoid attracting termites. Remove and destroy diseased plants, tree prunings or fallen fruit that might harbor pests.

Breeding Sites

Pet manure attracts flies; litter encourages rodents; and mosquitoes just love standing water for breeding.

Besides eliminating all the comforts of home that *pests love and need*, you also want to make your plants, both inside and out, as healthy and resistant to pests as possible. There are a number of simple steps to take:

- Plant at the best time of the year for the particular plant.
- Use mulch to stifle weed growth and maintain even soil temperature and moisture.
- Check in a gardening book or consult your local nursery for seeds or plants that are resistant to disease.

IS THERE A PROBLEM?

Despite your precautions, it may become obvious that you have a pest problem. You notice sawdust under the porch railing. A closer examination reveals damage to the wood. Suddenly the vegetables in your garden are no longer flourishing and look diseased. While the existence of a problem may be obvious, its cause may not be. For example, the problems you're having in your flowerbed or vegetable garden may not be caused by an infestation of insects. Instead, insufficient nutrients in the soil may be to blame.

If you are unable to determine the cause of the problem, or how widespread it is, or both, there are a number of different things you can do. A reference book on insects or gardening may help you identify the specific bug or disease that could be causing the problem. You can also call your local agricultural extension agent, a pesticide dealer or your state agency. (See end of chapter for state phone numbers.)

Once you've determined the extent of your problem, the next question is what to do about it. There are a number of factors that enter into that decision, including the expense of treatment, the time involved, and the possible risks associated with some exposure to pesticides. These considerations must be weighed against the potential damage the problem may cause. You may decide that you can put up with a less than perfect lawn and some possible glaring looks from your neighbors. Of course there are some problems that leave you no choice—they must be dealt with. (Termite infestation is the most obvious example.)

The extent of the problem, and its cause, will determine the appropriate response.

NON-TOXIC PEST ELIMINATION

There are some steps you can take that require no pesticides at all. You may use these methods alone or in combination with a pesticide.

Picking weeds by hand can be time consuming and hard work, but it will eliminate the need for a chemical weed killer, or at least the amount you'll have to use. The only precautions you'll have to take are wearing a hat and using some kind of protection from the sun.

Traps can be set for mice and other rodents, larger pests such as squirrels and raccoons, as well as for some insects. If you are interested in "humane" traps tell your hardware store your concerns. You can also call the ASPCA or Humane Society for information on traps.

Screens can be very effective in keeping flies, wasps and mosquitoes out of the house. Make sure the screens have no holes. Tears or holes are easy to repair, and the screens usually don't have to be replaced, unless you are doing it for cosmetic reasons. Chimneys should always be covered with a chimney cap to keep larger pests, such as squirrels and raccoons, from making a visit. Check regularly to make sure it's in place. Never leave food out in the open. Even if garbage is in a "tamper-proof" can, it should be kept in an enclosed area, like a garage.

If these methods are not practical, appropriate or appealing, you may have to use some kind of pesticide. Even so, a natural, healthy alternative may exist.

Biological pesticides, which do not use chemicals, can be used. This is a relatively new field, and one that is developing rapidly. Among the biological pesticides available are predators such as purple martins, praying mantises and lady bugs; parasites; and some pathogens such as bacteria, viruses and other organisms like milky spore disease. Many of these pesticides are now on the market. Fred Definis, the marketing director for Safer, Inc., a large company that has been manufacturing biological pesticides since 1976, notes that usage is increasing as the EPA bans more chemicals and as consumers become more concerned about their possible health hazards and more aware of the existence of this alternative. Safer's products are now available throughout the United States. You'll find them in hardware and gardening stores and home centers. Safers is at 60 William Street, in Wellesley, Massachusetts 02181.

Biological pesticides generally cost as much as the chemical pesticides. Some of them may not have immediate results, and some of them have a shorter residual effect, so they have to be applied more frequently. On the plus side, they do not cause the pest population to become pesticide-resistant as often happens with chemical pesticides, and they can be used without safeguards because they pose virtually no threat to human health or the environment.

At the time of publication, there was no effective biological treatment for termites, but efforts were underway to create one.

THE TRADITIONAL PESTICIDES

Choosing the best pesticide for your specific problem is very important. You first want to determine, if possible, that neither you nor any member of your family is allergic or sensitive to any of the chemicals in a particular pesticide. After you've checked that out, you'll want to find the most efficient and least toxic product. There are thousands of pesticides on the market from which to choose. You'll probably find the largest selection in a gardening/farm supply store or hardware store.

First find the pesticides that deal with your problem. Read the labels carefully. Will the product affect wildlife that you don't want to harm? Is it toxic to pets? Are any of the chemicals listed suspected of causing any health problems? The label will also tell you the specific pest the product eliminates and the specific area where the product should be used (e.g., lawns, roses, swimming pools etc.). Be sure the place where you plan to use the pesticide is listed. If your pest problem is severe and you will be using a large amount of a pesticide, you may find it helpful to speak with a pesticides dealer or your state pesticides agency (see listing at the end of this chapter) before making a decision on treatment.

Pesticides can be categorized in a number of different ways. Broad spectrum pesticides are effective against a wide range of pests. Selective pesticides are just that, selective. They are made to control specific pests. Pesticides also come in a variety of forms and are applied in different ways. Following are some of the more common types:

- **Aerosols:** These contain one or more active ingredients and a solvent. They are ready for immediate use without further preparation.
- **Solutions:** Solutions are concentrated. They contain the active ingredient and one or more additives. They must be mixed with water.
- **Dusts:** Dusts contain active ingredients plus a very fine, dry, inert carrier such as clay, talc or volcanic ash. Dusts are ready for immediate use and are applied dry.
- **Granulars:** These are similar to dusts but with larger and heavier particles for broader applications.
- **Baits:** Baits are active ingredients that are mixed with foods or other substances to attract the pest.
- **Wettable Powders** These powders are finely ground formulations that can also be used as dusts. They are generally mixed with water for spray application.

READING THE LABEL: DIRECTIONS/PRECAUTIONS

The importance of reading, and *following precisely*, the directions on the label cannot be stressed enough.

According to a survey done by the EPA in the late '70s, nine out of 10 households in the United States used pesticides. Of those people surveyed, less than 50% read the labels for information on how to use the pesticide—and only 9% used the pesticide with caution. Few sought additional information on pesticides from outside sources.

Reading that label can be a rather laborious task. Typically it's chock full of information, much of it in fine print, but it provides the essential EPA registration number; the active ingredients; the directions; and precautionary statements. Incorrect use of a pesticide can decrease its effectiveness. More important, incorrect use can be unhealthy. Pesticides are poisons. They are designed to kill. When using them, you want to be as cautious as possible so as to pose the minimal health threat to you, your family and your pets.

You should read the label not only before you buy the product, but also right before use. Do not trust your memory. There is too much at stake. Following is a brief explanation of the information contained on the label of a pesticide.

EPA Registration Number
The EPA registration number means the pesticide has been approved by the EPA for sale in the United States. All pesticides sold in the United States must have this approval.

Directions for Use

The directions tell you how to use the pesticide so that it does what it is supposed to do. Not following the directions and safety precautions is against the law. Granted, the chances of your being arrested and charged with a crime for incorrectly using a bug spray in your kitchen are just about nil, but it's important to remember that those directions are there to limit, as much as possible, any health risk of using a powerful chemical that is potentially harmful.

Ingredients

The pesticide contains active ingredients and inert ingredients. The active ingredients are those that kill, or otherwise control, the pests. Pesticides are regulated primarily on the basis of active ingredients. The inert ingredients are the other ingredients such as solvents carriers that are not active against the pests. However, inert ingredients are not necessarily innocuous. Again, it cannot be repeated often enough: Read the directions carefully and follow them precisely.

Precautionary Statements

This information will tell you when and how the pesticide could be harmful; what immediate action to take if there is the possibility of harm (e.g., if your child swallows some of the pesticide, the bottle breaks etc.); and how to dispose of the pesticide or empty container that remains. You'll get an immediate indication of how hazardous the pesticide is by seeing one of the following three words on the label:

Danger = highly poisonous
Warning = moderately poisonous
Caution = least hazardous

These words tell you how poisonous a pesticide is if swallowed, inhaled or absorbed through the skin.

First aid

The label will provide you with information on what steps to take in case some of the pesticide is swallowed, inhaled or touches your skin.

Restricted

This means the pesticide warrants special handling because of its toxicity. Some, or all of its use may be restricted. *Restricted-use pesticides may be applied only by trained, certified applicators, or those under their direct supervision.* Generally there is no "enforcement." Most stores aren't going to bother to question someone. However, it is in your own best interest not to buy a restricted pesticide.

DETERMINING THE AMOUNT OF PESTICIDE

If the pesticide you are using is concentrated, or in powder form, and must be mixed with liquid, you must determine how much to use. The label will give you some information, but as with so much of the other information on the label, you'll generally get very basic guides. You do not want to mix up more than you need because you then have a storage or disposal problem. It's not a good idea to store any pesticide that you have mixed. You also do not want to use more than is called for in the directions. More is not better and will not be any more effective. It can be harmful to you and your family.

When you are mixing the pesticide, do it in a well ventilated area. If possible, mix it outside. Keep children and pets away. If a small amount spills, cover with kitty litter, sawdust or vermiculite and sweep into a plastic bag. Close it tightly and throw out with the rest of the trash.

If the directions are for mixing up a gallon of the pesticide to cover a 5,000-cubic-foot area, and your area is smaller, you'll have to prepare and use a lesser amount. If the directions are only for a gallon and you know you need only a quart, again, you'll have to adjust for that. Following is a listing of equivalents which should help you do that:

1 gallon (gal.)	=	128 fluid ounces (fl. oz.)
	=	4 quarts (qt.)
	=	8 pints (pt.)
	=	16 cups
1 quart	=	32 fl. oz.
	=	2 pt.
	=	4 cups
1 pint	=	16 fl. oz.
	=	2 cups
1 cup	=	8 fl. oz.
1 tablespoon (tbsp.)	=	1/2 fl. oz.
	=	3 teaspoons (tsp.)
1 teaspoon	=	1/6 fl. oz.

When you are measuring the concentrated pesticide always use a level teaspoon, tablespoon or cup. Any measuring tool you use, whether it's a measuring cup or spoon, should not be used in food preparation. The same goes for the container in which the pesticide is prepared.

The following conversions should help you figure out how much pesticide you need for your particular area.

Units specified on pesticide label per gallon water		Units per quart water	Units per pint water	
8	=	2	1	
16	=	4	2	
32	=	8	4	
128	=	32	16	

Units specified on pesticide label per 1,000 sq.ft.		Units per 20,000 sq. ft.	Units per 10,000 sq. ft.	Units per 500 sq. ft.
1	=	20	10	1/2
2	=	40	20	1
5	=	100	50	2½
10	=	200	100	5

Aerosol cans specified on label per 10,000 cu.ft		Cans per 20,000 cu. ft.	Cans per 10,000 cu. ft.	Cans per 5,000 cu. ft.
1	=	2	1	Don't use
1	=	4	2	1
1	=	8	4	2

USING THE PESTICIDE

You've identified the problem and chosen the best pesticide. Now it is time to put it to work. But before you hit the spray button, take the following safety measures:

• Make sure you know what steps to take in case of an accidental poisoning.
• Make sure children and pets are out of the area to be treated. Remove toys from the area. Never place rodent or insect bait where small children or pets can reach them.
• If you are treating kitchen cabinets, remove all food, dishes, pots and pans and don't let pesticides get on the surfaces. Wait until shelves dry before putting items back.
• Wear whatever protective clothing is recommended. That could be long sleeves or pants, impervious gloves, vinyl or rubber footwear (not canvas or leather, which is permeable), hat, safety goggles and a

respirator. Protective clothing is usually available at a home building supply store.

- If using the pesticide inside, have as much ventilation as possible. Open windows. Stay away from the treated area for at least as long as advised on the label.
- If you're using a spray, remove birds and pets and cover aquariums and fish bowls. Most surface sprays should be applied only to limited areas. Entire walls, floors or ceilings should not be sprayed.
- When spraying or applying dust outside, cover fish ponds and avoid applying pesticides near wells. Close the windows of your home and car if they are anywhere in the line of fire. Avoid over-application when treating your lawn, shrubs or garden. Runoff or seepage from excess pesticides may contaminate water supplies or leave harmful residues on homegrown produce, or both. Avoid non-target or blooming plants, especially if you see honeybees or other pollinating insects around them. Avoid bird nests when spraying trees. Do not spray or dust outside on a windy day.
- Never smoke while applying pesticides. You could carry traces of the pesticides from your hand to your mouth. Also, some products are flammable.
- When you've finished, shower and shampoo thoroughly. Wash the clothing that you wore separately from the family laundry. Rinse boots and shoes to avoid tracking chemicals inside.
- In order to remove any residues, rinse three times any tools or equipment used in the application.

STORING THE PESTICIDE

Ideally, you should not store any pesticides. Once opened a pesticide will degrade over time. Containers, no matter how tightly sealed, can leak. Labels telling what is in the container as well as very important directions for use can come off. And the longer it is around the more opportunity there is for a child to stumble across it, no matter how carefully it's been stored. Try to buy only enough pesticide for the season. Mix only as much as you are going to use.

If you must store pesticides, put them in areas inaccessible to children and pets. A locked cabinet in a well-ventilated utility area is best. Never put pesticides in soda bottles or containers that children may associate with something to eat or drink. Always refasten child-proof covers properly.

Never put pesticides in cabinets with, or near food, medical supplies or cleaning materials.

Store flammable liquids outside living quarters and away from any area where they might be ignited. Do not store them in an area that could get flooded, or in an open place where they could spill or leak into the environment.

Always store pesticides in their original containers, complete with labels that list ingredients, directions for use and antidotes in case of accidental poisoning. Apply transparent tape over the label to keep it readable. If you have any doubt about what's in a container, get rid of it.

DISPOSING OF THE LEFTOVERS

Follow the directions for disposal on the container of the pesticide. If you have any doubts about disposing of the pesticides you have, contact your local health department.

If the container you're getting rid of still contains some of the pesticide, make sure the cap is on securely. Wrap it in several layers of newspaper and tie or tape it. Put it in a covered trash container for routine pickup. Dry pesticides should also be wrapped in newspaper, or you can place the container in a tight carton or bag and tape or tie it closed, then put it in a covered trash container for pickup. Treated this way, small quantities of the pesticide pose no threat to trash collectors or to the environment. If the container is empty, rinse it out three times, then punch holes in the container, so that it can't be used again, and discard. In a properly operated landfill, the pesticides will be sufficiently diluted and contained so that any hazardous effects will be eliminated.

Pesticide boxes or sacks should not be burned outside, or in apartment incinerators. Burning the container could cause an explosion or release toxic fumes or gasses.

Do not pour leftover pesticides down the sink or into the toilet. Chemicals in the pesticide could interfere with the operation of septic tanks or pollute waterways. Many wastewater treatment systems cannot remove all pesticide residues.

CHLORDANE AND TERMITICIDES

Most often it is the discovery of termites that sends homeowners into a panic. And well it should. Termites can virtually destroy your home as they eat their way through wood beams, fences, windowsills, floors, exteriors—anything made of wood!

Termiticides are pesticides used to eliminate termites. Chlordane is the most well known and widely used. The other organic chemicals in the chlorinated cyclodienes family used as termiticides are heptachlor, aldrin and dieldrin. For the sake of simplicity, cyclodienes will refer to all four, unless otherwise noted.

Chlordane was registered as a pesticide in this country in 1948. Heptachlor, aldrin and dieldrin were registered over the next several years. These pesticides were used to control termites and other insects, in agriculture, crab grass and around the home.

It had been thought that when cyclodienes were applied correctly, the residents in the home would not suffer harmful exposure from the pesticide. New studies in 1987 revealed that *even with proper treatment*, below ground or subterranean termite control could result in low levels of cyclodienes in the air inside the home. They have great staying power in the soil (one reason why they're so effective) and in the air and have been found in the soil of areas treated 30 or more years earlier. Monitoring studies received by the EPA, of homes properly treated with chlordane, showed detectable levels of chlordane one year later in approximately 90% of the homes.

In 1983 the EPA restricted the use of the four cyclodienes for nearly everything, with the main exception of subterranean termite control. The EPA was concerned that long-term exposure to the chemicals could result in damage to the liver and nervous system. Laboratory animals exposed to the chemicals for extended periods of time developed tumors, and the EPA views cyclodienes as probable human carcinogens. When the EPA limited their use, there was no other effective chemical for controlling termites available. That is no longer the case.

Production of aldrin and dieldrin in the United States stopped in the 1970s. In 1985, product manufacturers stopped importing these termiticides. In August of 1987, the EPA announced that it was proceeding to cancel all registrations of aldrin and dieldrin.

At the same time, the EPA announced that it had reached an agreement with Velsicol Chemical Company, the largest manufacturer of chlordane and heptachlor, to immediately stop its sale and distribution of chlordane and heptachlor. In October 1987 the EPA established some strict requirements for the sale, distribution and use of Velsicol chlordane and heptachlor products. As of April 1988 the distribution and sale of chlordane and heptachlor manufactured by Velsicol was prohibited. However, if a professional still has it in stock, it can be used provided the customer gives approval. It may be applied only by certified applicators, in perimeter areas around homes or other buildings, using only low-pressure application techniques. Applications at construction sites are also permitted, with some additional restrictions.

Chlordane/heptachlor products marketed by other manufacturers may continue to be sold and used. Sound confusing? Yes, it is! And no doubt there will be other changes in the future as more studies are completed. The bottom line is, if you have a termite problem make sure you have it treated by a reputable, competent and certified company.

APPLYING A TERMITICIDE

The extermination of termites is much more complicated and hazardous than exterminating other household pests and requires the services of a professional. Greater quantities of the chemicals are needed, along with special equipment and training. Understanding termite behavior as well as understanding how a house is built are also necessary for the most successful treatment.

The termiticide works by acting as a barrier between the termites in the soil and the wood. Following are the different ways to apply the termiticide:

- A trench can be dug around the house and the termiticide poured into the trench.
- The termiticide can be "injected" into the soil around the house or in the inside perimeter of a crawl space.
- Holes can be drilled into the foundation or slab of the building. The termiticide is then injected into the holes.
- Holes can be drilled into hollow-block walls. The termiticide can be injected into those holes and then allowed to seep down through the hollow areas in the blocks.

TERMITICIDE HAZARDS

In the spring of 1984, Debbie Schick discovered that her house was infested with termites. She called in an exterminating company. Chlordane was used to get rid of the termites. Shortly after the extermination, Debbie, her husband and their three young sons came down with flu-like symptoms—headaches, nausea. One month later, tests revealed chlordane levels in the blood of all five family members. The family moved out of their home in April. Repair work on the house was halted when contractors said it could cost $100,000 to remove the chlordane—and there could be no guarantee that all of it would be removed. A year later Debbie had still not completely recovered.

The health risk associated with exposure to a termiticide is a result of several factors, including the concentration of the vapor, length of time of exposure and how chemically sensitive the individual is. Some of the symptoms associated with exposure to high levels of termiticides include headaches, dizziness, muscle twitching, weakness, tingling sensations and nausea. If you have these symptoms you should see a doctor (though they can also be an indicator of many other illnesses).

Even if the termiticide is applied properly, with all the necessary precautions taken, vapors can still get into the house through cracks in concrete floors and walls, floor drains, sumps, joints, cracks in hollow block walls, and air ducts (heating, cooling and ventilation). Of course, if the termiticide is improperly applied—by careless injection directly into the living space of a house or into air ducts located in, or below, the slab—there is a greater likelihood of vapors permeating the house, and in greater concentration. Surface-spraying the soil or the wood in a crawl space is illegal in most states. *Any indoor surface spraying is an improper application.*

Many termiticides are banned from any use in plenum construction, where air is circulated without ductwork through an open area below the house. This allows vapors to be drawn out of the soil and into the house.

CHOOSING A PEST CONTROL COMPANY

If your pest problem is severe, you may have to call in an exterminating company for the termites, roaches, mice, wasps or other annoying pests in your home. The following guidelines apply to any pest control company you call—whether for termites or other pests.

Finding an Exterminator
First check with friends in the area. They may have used someone they "swear by"; and if you consider their judgment credible, that may be the first, and only, company you'll have to call! If no one you know can recommend a pest control company, you may have to consult the yellow pages. Call the Better Business Bureau or the local consumer office or both and ask if they've had any information, or complaints, on the particular company. (See also the state pesticide agencies at the end of the chapter.) Ask the company for references and call them. Ask the previous customers how satisfied they were with the service. Did the exterminator come when he or she said they would? Were the results satisfactory? Did he or she stick to the price quoted?

Checking Credentials
Find out if the company has a license. Licenses are not required in all states, but in the state where a license is required, it is illegal to do business without one. The license requirements will vary from state to

state. In some cases, cities will also license an exterminating company. Check with the state pesticide agency or your local health department, or both, to see if a license is required; what qualifications are needed to get the license; how often it is renewed; and whether renewing the license is a mere formality.

Insurance

Found out if the company has insurance, and if so, what kind. Contractors' general liability insurance, including insurance for sudden and accidental pollution, gives you some protection should there be an accident when the pesticide is being applied. Workers' compensation insurance can protect you if an employee of the company is hurt while working in your home. Not many states require insurance, but there are good reasons for making it a priority in choosing a pest control company.

Guarantee

Find out what kind of guarantee the company will give you. Make sure any guarantee is in writing. Find out how long it is in effect and if there are any circumstances when the guarantee would not apply.

Treatment proposal

When you have chosen a company, its representatives will come to your home, determine the extent of the problem and describe, in detail, what they will do to solve it. The company should tell you what pesticide will be used and explain any hazards associated with that particular pesticide. You should also be told how long the work will take; what actions, if any, you should take before or during the application; whether you are required to leave your home during the application; and how soon after completion you can return. And last, but not least, you want an estimate, in writing. As with anything you are purchasing, whether it's a product or service, you may want to get several estimates. A fixed price, of course, is better.

CLEARING THE AIR

With the use of any pesticide inside the home, ventilation is important. Whenever possible open windows to allow fresh air in. Use fans to mix the air. If you have a crawl space, clear or add vents and install a fan to vent crawl space air outside.

Use grout, caulk or sealant to seal those areas that are in direct contact with the treated soil. Fill cracks in the basement, ground floors, walls, and openings around pipes, drains and sumps. Check those areas regularly for signs of new cracks or broken seals, since houses settle over time.

Install a system that enables appliances such as clothes dryers and furnaces to use outside air, rather than air inside the house, to avoid depressurization. When depressurization occurs termiticide vapors (and other pollutants as well) can be drawn into the house through the walls, floors and basement.

Use duct tape to seal openings and joints in the ducts in your crawl space or basement.

The importance of following the directions precisely when using a pesticide cannot be stressed enough. Pesticides can be very useful in ridding your home of pests. But their benefits disappear quickly if their use results in illness or death through carelessness.

EPA REGIONAL OFFICES FOR PESTICIDES

ALABAMA—4	KENTUCKY—4	OHIO—5
ALASKA—10	LOUISIANA—6	OKLAHOMA—6
ARIZONA—9	MAINE—1	OREGON—10
ARKANSAS—6	MARYLAND—3	PENNSYLVANIA—3
CALIFORNIA—9	MASSACHUSETTS—1	PUERTO RICO—2
COLORADO—8	MICHIGAN—5	RHODE ISLAND—1
CONNECTICUT—1	MINNESOTA—5	SOUTH
DELAWARE—3	MISSISSIPPI—4	CAROLINA—4
DISTRICT OF	MISSOURI—7	SOUTH DAKOTA—8
COLUMBIA—3	MONTANA—8	TENNESSEE—4
FLORIDA—4	NEBRASKA—7	TEXAS—6
GEORGIA—4	NEVADA—9	UTAH—8
GUAM—9	NEW HAMPSHIRE—1	VERMONT—1
HAWAII—9	NEW JERSEY—2	VIRGINIA—3
IDAHO—10	NEW MEXICO—6	VIRGIN ISLANDS—2
ILLINOIS—5	NEW YORK—2	WASHINGTON—10
INDIANA—5	NORTH	WEST VIRGINIA—3
IOWA—7	CAROLINA—4	WISCONSIN—5
KANSAS—7	NORTH DAKOTA—8	WYOMING—8

REGION 1
Air Management Division
JFK Federal Building
Room 2311-AAA
Boston, Massachusetts 02224
(617)223-2226

REGION 2
Pesticides & Toxic Substances
Woodbridge Avenue
Building 209
Edison, New Jersey 08837
(201)321-6768

REGION 3
TSCA/FIFRA Enforcement Section
841 Chestnut Street
Philadelphia, Pennsylvania 19107
(215)597-8598

REGION 4
Pesticides & Toxic Substances
345 Courtland Street, NE
Atlanta, Georgia 30365
(404)881-4727

REGION 5
Pesticides & Toxic Substances
  Branch
536 South Clark Street
Chicago, Illinois 60605
(312)353-2291

REGION 6
Air & Waste Management
  Division
1201 Elm Street
Dallas, Texas 75270
(214)767-2600

REGION 7
Case Preparation & Technical
  Assistance Section Branch
727 Minnesota Avenue
Kansas City, Kansas 66101
(913)236-2800

REGION 8
EPA
One Denver Place
999 18th Street, Suite 1300
Denver, Colorado 80202
(303)293-1603

REGION 9
Pesticides & Toxics Branch
215 Fremont Street
San Francisco, California 94105
(415)974-8071

REGION 10
Pesticides & Toxic
  Substances Branch
Mail Stop 524
1200 6th Street
Seattle, Washington 98101
(206)442-5810

STATE AGENCIES FOR PESTICIDES/TERMITICIDES (CHLORDANE)

ALABAMA
Department of Agriculture &
  Industries
Agriculture Chemistry/Plant
  Industry Division
P.O. Box 3336
Montgomery, Alabama 36193
(205)261-2656

ALASKA
Department of Environmental
  Conservation
Division of Environmental Quality
Southeast Regional Office
P.O. Box 2420

Juneau, Alaska 99803
(907)745-3151

ARIZONA
Department of Health Services
Office of Risk Assessment &
  Investigation
3008 North Third Street
Phoenix, Arizona 85012
(602)230-5861

Commission of Agriculture &
  Horticulture
Agricultural Chemicals & Environ-
  mental Services Division

1688 West Adams Street
Phoenix, Arizona 85007
(602)255-4373

Structural Pest Control Board
2207 South 48th Street, Suite M
Tempe, Arizona 85282
(602)255-3664

ARKANSAS
Contact regional EPA office

CALIFORNIA
Department of Health Services
Hazard Evaluation System &
  Information Service
2151 Berkeley Way, Room 504
Berkeley, California 94704
(415)540-2662

Department of Food and
  Agriculture
Division of Pest Management,
  Environmental Protection
  and Worker Safety
1220 N Street
Sacramento, California 95814
(916)322-6315

Dept. of Industrial Relations
Division of Occupational Safety
  & Health
525 Golden Gate Avenue
San Francisco, California 94102
(415)557-2037

COLORADO
Department of Health
Consumer Protection Division
4210 East 11th Avenue
Denver, Colorado 80220
(303)331-8250

CONNECTICUT
Department of Health Services
Toxic Hazards Section
150 Washington Street
Hartford, Connecticut 06106
(203)566-8167

Department of Environmental
  Protection
Hazardous Materials
  Management Unit
165 Capitol Avenue
Hartford, Connecticut 06115
(203)566-5148

DELAWARE
Department of Agriculture
2320 South DuPont Highway
Dover, Delaware 19901
(302)736-4811

Department of Health & Social
  Services
Bureau of Environmental Health
802 Silver Lake Boulevard
Robbins Building
Dover, Delaware 19901
(302)736-4731

DIST. OF COLUMBIA
Contact regional EPA office

FLORIDA
Dept. of Health & Rehabilitative
  Services
Office of Entomology
Pest Control Program
P.O. Box 210
Jacksonville, Florida 32231
(904)354-3961

GEORGIA
Department of Agriculture
Entomology & Pesticides Division
19 M.L. King Jr. Drive, S.W.
Atlanta, Georgia 30334
(404)656-4958

GUAM
Contact regional EPA office

HAWAII
Department of Agriculture
Division of Plant Industry
1428 South King Street

Honolulu, Hawaii 96814
(808)548-7124

Department of Health
Environmental Protection & Health
    Services Div.
1250 Punchbowl Street
Honolulu, Hawaii 96813
(808)548-4139
or 4159

IDAHO
Department of Agriculture
Bureau of Pesticides
P.O. Box 790
Boise, Idaho 83701
(208)334-3243

Department of Health & Welfare
Bureau of Preventative Medicine
Statehouse Mall
Boise, Idaho 83720
(208)334-5933

ILLINOIS
Department of Public Health
Division of Environmental Health
Pesticides and Vector Control
Environmental Toxicology
525 West Jefferson Street
Springfield, Illinois 62761
(217)782-5830

For termiticides/chlordane:
Department of Labor
Division of Safety, Inspection &
    Education
One West Old State Capitol Plaza
Springfield, Illinois 62701
(217)782-9386

INDIANA
For pesticides contact regional EPA
office

For termiticides/chlordane:
State Board of Health
Environmental Epidemiology
1330 West Michigan Street
P.O. Box 1964

Indianapolis, Indiana 46206
(317)633-8554

IOWA
Department of Agriculture
Pesticide Bureau
Wallace State Office Building
Des Moines, Iowa 50319
(515)281-8591

KANSAS
Board of Agriculture
Plant Health Division
109 S.W. 9th Street
Topeka, Kansas 66612
(913)296-5192
or 2263

KENTUCKY
Cabinet for Labor
Occupational Safety & Health
    Administration
Division of Compliance
U.S. Highway 127 South
Frankfort, Kentucky 40601
(502)564-7360

Cabinet for Labor
Occupational Safety & Health
    Administration
Division of Education and Training
U.S. Highway 127 South
Frankfort, Kentucky 40601
(502)564-6895

LOUISIANA
Department of Health & Hospitals
Office of Preventive & Public
    Health Services
Environmental Epidemiology
P.O. Box 60630
New Orleans, Louisiana 70160
(504)568-5053

Department of Agriculture &
    Forestry
P.O. Box 11453
Baton Rouge, Louisiana 70804
(504)925-3763

MAINE
Department of Agriculture
Division of Food & Rural Resources
Board of Pesticides Control
Statehouse Station 28
Augusta, Maine 04333
(207)289-2731

MARYLAND
For pesticides contact regional EPA
office

For termiticides/chlordane:
Department of the Environment
Center for Environmental Health
201 West Preston Street
Baltimore, Maryland 21201
(301)225-5753

MASSACHUSETTS
Department of Food and
  Agriculture
Pesticides Bureau
100 Cambridge Street, 21st floor
Boston, Massachusetts 02202
(617)727-7712

Department of Public Health
Division of Community Sanitation
Environmental Hygiene
150 Tremont Street
Boston, Massachusetts 02111
(617)727-2670

For termiticides/chlordane:
Department of Public Health
(same address as above)
(617)727-7035

MICHIGAN
Department of Agriculture
Pesticides & Plant Pest Management
  Division
611 West Ottawa, Ottawa Building
P.O. Box 30017
Lansing, Michigan 48909
(517)373-1087

Department of Public Health
Center for Environmental Health

Sciences
3500 North Logan Street
P.O. Box 30035
Lansing, Michigan 48909
(517)335-8350

MINNESOTA
Department of Agriculture
Division of Agronomy Services
90 West Plato Boulevard
St. Paul, Minnesota 55107
(612)296-6121

MISSISSIPPI
Department of Agriculture &
  Commerce
Division of Plant Industry
P.O. Box 5207
Mississippi State, Mississippi 39762
(601)325-3390

For termiticides/chlordane
Department of Health
Preventative Health Services
P.O. Box 1700
Jackson, Mississippi 39215-1700
(601)960-7725

MISSOURI
Department of Agriculture
Bureau of Pesticide Control
P.O. Box 630
Jefferson City, Missouri 65102
(314)751-2462

Department of Health
Division of Environmental Health &
  Epidemiology
1730 East Elm Street
P.O. Box 570
Jefferson City, Missouri 65102-0570
(314)751-6102

MONTANA
Department of Health &
  Environmental Services
Occupational Health Bureau
Cogswell Building, Room A113

Helena, Montana 59620
(406)444-3671

NEBRASKA
Department of Agriculture
Bureau of Plant Industry
301 Centennial Mall South
Lincoln, Nebraska 68509
(402)471-2341

Department of Health
Division of Environmental Health &
  Housing Surveillance
301 Centennial Mall South
P.O. Box 95007
Lincoln, Nebraska 68509
(402)471-2541

NEVADA
Department of Agriculture
Division of Plant Industry
350 Capital Hill Avenue
P.O. Box 11100
Reno, Nevada 89510
(702)789-0180

NEW HAMPSHIRE
Department of Agriculture
Division of Pesticide Control
Caller Box 5042
Concord, New Hampshire 03301
(603)271-3550

NEW JERSEY
Department of Environmental
  Protection
Bureau of Pesticide Control
380 Scotch Road, CN 411
Trenton, New Jersey 08625
(609)530-4123

Department of Environmental
  Protection
Division of Science & Research
401 East State Street, 6th Floor,
  CN 409
Trenton, New Jersey 08625
(609)984-3889

Department of Health
Division of Occupational &
  Environmental Protection
CN 360
Trenton, New Jersey 08625
(609)633-2043

NEW MEXICO
Agriculture Department
Agricultural & Environmental
  Service Division
P.O. Box 30005, Dept. 3150
New Mexico State University
Las Cruces, New Mexico 88003-0005
(505)646-3208

NEW YORK
Department of Environmental
  Conservation
Bureau of Pesticide Management
50 Wolf Road, Room 404
Albany, New York 12233
(518)457-7482

Department of Health
Division of Environmental
  Health Assessment
Bureau of Toxic Substance
  Assessment
2 University Place, Room 240
Albany, New York 12203-3313
(518)458-6376

Division of Occupational Health &
  Environmental Epidemiology
2 University Place, Room 375
Albany, New York 12203-3313
(518)458-6433

NORTH CAROLINA
Department of Human Resources
Division of Health Services
Environmental Epidemiology
  Branch
225 North McDowell Street
Raleigh, North Carolina 27602
(919)733-3410

Department of Human Resources
Division of Health Services

Occupational Health Branch
P.O. Box 2091
Raleigh, North Carolina 27602
(919)733-3680

Department of Labor
Division of Occupational Safety and
  Health
4 West Edenton Street
Raleigh, North Carolina 27603
(919)733-4880

For termiticides/chlordane:
Department of Agriculture
Food and Drug Protection Division
Consumer Product Safety
4000 Reedy Creek Road
Raleigh, North Carolina 27607
(919)733-7366

NORTH DAKOTA
Department of Agriculture
Plant Industries Division
State Capitol, 6th Floor
Bismarck, North Dakota 58505
(701)224-4756

Department of Health &
  Consolidated Labs
Consolidated Laboratories Branch
Consumer Protection Section
P.O. Box 637
Bismarck, North Dakota 58501
(701)221-6140

OHIO
Department of Health
Bureau of Environmental Health
246 North High Street
Columbus, Ohio 43266-0588
(614)466-1450

OKLAHOMA
Department of Agriculture
Plant Industry Division
Pest Management Section
2800 North Lincoln Boulevard
Oklahoma City, Oklahoma
  73105-4298
(405)521-3864

Department of Health
1000 Northeast Tenth Street
P.O. Box 53551
Oklahoma City, Oklahoma 73152
(405)271-7353

OREGON
Department of Agriculture
Plant Division
635 Capitol Street, North East
Salem, Oregon 97301
(503)378-3776

Department of Agriculture
Laboratory Services Division
Pesticide Analytical & Response
  Center
635 Capitol Street, N.E.
Salem, Oregon 97310-0110
(503)378-3793

Department of Insurance & Finance
Accident Prevention Division
Resource Center
Labor & Industries Building
Salem, Oregon 97310
(503)378-3272

PENNSYLVANIA
Department of Environmental
  Resources
Bureau of Air Quality Control
Third & Locust Street, Fulton Bank
  Building
P.O. Box 2063
Harrisburg, Pennsylvania 17120
(717)787-4310

PUERTO RICO
Contact regional EPA office

RHODE ISLAND
Contact regional EPA office

SOUTH CAROLINA
Dept. of Fertilizer & Pesticide
  Control
256 P & AS Building, Clemson
  University

Clemson, South Carolina
29634-0394
(803)656-3171

SOUTH DAKOTA
Department of Health
Division of Public Health
Joe Foss Building
523 East Capitol Avenue
Pierre, South Dakota 57501
(605)773-3364

TENNESSEE
Department of Agriculture
Plant Industries Division
P.O. Box 40627, Melrose Station
Nashville, Tennessee 37204
(615)360-0130

Department of Health &
   Environment
Bureau of Environment
Division of Air Pollution Control
Customs House
701 Broadway
Nashville, Tennessee 37219-5403
(615)741-3931

TEXAS
Department of Health
Occupational & Health Division
1100 West 49th Street
Austin, Texas 78756
(512)458-7521

Department of Agriculture
Div. of Agricultural &
   Environmental Sciences
P.O. Box 12847
Austin, Texas 78711
(512)463-7534

Structural Pest Control Board
1300 East Anderson Lane
Building C, Suite 250
Austin, Texas 78752
(512)835-4066

UTAH
Department of Agriculture

Division of Plant Industries
350 North Redwood Road
Salt Lake City, Utah 84116
(801)533-4107

VERMONT
Department of Agriculture
Plant Industry Division
116 State Street
State Office Building
Montpelier, Vermont 05602
(802)828-2431

VIRGINIA
Department of Agriculture &
   Consumer Services
Division of Product & Industry
   Regulation
Office of Pesticide Regulation
P.O. Box 1163
Richmond, Virginia 23209
(804)786-3798

Department of Health
Division of Health Hazards Control
James Madison Building
109 Governor Street
Richmond, Virginia 23219
(804)786-3798

WASHINGTON
Department of Social & Health
   Services
Health Services Division
Environmental Health Programs
Toxic Substances Section
Mail Stop LD-11
Olympia, Washington 98504
(206)753-5965

WEST VIRGINIA
Department of Agriculture
Regulatory and Inspection Division
Capitol Building
Charleston, West Virginia 25305
(304)348-2206

Department of Health
Office of Environmental Health

Services
Indoor Air Quality Program
4873 Brenda Lane
Charleston, West Virginia 25312
(304)348-0696

WISCONSIN
Dept. of Agriculture, Trade &
   Consumer Protection
Agricultural Resource Management
   Division
Groundwater & Regulatory Services

Section
801 West Badger Road
Madison, Wisconsin 53713
(608)266-7137 or 7756 or 0197

WYOMING
Department of Agriculture
Division of Standards & Consumer
   Services
2219 Carey Avenue
Cheyenne, Wyoming 82002-0100
(307)777-7321

6

FORMALDEHYDE

You remember formaldehyde—that foul smelling fluid in biology class that made you feel a bit queasy. You may not have seen the end of formaldehyde when you finally graduated. It may now be residing in parts of your home—making you sick all over again.

Formaldehyde is a colorless, toxic, water-soluble gas with a strong, pungent, pickle-like smell. Besides preserving dead frogs for dissection, it is used widely in manufacturing. About five billion pounds are produced annually in the United States. Its primary use is in the manufacturing of synthetic resins. These synthetic, formaldehyde-based resins are the binders and adhesives for the plywood, particleboard and chipboard found in many homes.

Formaldehyde may be present in the home primarily in two forms: as urea-formaldehyde foam insulation (UFFI) and/or in particleboard, plywood and chipboard. The smoother surface of particleboard makes it a good material for floors that will be carpeted. Some 10 million homes in the United States have particleboard subflooring.

Formaldehyde may also be found, in very small and generally insignificant amounts, in drapes, carpets, rugs, tobacco smoke, cosmetics, cleaning products and disinfectants, clothing (particularly permanent press or other treated fabrics), paper products (newsprint, wax paper, grocery bags, facial tissue, "wet strength" towels) and some plastics used in plumbing fixtures and appliances. (Because so many of these materials are used in mobile homes, which are so well sealed with "airtight" construction, mobile homes are especially susceptible to formaldehyde contamination.)

UREA-FORMALDEHYDE FOAM INSULATION

In the '70s and early '80s UFFI was used as an insulation in half a million homes in the United States. It is made at the job site by the installer, who mixes urea-formaldehyde-based resin, a foaming agent and compressed air in special equipment. A foam, with the consistency of shaving cream, is produced. It is pumped through a hose into a wall cavity where it hardens.

By the end of 1980, the Consumer Product Safety Commission (CPSC) had received more than 1,500 complaints of adverse health effects resulting form UFFI. Because of concerns over possible health hazards, in August of 1982 the CPSC banned the use of UFFI in homes. The ban was overturned in April of the following year by the Fifth Circuit Court of Appeals on the grounds that the data from animal studies supplied by the CPSC did not justify the ban. However, some states have banned its use or imposed restrictive measures. What was a booming business is now virtually dead.

While UFFI has gotten a lot of publicity, and for all practical purposes is no longer being used, formaldehyde is still being used extensively in particleboard subflooring, paneling, cabinets and furniture and in hardwood and plywood paneling.

THE HAZARDS OF FORMALDEHYDE

When UFFI is installed, and afterwards as well, formaldehyde gas can be released. Wood products made with urea-formaldehyde give off formaldehyde vapors when they are exposed to water and heat.

Formaldehyde gas can cause a variety of unpleasant symptoms, including irritation to eyes, the nose and throat; a persistent cough, respiratory distress; skin irritation; nausea, headaches, and dizziness. The symptoms can last a short time with minimal discomfort; or they can result in serious adverse health effects. How a person is affected by inhaling formaldehyde gas depends on a number of factors: the concentration of the gas in the air; the length of time exposed to that air; and the age and health of the person exposed.

An existing respiratory illness can be made worse by the exposure and result in hospitalization. Some people are allergic to formaldehyde and will get skin rashes or asthma.

Formaldehyde inhalation has caused cancer in laboratory animals. If the data from the animal studies is relevant to humans, the risk of getting cancer is small, yet some leading health scientists and scientific groups have advised the CPSC to presume that formaldehyde poses a risk to people. The 1982 decision to ban UFFI was based on all adverse health effects, acute as well as chronic.

FORMALDEHYDE LEVELS

There is no safe level of formaldehyde in the home, no level at which everyone can be assured of no adverse health effects. The National Academy of Sciences has suggested that somewhat less than 20% of healthy adults may experience reactions to formaldehyde levels at less than 0.25 ppm. The American Society of Heating, Refrigerating and Air Conditioning Engineers (ASHRAE) has recommended that indoor residential exposure be limited to 0.1 ppm. It appears that most healthy adults would not be expected to experience acute toxic effects from exposure below 0.1 ppm, but the CPSC has gotten complaints from homeowners who reported adverse effects with levels below that. Infants, people with allergies, the elderly, and people with respiratory problems may respond more severely to lower levels.

REPORTED HEALTH EFFECTS OF FORMALDEHYDE AT VARIOUS CONCENTRATIONS

EFFECTS	FORMALDEHYDE CONCENTRATION (ppm)
None reported	0.00 - 0.05
Neurophysiologic effects	0.05 - 1.50
Odor threshold	0.05 - 1.00
Eye irritation	0.01 - 2.00
Upper airway irritation	0.10 - 25.00
Lower airway and pulmonary effects	5.00 - 30.00
Pulmonary edema, inflammation, pneumonia	50.00 - 100.00
Death	100 +

Source: National Resource Council

HOW TO TELL IF YOUR HOME HAS UFFI

Since UFFI was used in the 1970s and early '80s, if you bought your home before 1970, in all probability you do not have UFFI. If you purchased your home after 1970 you can check with the previous owner, the real estate agent or the builder. If you did have insulation put in and you think it may contain formaldehyde, check with the installer or read the contract or the bill of sale.

   If you cannot find out by any of the ways above, you can make a physical check of the house. When UFFI was put into existing homes, it was pumped through a hole into the outer wall cavity. You may be able to find evidence of the holes where they've been patched. Look at the outside wall at different angles. The area just below a window, is a good place to check. If the installer has removed the siding and then replaced it, you will not find holes. Though finding patched holes does not necessarily mean that UFFI was pumped in (it is possible that other types of insulation, such as cellulose, mineral etc. may have been blown in), finding holes should alert you to the possibility.

It is also possible that the UFFI was installed through holes in the inside of the house. If you find patched holes in interior walls, or wallpaper borders where the wall and ceiling meet (placed there, perhaps, to cover the holes), it warrants further investigation.

There is yet another way to look for UFFI. The electrical outlets or switch plates on the outer wall can be examined. *The power must be turned off* when you do this, and it is really advisable to have someone knowledgeable about electrical wiring to do it. The presence of foam may be evident around the electrical switch or outlet once the coverplate is removed. Examination with a flashlight may reveal foam in the wall cavity, or in the electrical box where the outlet or switch is located.

If your house is insulated with UFFI, but no one in the family displays any "symptoms," there may be no point in testing for levels inside.

Measurements that have been made in homes indicate that some formaldehyde off-gassing from UFFI continues for years—but that the levels generally decline, rapidly over the first year and then gradually over the following years. In virtually any home with UFFI, the material has been in place for over 10 years. Formaldehyde levels in homes with particleboard subflooring have had peak levels in the range of 0.20-0.03 ppm up to five years after installation.

If you *do* have some of the symptoms, particularly if they disappear when you are away from your home, you may want to test for formaldehyde. (You may also want to check with your doctor for other causes, but you do want to tell your doctor that you suspect the possibility of formaldehyde.)

FORMALDEHYDE IN MOBILE HOMES

Although UFFI has gotten all the publicity, and most people associate formaldehyde with home insulation, the formaldehyde problem in mobile homes is much greater. Dr. Thad Godish, director of the Indoor Air Pollution Laboratory at Ball State University in Indiana, says over four million mobile homes have formaldehyde levels higher than levels found in UFFI homes. A typical formaldehyde level in a mobile home can be 0.35 ppm. In a study of workers exposed to that level of formaldehyde in Denmark, a significantly high prevalence of symptoms was reported—eye, ear and throat irritation, headaches, abnormal tiredness, menstrual irregularities and unnatural thirst—compared to a control population not exposed to formaldehyde. Mobile homes have the worst problem because materials with formaldehyde are extensively used in them. They frequently have particleboard flooring, paneling, cabinets and shelving in a relatively smaller amount of space than in an average house, leading to a greater concentration. In a mobile home there is relatively more surface area where formaldehyde-containing products are likely to be than in a traditional home.

TESTING FOR FORMALDEHYDE

To test for formaldehyde in your home, first check with your local or state health department. Some will conduct a test at no charge or for a nominal fee (see list at end of chapter). If your state doesn't test, it should be able to give advice on where to find a reliable testing service. If the state agency is unable to help you, check the yellow pages under laboratories that test for formaldehyde. It is important to make sure the lab is reliable and capable of doing the testing. Ask the lab how long it's been testing for formaldehyde; how frequently it does the test; the reliability of the testing procedure; whether several different areas of the home will be tested; and if you should do anything in preparation for the test. There are also do-it-yourself testing devices that sell for under $50.

There are basically two ways of testing: checking the air for levels of formaldehyde gas or testing some items in your home for formaldehyde content. It can be done actively, with a professional who comes to the house, or passively, by getting a measuring tool and putting it in a spot in the house. In active testing, a technician comes to your house and draws air through distilled water. The solution can then be analyzed.

Another method, which is faster but less accurate, uses a glass tube containing a material that reacts with formaldehyde when air is drawn through the tube. If formaldehyde is present, the material changes color. The PF-1 device made by Air Quality Research in Research Triangle Park, North Carolina, is more accurate. It has been on the market since 1982. The PF-1 is a small glass vial that is left in one place for one week and then sent back to the company for analysis. Two sell for about $60 with analysis and $36 without analysis. (AQR's phone number is [919] 941-5509.)

To test for formaldehyde content in items in your home, you have to remove some of the material and have it analyzed by a lab. Getting a

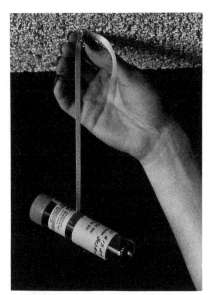

Installed as shown, the PF-1 detects the presence of formaldehyde in the home. Air Quality Research, Inc.

sample of sub-flooring may be difficult; a small sample of carpeting, or a kitchen cabinet may be a little easier.

WHAT TO DO ABOUT A FORMALDEHYDE PROBLEM

There are a number of ways to deal with formaldehyde contamination from UFFI or from wood products made with formaldehyde. The major remedies are ventilation/air filtration; sealing; and removal of the source. Frequently, a combination of methods is used. Determining which method or methods to use is the first step and will depend on the source of the formaldehyde, the extent of the problem and its effect on household members.

Ventilation/Air Filtration
This method is used to get contaminated air out of the house and can be done in a number of different ways.

- Whenever weather permits, open windows in your home to get as much natural ventilation as possible. This enables air contaminated with formaldehyde (as well as other toxic substances) to be replaced by fresh air from outside. (This is always a good practice, whether you have a known indoor air pollution problem or not.) This is certainly the easiest method. The costs involved are bigger bills for heating in the winter and cooling in the summer. To mitigate the cost, you can use an air- to-air heat exchanger, which can be installed centrally within your home or applied to limited room areas. Heat exchangers allow the recovery of heat otherwise discharged to the outside. As the hot air exits, it warms the air coming in. You may recover as much as 80% of the heat during the heating season.

- Heat your house to at least 80 degrees, have fans going, close all the windows and outside doors, and stay out of the house for 12 hours. When you return home, open all the windows and ventilate thoroughly. Keep the fans going to rid the house of the outgassed formaldehyde as quickly as possible. Depending on the severity of the problem, how new the formaldehyde is and how many sources there are, you may have to repeat this several times.
- Air conditioners should operate with outside air rather than recycling the inside air. That way fresh air is replacing inside air, which contains the contaminants.
- When you use a fireplace and have all the windows closed, a negative pressure is created that promotes outgassing of formaldehyde inside the home. To eliminate the negative pressure, leave at least one window slightly open.
- Use exhaust fans in combination with open windows. However, in homes with UFFI it may be more beneficial instead to blow air into the building. If you blow the air out, a negative pressure may result which will draw more of the formaldehyde out from wall cavities and into your home.
- If your home has hot air circulation or central air conditioning, duct the air to the suction (low pressure side) side of the fan. That will provide an increase in the air exchange rate with outside air and dilute any increase in formaldehyde concentrations.
- You can vent wall cavities to the outside by installing ventilator outlets.
- To minimize drafting of air to the interior, seal or cover electrical ceiling fixtures, switch boxes, and outlets. You can also apply styrofoam insulation materials in back of the cover plate in order to prevent outgassing of formaldehyde into the house.

For more information on how to do any of these measures call the state agency that handles formaldehyde (see end of chapter).

Sealing/Covering

Sealing and covering are done to prevent, to as great an extent as possible, formaldehyde vapors from getting into the air in your home, whether the source is UFFI or man-made wood products. There are a number of ways you can seal or cover areas to reduce the outgassing of formaldehyde vapors in your home.

- For UFFI, check carefully for any holes, cracks or gaps in the walls where the vapors may enter. The junction of the wall and floor, or the place where panel boards meet, may also allow vapors to leak into the room. Seal any openings or junctions with caulking or spackling compounds such as butyl or acrylic latex. You can also use weatherstripping or special foam-backed tapes for sealing.
- For paneling, plywood or other man-made wood in the home apply a sealant like polyurethane, shellac, lacquer, wax or latex-based paints. Use at least two coats.
- You can cover surfaces of man-made wood products with high density materials such as polyethylene vapor barriers, floor tile, linoleum or other floor coverings. Vinyl contact paper may also reduce emissions from surfaces containing formaldehyde.

Removal

This involves removing the UFFI from the walls or removing the man-made wood products from your home—products like cabinets or particleboard subflooring. This is the most difficult and costly method, and should be considered as a last resort. This is also the most foolproof method. Removing UFFI from walls requires removal of the inner or outer wall panels or siding, removal of the foam, installation of new insulation, and installation of new panels or siding. When the foam is removed, interior wall cavity surfaces must be sealed, or the residual foam chemically treated. Wood surfaces that have been in contact should be treated with a chemical stabilizing agent, such as sodium bisulfite. This must be done very carefully. If you are going to do this you may want to consult with an architect or engineer. The National Research Council (NRC) of Canada, which has looked into this method, reports that there have been cases where UFFI was removed, but adverse health effects continued. It is therefore *very important that removal is done properly.*

There are other methods of controlling formaldehyde contamination in the home that are not used as frequently, but may be appropriate in your situation. Following is a brief explanation of those methods.

Reducing Moisture Concentration

This method involves controlling humidity in the house in order to lower the amount of moisture that gets inside the wall, since moisture can increase outgassing of UFFI. Another way to reduce moisture is to use low permeability paints and vinyl wall coverings. Outside of the home, any place where water may be able to get in, such as the uncaulked perimeters of windows and doors, should be eliminated. Poor roof draining may also promote wet exterior surfaces.

Ammonia Treatment

Ammonia has been used to reduce formaldehyde levels in UFFI homes, and some data provided to the CPSC, although it's not conclusive, has indicated that high concentrations pumped through all cavities can be effective. *This should only be done by a trained professional.* Ammonia at high concentrations can be hazardous. If this method is used, special precautions should be taken to protect gas and electrical fittings made of brass, even if they are inside the wall. Ammonia can cause rapid corrosion of those fittings and create a fire hazard.

Ammonia has also been used to treat inside air when the primary source of formaldehyde is man-made wood products and furnishings. This method has typically been used in mobile homes. An ammonia solution is placed in pans with large surface areas within an enclosure. The temperature is raised to evaporate the ammonia and to generate off-gassing of formaldehyde. This speeds up the curing or neutralizing process of the materials that contain formaldehyde.

The number of times the process is repeated depends on how effective the previous treatment was in eliminating the formaldehyde. It is IM-PERATIVE that the space treated be thoroughly ventilated between treatments.

FORMALDEHYDE PREVENTION

If you don't have a formaldehyde problem now, you could end up with one very easily. Formaldehyde is still being used in a great many household products. As mentioned earlier, it is used as binders and adhesives for plywood, chipboard and particleboard. These materials are frequently used on floors, walls, cabinets and furniture. Formal-dehyde is also used in, among other things, drapes, carpets, rugs, cosmetics, and some plastics used in plumbing and appliances. If you have any questions about a carpet you are buying or a sofa or drapes, call the manufacturer and ask what has been used in the product. You can ask for the material safety data sheet (MSDS), which manufacturers are required to have for the safety of workers. The manufacturer is under no obligation to give that to you, but you may wonder why he is refusing to do so. You can get it under the Freedom of Information Act. The sensitivity of you and your family to chemicals will dictate how earnestly you want to pursue this. However, with a reasonable degree of effort you can control the amount of formaldehyde, if any, you and your family are exposed to in the future.

EPA REGIONAL OFFICES FOR FORMALDEHYDE

ALABAMA—4	KENTUCKY—4	OHIO—5
ALASKA—10	LOUISIANA—6	OKLAHOMA—6
ARIZONA—9	MAINE—1	OREGON—10
ARKANSAS—6	MARYLAND—3	PENNSYLVANIA—3
CALIFORNIA—9	MASSACHUSETTS—1	PUERTO RICO—2
COLORADO—8	MICHIGAN—5	RHODE ISLAND—1
CONNECTICUT—1	MINNESOTA—5	SOUTH
DELAWARE—3	MISSISSIPPI—4	CAROLINA—4
DISTRICT OF	MISSOURI—7	SOUTH DAKOTA—8
COLUMBIA—3	MONTANA—8	TENNESSEE—4
FLORIDA—4	NEBRASKA—7	TEXAS—6
GEORGIA—4	NEVADA—9	UTAH—8
GUAM—9	NEW HAMPSHIRE—1	VERMONT—1
HAWAII—9	NEW JERSEY—2	VIRGINIA—3
IDAHO—10	NEW MEXICO—6	VIRGIN ISLANDS—2
ILLINOIS—5	NEW YORK—2	WASHINGTON—10
INDIANA—5	NORTH	WEST VIRGINIA—3
IOWA—7	CAROLINA—4	WISCONSIN—5
KANSAS—7	NORTH DAKOTA—8	WYOMING—8

REGION 1
Air Management Division
JFK Federal Building
Room 2311-AAA
Boston, Massachusetts 02224
(617)223-2226

REGION 2
Pesticides & Toxic Substances
Woodbridge Avenue
Building 209
Edison, New Jersey 08837
(201)321-6768

REGION 3
TSCA/FIFRA Enforcement Section
841 Chestnut Street
Philadelphia, Pennsylvania 19107
(215)597-8598

REGION 4
Pesticides & Toxic Substances
345 Courtland Street, NE
Atlanta, Georgia 30365
(404)881-4727

REGION 5
Pesticides & Toxic Substances
   Branch
536 South Clark Street
Chicago, Illinois 60605
(312)353-2291

REGION 6
Air & Waste Management
   Division
1201 Elm Street
Dallas, Texas 75270
(214)767-2600

REGION 7
Case Preparation & Technical
   Assistance Section Branch
727 Minnesota Avenue
Kansas City, Kansas 66101
(913)236-2800

REGION 8
EPA
One Denver Place
999 18th Street, Suite 1300
Denver, Colorado 80202
(303)293-1603

REGION 9
Pesticides & Toxics Branch
215 Fremont Street

San Francisco, California 94105
(415)974-8071

REGION 10
Pesticides & Toxic
  Substances Branch
Mail Stop 524
1200 6th Street
Seattle, Washington 98101
(206)442-5810

STATE AGENCIES FOR FORMALDEHYDE

ALABAMA
Department of Public Health
Division of Environmental
  Health/Indoor Air Quality
  Section
434 Monroe Street, Room 254
Montgomery, Alabama 36130-1707
(205)261-5007

ALASKA
Department of Health & Social
  Services
Division of Public Health
Section of Epidemiology
P.O. Box 240249
Anchorage, Alaska 99524-0249
(907)561-4406

ARIZONA
Department of Health Services
Office of Risk Assessment &
  Investigation
3008 North Third Street
Phoenix, Arizona 85012
(602)230-5865

ARKANSAS
Department of Health
Division of Health Maintenance
4815 West Markham Street
Little Rock, Arkansas 72205
(501)661-2597

Department of Health
Division of Sanitarian Services
4815 West Markham Street
Little Rock, Arkansas 72205
(501)661-2171

CALIFORNIA
Department of Health Services
Indoor Air Quality Program
Air & Industrial Hygiene
  Laboratory
2151 Berkeley Way
Berkeley, California 94704
(415)540-2469

Department of Industrial Relations
Division of Occupational Safety &
  Health
525 Golden Gate Avenue
San Francisco, California 94102
(415)557-2037

Department of Consumer Affairs
Bureau of Home Furnishings &
  Thermal Insulation
3485 Orange Grove Avenue
North Highlands, California 95660
(916)920-6951

COLORADO
Department of Health
Consumer Protection Division
4210 East 11th Avenue
Denver, Colorado 80220
(303)331-8250

Department of Health
Disease Control & Environmental
  Epidemiology
(same address as above)
(303)331-8330

CONNECTICUT
Department of Health Services
Toxic Hazards Section
150 Washington Street
Hartford, Connecticut 06106
(203)566-8167

Department of Consumer
  Protection
Product Safety Division
165 Capitol Avenue
Hartford, Connecticut 06106
(203)566-2816

DELAWARE
Department of Health & Social
  Services
Division of Public Health
Bureau of Environmental Health
802 Silver Lake Boulevard
Robbins Building
Dover, Delaware 19901
(302)736-4731

DISTRICT OF COLUMBIA
Dept. of Consumer Affairs &
  Regulatory Affairs
Environmental Control Division
Air Branch
5010 Overlook Avenue, S.W.
Washington, D.C. 20032
(202)767-7370

Department of Employment
  Services
Occupational Safety & Health
950 Upshur Street, N.W.
Washington, D.C. 20011
(202)576-6339

FLORIDA
Department of Health & Rehabilitative Services

Health Programs
1323 Winewood Boulevard
Tallahassee, Florida 32301
(904)488-4070

GEORGIA
Department of Human Resources
Division of Public Health
47 Trinity Avenue, S.W.
Atlanta, Georgia 30334
(404)894-6644

Department of Natural Resources
Environmental Protection Division
Floyd Towers East, Suite 1166
205 Butler Street, S.E.
Atlanta, Georgia 30334
(404)656-2060

GUAM
Environmental Protection Agency
Government of Guam
P.O. Box 2999
Agana, Guam 96910
(671)646-8865

HAWAII
Department of Health
Environmental Protection/Health
  Services Branch
Pollution Investigation &
  Enforcement Branch
1250 Punchbowl Street
Honolulu, Hawaii 96813
(808)548-4139
or 4159

Office of Consumer Protection
250 South King Street
Honolulu, Hawaii 96813
(808)548-2560

IDAHO
Department of Health and Welfare
Health Promotion & Disease
  Prevention
Bureau of Preventive Medicine
Statehouse Mall
Boise, Idaho 83720

(208)334-5939
or 4370

ILLINOIS
Department of Public Health
Division of Environmental Health
Environmental Toxicology
525 West Jefferson Street
Springfield, Illinois 62761
(217)782-5830
or 2060

INDIANA
State Board of Health
Division of Industrial Hygiene
1330 West Michigan Street
P.O. Box 1964
Indianapolis, Indiana 46206
(317)633-0692

IOWA
Department of Public Health
Bureau of Compliance/Health Care
  Services
Lucas State Office Building
Des Moines, Iowa 50319
(515)281-7782

Department of Public Health
Division of Disease Prevention
Lucas State Office Building
Des Moines, Iowa 50319
(515)281-4928
or 7785 or 5787

KANSAS
Department of Health and
  Environment
Bureau of Air Quality and
  Radiation Control
Environmental Toxicology Section
Forbes Field
Topeka, Kansas 66620
(913)296-1543
or 1542

Department of Health and
  Environment
Bureau of Epidemiology

109 Southwest Ninth Street,
Suite 605
Topeka, Kansas 66612-1274
(913)296-5586

Department of Health and
  Environment
Bureau of Food, Drug and Lodging
Consumer Product Safety Officer
109 Southwest Ninth Street,
  Suite 604
Topeka, Kansas 66612-1274
(913)296-5602

KENTUCKY
Cabinet for Labor
Division of Education and Training
U.S. Highway 127 South
Frankfort, Kentucky 40601
(502)564-6895

Cabinet for Labor
Division of Compliance
U.S. Highway 127 South
Frankfort, Kentucky 40601
(502)564-7360

Department of Housing, Buildings
  & Construction
Division of Building Code
  Enforcement
The 127 Office Building
Frankfort, Kentucky 40601
(502)564-8090

LOUISIANA
Department of Health and
  Hospitals
Office of Preventative & Public
  Health Services
Environmental Epidemiology
P.O. Box 60630
New Orleans, Louisiana 70160
(504)568-5053
or 5181

MAINE
Department of Human Services
Occupational and Residential
  Health Program

Consumer Product Safety
State House Station 10
Augusta, Maine 04333
(207)289-3826

Office of Energy Resources
Energy Extension Service
233 Oxford Street
Portland, Maine 04101
(207)879-4199

MARYLAND
Department of the Environment
Toxics, Environmental Science &
  Health
Center for Environmental Health
201 W. Preston Street
Baltimore, Maryland 21201
(301)225-5753

MASSACHUSETTS
Department of Public Health
Division of Community Sanitation
Environmental Hygiene
150 Tremont Avenue
Boston, Massachusetts 02111
(617)727-2660

MICHIGAN
Department of Public Health
Center for Environmental Health
  Sciences
3500 North Logan Street
P.O. Box 30035
Lansing, Michigan 48909
(517)335-8350
or 9241

Department of Public Health
3500 North Logan Street
P.O. Box 30035
Lansing, Michigan 48909
(517)335-9214

MINNESOTA
Department of Health
Division of Housing and
  Environmental Health

St. Paul, Minnesota 55411
(612)623-5100

MISSISSIPPI
Department of Health
Preventative Health Services
P.O. Box 1700
Jackson, Mississippi 39215-1700
(601)960-7725

Department of Health
Division of Sanitation
P.O. Box 1700
Jackson, Mississippi 39215-1700
(601)960-7689

Bureau of Buildings
1501 Walter Sillers Building
Jackson, Mississippi 39202
(601)359-3621

MISSOURI
Department of Health
Division of Environmental Health &
  Epidemiology
1730 Elm Street
P.O. Box 570
Jefferson City, Missouri 65102-0570
(314)751-6102

MONTANA
Department of Health &
  Environmental Sciences
Occupational Health Bureau
Cogswell Building, Room A-113
Helena, Montana 59620
(406)444-3671
or 4740

Department of Health &
  Environmental Sciences
Food and Consumer Health Bureau
Cogswell Building
Helena, Montana 59620
(406)444-2408

NEBRASKA
Department of Health
Division of Environmental Health
  and Housing Surveillance

301 Centennial Mall South
P.O. Box 95007
Lincoln, Nebraska 68509
(402)471-2541

Department of Health
Bureau of Health Protection
Consumer Product Safety
301 Centennial Mall South
Lincoln, Nebraska 68509
(402)471-3979

NEVADA
Department of Human Resources
Division of Health
505 East King Street
Carson City, Nevada 89710
(702)885-4740

Department of Commerce
Manufactured Housing Division
1923 North Carson Street, Capitol
  Complex
Carson City, Nevada 89710
(702)678-4298

NEW HAMPSHIRE
Department of Health and Human
  Services
Division of Public Health
Bureau of Environmental Health
Consumer Product Safety
6 Hazan Drive
Concord, New Hampshire
  03301-6527
(603)271-4676
or 4587

NEW JERSEY
Department of Health
Division of Occupational &
  Environmental Health
CN-360
Trenton, New Jersey 08625
(609)984-1863
or 2043

Department of Community Affairs
Division of Housing and
  Development

South Broad & Front Streets,
  CN-804
Trenton, New Jersey 08625
(609)292-7899

NEW MEXICO
No specific state agency for
formaldehyde;
call the Consumer Product Safety
Commission;
1-800-638-CPSC.

NEW YORK
Department of Health
Division of Environmental Health
  Assessment
Bureau of Toxic Substance
  Assessment
2 University Place
Albany, New York 12203-3313
(518)458-6376
or 6402

NORTH CAROLINA
Department of Human Resources
Division of Health Services
Environmental Epidemiology
  Branch
225 North McDowell Street
Raleigh, North Carolina 27602
(919)733-3410

Department of Labor
Division of Occupational Safety &
  Health
4 West Edenton Street
Raleigh, North Carolina 27603
(919)733-4880

Department of Human Resources
Division of Health Services
Occupational Health Branch
P.O. Box 2091
Raleigh, North Carolina 27602
(919)733-3680

NORTH DAKOTA
Department of Health &
  Consolidated Laboratories

Environmental Health Section
1200 Missouri Avenue
P.O. Box 5520
Bismarck, North Dakota 58502-5520
(701)224-2374

Department of Health &
  Consolidated Laboratories
Consolidated Laboratories Branch
Consumer Protection Section
P.O.Box 937
Bismarck, North Dakota 58501
(701)221-6140

OHIO
Department of Health
Bureau of Environmental Health
246 North High Street
Columbus, Ohio 43266-0588
(614)466-1450
or 5190

OKLAHOMA
State Department of Health
Radiation & Special Hazards
  Service
P.O. Box 53551
1000 Northeast 10th Street
Oklahoma City, Oklahoma 73152
(405)271-5221

OREGON
Office of Health Status Monitoring
State Health Division
1400 Southwest Fifth Avenue
Portland, Oregon 97201
(503)229-5792

Department of Insurance & Finance
Accident Prevention Division
Resource Center
Labor & Industries Building
Salem, Oregon 97310
(503)378-3272

PENNSYLVANIA
Department of Health
Division of Environmental Health
P.O. Box 90

Harrisburg, Pennsylvania 17108
(717)787-1708

Department of Community Affairs
Division of Manufactured Housing
Forum Building, Room 508
Harrisburg, Pennsylvania 17120
(717)787-9682

PUERTO RICO
No specific state agency for
formaldehyde;
call the Consumer Product Safety
Commission:
1-800-638-CPSC.

RHODE ISLAND
Department of Health
Division of Occupational Health
206 Cannon Building
75 Davis Street
Providence, Rhode Island 02908
(401)277-2362

SOUTH CAROLINA
Dept. of Health & Environmental
  Control
Air Compliance & Management
  Division
Bureau of Air Quality Control
2600 Bull Street
Columbia, South Carolina 29201
(803)734-5429

Department of Labor
Occupational Safety and Health
  Division
3600 Forest Drive
P.O. Box 11329
Columbia, South Carolina 29211
(803)734-9644

SOUTH DAKOTA
Department of Health
Division of Public Health
Joe Foss Building
523 East Capitol Avenue
Pierre, South Dakota 57501
(605)773-3364

TENNESSEE
Department of Health &
   Environment
Bureau of Environment
Division of Air Pollution Control
701 Broadway
Nashville, Tennessee 37219-5403
(615)741-3931

TEXAS
Department of Health
Occupational & Health Division
1100 West 49th Street
Austin, Texas 78756
(512)458-7254
or 7269

Department of Labor and Standards
Manufactured Housing Division
Capitol Station
P.O.Box 12157
Austin, Texas 78711
(512)463-5522

UTAH
Energy Office
365 West North Temple
Third Triad Center, Suite 450
Salt Lake City, Utah 84116
(801)538-5428

VERMONT
Department of Health
Division of Environmental Health
60 Main Street
Burlington, Vermont 05402
(802)863-7220

VIRGINIA
Department of Health
James Madison Building
109 Governor Street
Richmond, Virginia 23219
(804)786-1763

WASHINGTON
Department of Social & Health
   Services
Health Services Division

Environmental Health Programs
Toxic Substances Section
Mail Stop LD-11
Olympia, Washington 98504
(206)753-2556

Department of Labor & Industries
Division of Industrial Safety &
   Health
Mail Stop HC-412
P.O. Box 207
Olympia, Washington 98504
(206)586-8028

WEST VIRGINIA
Department of Health
Office of Environmental Health
   Services
Indoor Air Quality Program
4873 Brenda Lane
Charleston, West Virginia 25312
(304)348-0696

Department of Labor
Safety & Boiler Division
1800 Washington Street East
Charleston, West Virginia 25305
(304)348-7890

Fire Marshal's Office
2000 Quarrier Street
Charleston, West Virginia 25305
(304)348-2191

WISCONSIN
Department of Health & Social
   Services
Bureau of Community Health &
   Prevention
Environmental & Chronic Disease
   Epidemiology
P.O. Box 309
Madison, Wisconsin 53701-0309
(608)266-1253

Department of Industry, Labor &
   Human Relations
Division of Safety & Buildings
P.O. Box 7969

Madison, Wisconsin 53707
(608)266-1816

Division of Health
Section of Occupational Health
1414 East Washington Avenue,
Room 112
Madison, Wisconsin 53703
(608)266-8393

WYOMING
Department of Health & Social
  Services

Division of Health & Medical
  Services
Hathaway Building, Room 427
Cheyenne, Wyoming 82002
(307)777-6004

Department of Health & Social
  Services
Environmental Health Program
Consumer Product Safety
Hathaway Building, Room 482
Cheyenne, Wyoming 82002
(307)777-7957

7

OTHER INDOOR AIR POLLUTANTS

There are all kinds of substances and situations that can cause the air inside your home to become polluted. We've looked at the major ones—radon, asbestos, formaldehyde, pesticides, etc. But while the big ones do get the headlines and create alarm, frequently it's the little ones, from many different sources, that cause the most problems. Each pollutant, on its own, might not even be noticed. However, when they all get together, *the cumulative effect can be very unhealthy* and, at the very least, irritating and uncomfortable.

During the last 20 years, many homes have been made tighter to conserve energy, to decrease the amount of heated air that leaves the house in the winter, and likewise, decrease the amount of cooled air that escapes in the summer. At the same time, of course, there is less fresh, cold air getting into the house in the winter and less fresh hot air entering the house in the summer. This has several advantages. Less energy is used, and the bill for heating and air conditioning is reduced.

This may seem like a good idea; it isn't. Because the air inside your house is in an enclosed space, the concentration or level of pollutants can be much greater in the air inside than outside. A tighter house has a lower ventilation rate. As the rate of ventilation decreases, the concentration of pollutants inside your home increases.

THOSE AT GREATEST RISK

The people at the greatest risk are the ones who are the most exposed to indoor air pollution—those who are at home the most: babies, children, the elderly, and the chronically ill. As a whole, they are also the people *most susceptible* to pollution in the air.

Different people react differently to the pollutants. Some are simply more sensitive to chemicals and/or biologicals; others become chemically sensitive after repeated exposure.

Some of the indoor pollutants like asbestos and radon are life threatening. Others may not be life threatening, but can make your life miserable, causing eye, nose and throat irritation, shortness of breath, dizziness, lethargy, fever and digestive problems. Sometimes the only symptom is unremitting discomfort in a room that is stuffy and just doesn't smell right, but feeling uncomfortable in your home, where you spend a lot of your time, may be understandably unacceptable.

WAYS TO REDUCE INDOOR AIR POLLUTION

There are three basic ways to alleviate indoor air pollution: elimination of the source; improved ventilation; and air cleaners.

Source Control
The goal here is removing the source of pollution, when possible, or decreasing the amount of pollutants coming from that source. When this can be done it is the most efficient solution.

Ventilation
Both natural ventilation (opening doors and windows) and mechanical ventilation (using a fan) will decrease the pollutants in your home. Ventilation will also boost your utility bill. Installing heat recovery ventilators is one way to keep energy bills from increasing significantly. These can be costly, however, and more involved than just going to your local hardware store and picking up a fan that's on sale. Before you purchase any device you should read up on what's available, how each device works, how efficient it is, and what maintenance it requires. If possible, a consultation with a mechanical engineer could be helpful—and in the long run, save you money.

Air Cleaners
Air cleaners, intended to remove pollutants without using ventilation, or in combination with it, are tricky. These devices come in many sizes and types. You can get a small, relatively inexpensive one, a portable that sits on a table top; or you can install an expensive, whole house system. Air cleaners generally remove particles from the air, but not gas pollutants. Their efficiency depends on how well they collect particle pollutants from the air and how much air they draw through the

cleaning element or filter in a given period of time. An air cleaner that collects a lot of pollutants but has a low air circulation rate will not be that effective; neither will an air cleaner that has a high air circulation rate but a less efficient collection of pollutants. How well the air cleaner works is also a function of how strong the source of pollution is. Air cleaners must be operated and maintained according to the manufacturer's directions to stay maximally effective. Failure to do so could result in an even bigger pollution problem.

INDOOR POLLUTANTS

The major indoor pollutants not discussed in previous chapters but which we'll look at here are: the by-products of combustion, including environmental tobacco smoke; respirable suspended particles; carbon monoxide; nitrogen dioxide; volatile organic compounds; biologicals; and electromagnetic fields. Another fairly recent source of indoor contaminants is consumer products that release or gas-out, pollutants— many cleaning products, materials used in construction, insulation and home furnishings.

Following is a brief description of these pollutants: what they are, where they're from, how they can affect you and what you can do about them.

ENVIRONMENTAL TOBACCO SMOKE (ETS)

Environmental tobacco smoke is actually a combination of many pollutants, including chemicals, respirable particles and various combustion gases such as carbon monoxide and nitrogen dioxide. When present indoors, tobacco smoke can be the major source, or a significant part, of indoor air pollution.

ETS HEALTH HAZARDS

It's well known that people who smoke are at a much higher risk of getting lung cancer, heart disease and other life-threatening illnesses. Let's take a look at how members of the household, who do not smoke, can be affected by inhaling someone else's smoke.

Every time someone lights up a cigarette, pipe or cigar, two types of smoke are generated. Mainstream smoke is the smoke that is inhaled and then exhaled by the smoker. The non-smoker is exposed to it when the smoker exhales. Sidestream smoke, which goes directly into the air from the burning tobacco, is a far more dangerous source of smoke for the non-smoker and is much more prevalent.

Research into the effect of passive smoking (exposure to the smoke generated by an active smoker, also referred to as "second hand smoking" or "involuntary smoking"), began in the 1970s. There have been many studies, worldwide, that indicate a link between passive smoking and the same diseases and side effects experienced by the active smoker, although generally to a lesser degree.

In 1986, reports from the U.S. Surgeon General's office and the National Academy of Sciences indicated environmental smoke as a cause of lung cancer in smokers and healthy non-smokers. There are studies that indicate that the passive smoking of a spouse may increase one's own risk of lung cancer by 30%. Studies have also shown that passive smoking can increase the risk of pneumonia, bronchitis, middle ear disease, chest colds and allergic reactions, as well as adversely affect angina, asthma, Raynaud's Phenomenon and pulmonary function.

Secondhand smoke is especially bad for young children. Studies show that during their first two years of life, children whose parents smoke at home have a higher rate of lung diseases such as bronchitis and pneumonia; and as a result are more likely to be hospitalized.

Though the risk for serious illness is smaller for the adult passive smoker, he or she can suffer many irritating side effects, such as eye, nose and throat irritation, coughing and headaches. Many people are sensitive to tobacco smoke, or find the smell unpleasant and just plain annoying.

ETS REDUCTION

Tobacco smoke is a pollutant that is very easy to eliminate from your home. You just stop smoking! If stopping is not something you or a family member is willing to do, another alternative is to smoke outside the house. This will eliminate exposure to family members inside the house—and only the smoker will be exposed to the potentially unhealthy effects. Smoking in just one room not used frequently by family members will mean less smoke in the rest of the house, but is not nearly as effective as not smoking at all, inside.

Ventilation will also reduce the smoke in the air. But because smoking produces such large amounts of pollutants, natural or mechanical ventilation will not remove it as quickly as it builds up!

RESPIRABLE SUSPENDED PARTICLES (RSP)

The term "respirable suspended particles" refers to a large collection of minute particles from many different sources, in many different sizes and forms—liquids, aerosols and solid particles. To qualify as RSPs they must be capable of being suspended, or remaining aloft, in air.

Many respirable suspended particles are formed during combustion from fireplaces, wood stoves, kerosene heaters and cigarettes. (Other sources such as lead or asbestos are discussed in other chapters.)

RSP HEALTH HAZARDS

RSPs are hazardous because if they are small enough to remain airborne, they can be inhaled into the respiratory system. Minute particles, under 15 microns in diameter (one micron is about one millionth of a yard) can settle on the tissues of the respiratory tract (larger particles are filtered out by the nose). The smallest particles, those under 2.5 microns, can penetrate the small air sacs in the lungs. The particles can remain for months and can cause eye, nose and throat irritation, respiratory infections, bronchitis and lung cancer. If a major part of the RSP is tobacco smoke it can have the same health effects listed earlier under "tobacco smoke."

REDUCING THE RSPS

There are a number of ways to reduce the RSP level in your home:

- If you smoke: either stop smoking or only smoke outside.
- Vent the furnace out of doors. When you are using an unvented space heater, keep the doors to the rest of the house open.
- Choose wood stoves that are the appropriate size for the room being heated and are certified to meet EPA emission standards.
- Make sure that doors on all wood stoves fit tightly.
- Have a trained professional inspect, clean and tune-up your central heating system (furnace, flues and chimneys) annually and repair any leaks promptly.
- Change filters on central heating and cooling systems and air cleaners according to manufacturer directions.

CARBON MONOXIDE (CO)

Carbon monoxide is a colorless, odorless, tasteless and nonirritating gas that can interfere with the supply of oxygen to body tissues. It is produced when carbon containing organic material such as wood, coal or natural gas is burned in an atmosphere that provides insufficient oxygen to allow for complete combustion. Its sources include unvented kerosene and gas heaters, leaking chimneys and furnaces, down-drafting from wood stoves and fireplaces, gas stoves, car exhaust from attached garages, and tobacco smoke.

CO HEALTH HAZARDS

Carbon monoxide enters the body through the respiratory system and reacts primarily with the hemoglobin in the blood, interfering with the supply of oxygen to body tissues. At low concentrations, exposure can result in fatigue and shortness of breath in healthy people, and chest pains in people with heart disease, who are the most susceptible. Higher concentrations can result in impaired vision and coordination, headaches, dizziness, confusion, nausea and flu-like symptoms that clear up when you leave the house. At very high concentrations CO can cause arrhythmia of the heart, myocardial infarction, impaired mental functioning, behavior alternations, coma and death. Even low levels of exposure can affect the heart and brain.

REDUCING CO LEVELS

There are a number of ways to reduce the carbon monoxide level in your home:

- Keep gas appliances properly adjusted.
- Consider buying ventilated gas space heaters and furnaces.
- Always use proper fuel in kerosene space heaters.
- Install and use an exhaust fan vented to the outside over gas stoves.
- Open flues when gas fireplaces are being used.
- Choose properly sized wood stoves that are certified to meet EPA emission standards; make sure that the doors on all wood stoves close tightly.
- Have a trained professional inspect, clean and tune-up your central heating system (furnaces, flues and chimneys) annually; repair any leaks promptly.
- Do not idle a car inside your garage.

NITROGEN DIOXIDE

Nitrogen dioxide is a red to brown gas with a pungent, acrid odor. It is a by-product of combustion. Its sources are kerosene heaters, unvented gas stoves and environmental tobacco smoke. Various materials, including fabrics, paints and metals, can absorb nitrogen dioxide and prolong its effects.

NITROGEN DIOXIDE HEALTH HAZARDS

There have been many studies on the health effects of exposure to nitrogen dioxide. Symptoms include eye, nose and throat irritation.

Exposure to 5 parts per million (ppm) can cause respiratory distress; concentrations around 50 ppm can cause chronic lung disease; levels greater than 150 ppm, while rarely found in the home, can cause death.

People with chronic respiratory problems will be affected by low levels. Children also appear to be more susceptible. Early results in one ongoing study indicate that children raised in homes with gas stoves show signs of respiratory illness before age two more frequently than children raised in homes where an electric stove is used.

To reduce the level of nitrogen dioxide in your home you should take the same steps as you would for carbon monoxide.

VOLATILE ORGANIC COMPOUNDS (VOC)

The term volatile organic compounds refers to a large number of organic vapors that contaminate the air. Over 250 VOCs have been identified in indoor air at concentrations exceeding 1 ppb. Among the most common are ethylbenzene, benzene, o-, m- and p-xylenes, styrene, chlorinated solvents (including 1,1,1, trichloroethane, tetrachloroethylene, and trichloroethylene), p-Dichlorobenzene, methylene chloride, carbon tetrachloride and chloroform. Each compound has physical and chemical properties that can cause it to interact with biological systems and materials, like nitrogen being absorbed by fabrics, paints or metals. Most of the time the VOC level is higher inside the home than outside.

There are numerous sources of VOC, including household products (paints, paint strippers and other solvents); new carpeting, drapes and furnishings; wood preservatives; aerosol sprays; cleansers and disinfectants; moth repellents and air fresheners; stored fuels and car supplies; hobby supplies; dry-cleaned clothing; and environmental tobacco smoke. Following is a list of just a few common sources of VOCs:

SOURCE OF VOC	COMPOUND
moth crystals, room deodorants	p-dichlorobenzene
paint removers	methylene chloride, n-hexane, heptone, toluene, methylene chloride, methanol, propylene dichloride
plastics, paints	styrene, xylenes
polyurethane foam aerosols	toluene, diisocyanate
carpet shampoo	sodium dodecyl sulfate
vinyl tiles plasticized with butyl benzyl phthalate	benzyl chloride, benzal chloride
sterilizers (hospitals)	ethylene oxide

SOURCE OF VOC	COMPOUND
printed material	n-decane, n-dodecane
cleaners/waxes	toluene, perchloroethylene, methylene chloride, 1, 1, 1-trichloroethane, carbon tetrachloride, isopropanol, ethanol, acetone
hobbies	n-hexane, heptane, methylene chloride, ethylene dichloride, ethanol, methanol, benzyl alcohol
automotive products	kerosene, mineral spirits, toluene, isopropanol, ethylene glycol
cosmetics	trichloroethylene, isopropanol, ethanol, acetone

VOC HEALTH HAZARDS

Ill effects from VOCs include eye, nose and throat irritation, headaches, loss of coordination and nausea. More serious health problems related to VOC exposure include damage to the liver, kidney and central nervous system, vertigo, visual disorders and, less frequently, tremors, fatigue, anorexia, weakness, memory impairment and mental confusion. Some VOCs are carcinogenic.

REDUCING VOC LEVELS

To keep VOC levels in your home as low as possible there are some precautionary measures you can take. During and following new construction, renovation or refurbishing, VOC levels can shoot up, temporarily. If you are doing any renovating or reconstruction in your home, try to work when household members (especially young children, pregnant women and the elderly) can be away from home. Increase ventilation as much as possible during and following the renovation.

When using household products such as paint, stripper, varnish or wax, always read and follow the manufacturer's directions carefully. If the label says to use the product in a well ventilated area, use it outside, if possible. If you must use it inside, use in an area where there is an exhaust fan, or open as many windows and doors as you can to increase ventilation.

Buy in quantities close to the amount that you will be using. You don't want to keep toxic substances around for a long period of time. Although the larger size may be more economical, it's better to pay a little more and not store any that's left over. Containers can leak. If you have just a small amount left, get rid of it; if you must store the leftovers, be sure the storage area is well ventilated and out of reach of small children.

When you are getting rid of small amounts of a toxic substance, or an empty container, it is very important to dispose of it safely. Never just toss it in a garbage can! Check with your local sanitation department for any special instructions and times for pickup.

BIOLOGICALS

Biological contaminants inside the home (also called bioaerosols, air-borne allergens or pathogens) include bacteria, mold and their spores, fungus, viruses, animal dander, dust mites (microscopic animals found in household dust), protozoa, algae and pollens.

There are various sources for these pollutants. Pollens, bacteria and viruses can be brought into the home on people or animals, or by contamination of many materials and surfaces in the home. Algae, amoebas and fungi come from outdoors—but under the right conditions in your home, they can prosper and grow tremendously. Those right conditions are moisture, humid air and warm temperatures. Moist surfaces or water in a humidifier or air conditioning system are ideal breeding grounds for fungi, bacteria and algae. Those conditions are also ideal for mold and mildew, which can be found in other damp areas such as the bathroom, the basement and the kitchen.

Pollen can get inside your home through cracks and crevices, doors, windows, and air conditioning systems and fans that bring in fresh air.

Animal dander and excreta come from pets in the house as well as from birds like pigeons, which often roost near the air inlets of buildings.

BIOLOGICALS HEALTH HAZARDS

Health effects from biologicals vary. Some biologicals, like pollen, fungi and animal dander can trigger allergic reactions that range from the minor, but annoying (sneezing, watery eyes, coughing, shortness of breath, dizziness, lethargy, fever and digestive problems) to the not only annoying but much more serious (including hypersensitivity, pneumonitis [inflammation of lung tissue], allergic rhinitis [often called hay fever] and some types of asthma). Some allergic reactions occur immediately; others can be a result of the effects of previous exposures, which you may not be aware of and which have built up, over time. Exposure to dust mites, animal-related allergens like animal dander and cat saliva, and mold send about 200,000 asthma patients a year to hospital emergency rooms.

Other biologicals are pathogenic. One well known example is the bacterium *Legionella,* which is found in the soil and can flourish in organically rich water and then become airborne. It can cause Legionnaires disease, a form of pneumonia that can be fatal. Viral diseases spread by biologicals include chicken pox and German measles.

REDUCING BIOLOGICALS

To eliminate or minimize the biologicals in your home, there a number of things you can do. The two major actions are controlling the moisture and keeping your home as clean as possible. Following is a brief description of ways to reduce biological contamination.

Controlling the Moisture

Humidity. Controlling humidity is a major preventative step in stemming indoor contaminants. The American Society of Heating, Refrigeration and Air-Conditioning Engineers recommends humidity levels not higher than 60% or 70%. The EPA recommends that the humidity in your home not be higher than 45% to 50%! Higher levels of humidity tend to encourage the growth of fungi, molds and dust mites. To measure humidity in your home purchase a device in a hardware store. These devices are common, inexpensive and usually measure the temperature and barometric pressure as well as the humidity.

Humidifiers. Humidifiers, which add moisture to dry air, can be a breeding ground for biological contaminants. Be sure to clean water trays daily. They should be filled with distilled water. Evaporation trays in air conditioners, dehumidifiers, cool misters, refrigerators and any place where water is likely to collect should be cleaned whenever moisture accumulates.

Dehumidifiers. Where necessary, dehumidifiers may be used to lower and keep the humidity at between 30% and 50%.

Fans. Using an exhaust fan in the kitchen and bathroom, and venting the clothes drier outside will eliminate a lot of the moisture that tends to build up.

Ventilation. If you have an attic and/or crawl space, be sure to keep them ventilated, regularly, in order to prevent any buildup of moisture. Water condensation can damage building materials. Since outdoor air can be a significant source of contamination, filtration of air coming into the house may be necessary.

Water damage. Any water damage in your home, especially to carpets and building materials, should be dried and cleaned as quickly as possible—preferably within 24 hours. It may be necessary to replace items damaged by water since it is sometimes virtually impossible to totally eliminate the mold and bacteria.

Water leaks. Any water leaks should be repaired immediately. Those leaks can cause water damage and create ideal breeding grounds for pollutants.

Cleanliness

The house. Contaminants such as dust mites, pollens, animal dander and other allergens can be reduced through regular cleaning. Anyone who is allergic to the pollutants should not vacuum since vacuuming can stir up and temporarily raise the level of airborne contaminants and lead to inhalation of a greater amount of allergens before most are removed and the rest settle down. Depending on the level of pollutants and the sensitivity of the individual, the best thing for that person may be to leave the house, during vacuuming. Central vacuum systems that are vented outside may also help reduce the level of allergens in your home.

The basement. Any floor drain in the basement should be cleaned and disinfected regularly. Before a subsurface basement is finished, make sure that all water leaks are fixed and that there is adequate ventilation and heat to prevent condensation.

Carpets, upholstered furniture, drapes etc. Any items in the house that can harbor biological contaminants should be cleaned regularly.

Pest control. Any insect problem should be taken care of by extermination. (See chapter on pesticides.)

Heating/air conditioning units. Furnace and air conditioning filters should be cleaned and/or replaced whenever necessary. They should be checked each month. All air cleaning devices should be regularly cleaned and maintained. Follow the maintenance instructions for the model you have.

ELECTROMAGNETIC FIELDS (EMF)

Electromagnetic fields are a combination of electric fields and magnetic fields that radiate from electric cables, wires, fixtures and appliances. There are many sources of electromagnetic fields and they include any appliance that has an electric motor, such as a refrigerator, freezer, clothes washer, hair-drier, shaver, food mixer, blender, vacuum etc.; an electric heating element, such as a clothes drier, iron, electric blanket, stove/oven etc.; or uses electric bulbs. For many years, scientists had thought this form of radiation was harmless and that EMF could not damage body cells the way X rays (which have more energy) and microwaves (which cause damage with heat) can.

It is looking more and more likely that this theory is incorrect. In June of 1989, the Congressional Office of Technology Assessment concluded that "emerging evidence no longer allows one to categorically assert that there are no risks" from exposure to EMFs. That emerging evidence comes from epidemiological studies and biological research (lab experiments on living cells and animals) in the United States and other countries. The focus had been on high voltage lines transmitting electricity. The congressional study, done by Carnegie Mellon University, concluded that electromagnetic fields could play a "far greater role than transmission lines, in any public health problem."

EMF HEALTH HAZARDS

Although the available data at the time of the congressional study were not conclusive, they indicated that the most likely health effects of exposure to EMF would be in the areas of cancer and reproduction. While a cause and effect relationship has yet to be established, a statistical association has emerged between exposure to EMF and cancer risks and reproduction malfunctions.

A study done in 1988 of pregnant women by the Kaiser-Permanente Medical Care Center in Oakland, California, found that women who used video display terminals for more than 20 hours a week during the first three months of pregnancy suffered almost twice the number of miscarriages as women doing other office work.

Another study, done in 1979 in Colorado by two epidemiologists, found that a greater percentage of children who lived near power distribution lines had cancer, compared with a control group. A study in 1986 was commissioned by the New York State Power Lines Project to see if the results could be repeated using a different group of children in Colorado. The findings in that study substantiated the earlier findings.

Research in experimental work with animals and human cells suggest that EMFs can interfere with the functioning of DNA (deoxyribonucleic acid) and RNA (ribonucleic acid), the two acids found in all cells. Other laboratory findings suggest that EMF exposure may reduce the immune response, cause reproductive disorders and birth defects (in chicks), stimulate activity in the biochemicals linked to cancer, and affect substances that are critically involved in the central nervous system. There is also data that suggest exposure could cause greater sensitivity to drugs and toxins, mood and sleep disorders, and chronic depression.

At the time of writing, risk standards had not been set and it appears that setting safe levels is a long way off. There are still many questions about exposure to EMFs: how important is the level of intensity; does greater intensity mean greater risk; what role does length of exposure time play—to name just a few. However, even as more extensive research is being conducted and planned, control mitigation measures are being investigated.

CONTROL AND MITIGATION OF EMF

It is certainly not practical to stop using electricity in your home, but until more is known about the possible health hazards of EMF exposure, researchers at Carnegie Mellon suggest some simple precautions you can take that will cause little, if any, inconvenience. Try to keep some distance from electrical appliances that are on all the time, like an electric clock radio. Move it as far from the bed as practical. If you have an electric blanket, use it to warm the bed and turn it off before you get into bed.

Other options which require a much greater effort and commitment, include redesigning appliances so that the emission of EMFs is reduced or eliminated (for example, appropriate shielding of television screens and computer terminals might reduce EMFs), finding ways to do electrical wiring in homes so as to limit EMFs, and planning routes for outside transmission lines so that they are as far from people as possible.

Research into electromagnetic fields is still in the initial stages. Dr. Leonard Sagan was a director of radiation studies for the power industry-supported Electric Power Research Institute of Palo Alto, California in June 1989, when the congressional report came out. At that time he said that until the mid-1980s, it had looked like there was no risk from EMFs. While the report did not convince him that they pose any risk to human health, he conceded that the possibility cannot be ignored. Stay tuned.

EPA REGIONAL OFFICES FOR INDOOR AIR POLLUTANTS

ALABAMA—4	GEORGIA—4	MARYLAND—3
ALASKA—10	GUAM—9	MASSACHUSETTS—1
ARIZONA—9	HAWAII—9	MICHIGAN—5
ARKANSAS—6	IDAHO—10	MINNESOTA—5
CALIFORNIA—9	ILLINOIS—5	MISSISSIPPI—4
COLORADO—8	INDIANA—5	MISSOURI—7
CONNECTICUT—1	IOWA—7	MONTANA—8
DELAWARE—3	KANSAS—7	NEBRASKA—7
DISTRICT OF	KENTUCKY—4	NEVADA—9
COLUMBIA—3	LOUISIANA—6	NEW HAMPSHIRE—1
FLORIDA—4	MAINE—1	NEW JERSEY—2

NEW MEXICO—6	PENNSYLVANIA—3	UTAH—8
NEW YORK—2	PUERTO RICO—2	VERMONT—1
NORTH	RHODE ISLAND—1	VIRGINIA—3
CAROLINA—4	SOUTH	VIRGIN ISLANDS—2
NORTH DAKOTA—8	CAROLINA—4	WASHINGTON—10
OHIO—5	SOUTH DAKOTA—8	WEST VIRGINIA—3
OKLAHOMA—6	TENNESSEE—4	WISCONSIN—5
OREGON—10	TEXAS—6	WYOMING—8

REGION 1
JFK Federal Building
Boston, Massachusetts 02203-2211
(617)565-3232

REGION 6
1445 Ross Avenue
Dallas, Texas 75202-2733
(214)655-7214

REGION 2
26 Federal Plaza
New York, New York 10278
(212)264-2517

REGION 7
726 Minnesota Avenue
Kansas City, Missouri 66101
(913)236-2893

REGION 3
841 Chestnut Street
Philadelphia, Pennsylvania 19107
(215)597-9090

REGION 8
999 18th Street, Suite 1300
Denver, Colorado 80202-2413
(303)293-1750

REGION 4
345 Courtland Street, NE
Atlanta, Georgia 30365
(404)347-2864

REGION 9
215 Fremont Street
San Francisco, California 94105
(415)974-8381

REGION 5
230 South Dearborn Street
Chicago, Illinois 60604
(312)475-8470

REGION 10
1200 6th Avenue
Seattle, Washington 98101
(206442-4226

STATE AGENCIES FOR INDOOR AIR POLLUTION

Following are numbers, by states, for specific indoor air pollutants. There may be more than one number for a particular pollutant. You should be able to tell which number will be most help to you by the department it is in. At times the same agency handles a number of different pollutants. It is noted when that is the case. If your state doesn't have a specific agency for one of the pollutants, call the state department of health or the regional EPA office for Indoor Air Quality.

Building Complaints is the place to call for health complaints commonly referred to as "sick building syndrome." Combustion Devices is the place to call for questions about kerosene and gas space heaters, wood stoves, fireplaces and gas stoves, as well as combustion gases, including particulars such as carbon monoxide, carbon dioxide, oxides of nitrogen, car exhaust, gas and diesel fumes.

ALABAMA
Tobacco smoke
Department of Health and Public
  Services
Health Promotion and
  Information
434 Monroe Street,
  Room 644
Montgomery, Alabama 36130-1701
(205)261-5095

Biologicals
N/A

Building complaints
Department of Public Health
Indoor Air Quality Section
434 Monroe Street,
  Room 254
Montgomery, Alabama 36130-1701
(205)261-5007

Combustion devices
N/A

Ventilation
N/A

ALASKA
Tobacco smoke
Department of Health and Social
  Services
Division of Public Health, Box H
Juneau, Alaska 99811-0613
(907)465-3090

Biologicals
Department of Health and Social
  Services
Epidemiology Section
P.O. Box 240249
Anchorage, Alaska 99524-0249
(907)561-4406

Building complaints
(same address as for biologicals)

Combustion devices
N/A

Ventilation
Division of Community

Development
Energy Program
949 East 36th Street
Anchorage, Alaska 99508
(907)563-1955

ARIZONA
Tobacco Smoke
Department of Health Services
Office of Risk Assessment
3008 North Third Street
Phoenix, Arizona 85012
(602)230-5865

Biologicals
Office of Risk Assessment
(same address as above)
(602)230-5858

Building complaints
Office of Risk Assessment
(same address as above)
(602)230-5865

Combustion devices
Office of Risk Assessment
(same address as above)
(602)230-5865

Ventilation
Office of Risk Assessment
(same address as above)
(602)230-5858

Energy Office
1700 West Washington Street
Phoenix, Arizona 85007
(602)255-4945

ARKANSAS
Tobacco smoke
Department of Health
Health Education Division
4815 West Markham Street
Little Rock, Arkansas 72205-3876
(501)661-2494

Biologicals
Department of Health
Bureau of Environmental Health
  Services

4815 West Markham Street
Little Rock, Arkansas 72205
(501)661-2574

Building complaints
Department of Health
Division of Sanitarian Services
(same address as above)
(501)661-2171

Combustion devices
Department of Health
Bureau of Environmental Health
  Services
(same address as above)
(501)661-2574

Ventilation
N/A

CALIFORNIA
Tobacco smoke
Department of Health Services
Human Population Lab
2151 Berkeley Way, Annex 2
Berkeley, California 94704
(415)540-2396

Department of Health Services
Cancer Prevention Section
5850 Shellmound Street, Suite 200
Emeryville, California 94608
(415)540-2913

Air Resources Board
Research Division/Indoor Air
  Quality
Box 2815
Sacramento, California 95812
(916)323-5043

Biologicals
Department of Health Services
Indoor Air Quality Program
2151 Berkeley Way
Berkeley, California 94704
(415)540-2469

Building complaints
(same address and phone number
for biologicals)

Combustion devices
(same address and phone number
as for biologicals)

Ventilation
(same address and phone number
as for biologicals)

Energy Commission
1516 9th Street
Sacramento, California 95814
(916)324-3383

COLORADO
Tobacco smoke
Department of Health
Consumer Protection Division
4210 East 11th Avenue
Denver, Colorado 80220
(303)331-8250

Department of Health
Division of Prevention Programs
4210 East 11th Avenue
Denver, Colorado 80220
(303)331-8300

Biologicals
Department of Health
Consumer Protection Division
(same address as above)
(303)331-8250

Department of Health
Disease Control/Environmental
  Epidemiology Division
4210 East 11th Avenue
Denver, Colorado 80220
(303)331-8330

Building complaints
(same addresses and phone
numbers as for biologicals)

Combustion devices
Department of Health
Disease Control/Environmental
  Epidemiology Division
(same address as above)
(303)331-8330

Department of Health
Consumer Protection Division
(same address as above)
(303)331-8250

Ventilation
Office of Energy Conservation
112 East 14th Avenue
Denver, Colorado 80203
(303)894-2144

Department of Local Affairs
Division of Housing
1313 Sherman Street
Denver, Colorado 80203
(303)866-2033

CONNECTICUT
Tobacco smoke
Department of Health Services
Preventable Diseases Division
150 Washington Street
Hartford, Connecticut 06106
(203)566-1292

Biologicals
(same address as for tobacco smoke)
(203)566-3186

Department of Health Services
Toxic Hazards Section
(same address as above)
(203)566-8167

Building complaints
Department of Health Services
Toxic Hazards Section
(same address as above)
(203)566-1260

Combustion devices
N/A

Ventilation
N/A

DELAWARE
Tobacco smoke
Department of Health/Social
  Services
Bureau of Environmental Health
802 Silver Lake Boulevard

Robbins Building
Dover, Delaware 19901
(302)736-4731

Biologicals
(same address and phone number
as above)

Building complaints
(same address and phone number
as above)

Combustion devices
(same address and phone number
as above)

Ventilation
(same address and phone number
as above)

Department of Administrative
  Services
Energy Office
P.O. Box 1401
Dover, Delaware 19903
(302)736-5644

DIST. OF COLUMBIA
Tobacco smoke
Department of Consumer and
  Regulatory Affairs
Air Branch
5010 Overlook Avenue, S.W.
Washington, D.C. 20032
(202)767-7370

Biologicals
(same address and phone number
as above)

Building Complaints
(same address and phone number
as above)

Combustion devices
N/A

Ventilation
N/A

FLORIDA
Tobacco smoke
Department of Health &

Rehabilitative Services
Office of Epidemiology
1317 Winewood Boulevard
Tallahassee, Florida 32301
(904)488-2901

Biologicals
Department of Health &
  Rehabilitative Services
Laboratory Services
1217 Pearl Street
Jacksonville, Florida 32202
(904)359-6125

Department of Environmental
  Regulation
2600 Blair Stone Road
Tallahassee, Florida 32399
(904)488-1344

Building complaints
Department of Health &
  Rehabilitative Services
Laboratory Services
(same address as above)
(904)359-6125

Department of Health &
  Rehabilitative Services
Office of Epidemiology
(same address as above)
(904)488-2905

Combustion devices
N/A

Ventilation
Department of Community Affairs
Energy Code Program
2740 Centerview Drive
Tallahassee, Florida 32399
(904)487-1824

GEORGIA
Tobacco smoke
Department of Human Resources
Division of Public Health
47 Trinity Avenue
Atlanta, Georgia 30334
(404)894-6527

Biologicals
(same address as above)
(404)894-6644

Building complaints
N/A

Combustion devices
N/A

Ventilation
(same address as above)
(404)894-6644

Department of Community Affairs
Building Codes and Safety Program
1200 Equitable Building
100 Peachtree Street
Atlanta, Georgia 30303
(404)656-1725

GUAM
Tobacco smoke
Department of Public Health &
  Social Services
Division of Public Health
P.O. Box 2816
Agana, Guam 96910
(671)734-2544

Biologicals
(same address and phone number
as above)

Building complaints
Department of Public Health &
  Social Services
Division of Environmental Health
P.O. Box 2816
Agana, Guam 96910
(671)734-2671

Combustion devices
N/A

Ventilation
(same address and phone number
as for building complaints)

HAWAII
Tobacco smoke
Department of Health

Medical Health Services Division
Chronic Disease Branch
P.O. Box 3378
Honolulu, Hawaii 96801
(808)548-5835

Biologicals
Department of Health
Pollution Investigation &
  Enforcement Branch
1250 Punchbowl Street
Honolulu, Hawaii 96813
(808)548-6355

Building complaints
N/A

Combustion devices
N/A

Ventilation
Department of Health
Environmental Protection & Health
  Services
1250 Punchbowl Street
Honolulu, Hawaii 96813
(208)548-3075 or 4883

IDAHO
Tobacco smoke
Department of Health & Welfare
Bureau of Preventive Medicine
Statehouse Mall
Boise, Idaho 83720
(808)334-5930 or 5933

Biologicals
N/A

Building complaints
N/A

Combustion devices
N/A

Ventilation
Department of Labor & Industrial
  Services
Building Division
277 North Sixth Street
Statehouse Mall

Boise, Idaho 83720
(208)334-3896

ILLINOIS
Tobacco smoke
Department of Public Health
Division of Environmental Health
525 West Jefferson Street
Springfield, Illinois 62761
(217)782-5830

Biologicals
(same address and phone number
as above)

Building complaints
(same address and phone number
as above)

Combustion devices
(same address and phone number
as above)

Ventilation
(same address and phone number
as above)

INDIANA
Tobacco smoke
State Board of Health
Division of Education
1330 West Michigan Street
P.O. Box 1964
Indianapolis, Indiana 46206-1964
(317)633-0267

Biologicals
State Board of Health
Department of Environmental
  Management
Office of Air Management
105 South Meridian Street
Indianapolis, Indiana 46225
(317)232- 8222

Building complaints
State Board of Health
Division of Industrial Hygiene
1330 West Michigan Street
P.O. Box 1964

Indianapolis, Indiana 46206-1964
(317)633-0692

Combustion devices
Department of Fire & Building
  Services
1099 North Meridian Street,
  Suite 900
Indianapolis, Indiana 46204
(317)232-1402

Ventilation
(same address and phone number
as for combustion devices)

IOWA
Tobacco smoke
Department of Public Health
Division of Disease Prevention
Lucas State Office Building
Des Moines, Iowa 50319
(515)281-7785

Biologicals
Department of Public Health
Bureau of Compliance & Health
  Care Services
Lucas State Office Building
Des Moines, Iowa 50319
(515)281-7782

Department of Public Health
Division of Disease Prevention
(same address as above)
(515)281-4928

Building complaints
Division of Labor Services
1000 East Grand Avenue
Des Moines, Iowa 50319
(515)281-3606

Combustion devices
N/A

Ventilation
(same address and phone number
as for building complaints)

KANSAS
Tobacco smoke
Department of Health &

Environment
109 Southwest Ninth Street
Topeka, Kansas 66612
(913)296-1216

Biologicals
(same address as above)
(913)296-1619

Building complaints
Department of Health &
  Environment
Air Quality & Radiation Control
  Board
Forbes Field
Topeka, Kansas 66620
(913)296-1543

Combustion devices
N/A

Ventilation
(same address and phone number
as for building complaints)

Kansas Corporation Commission
Dockings State Office Building, 4th
  Floor
Topeka, Kansas 66612
(913)296–5460

KENTUCKY
Tobacco smoke
N/A

Biologicals
Cabinet for Labor
Division of Compliance
U.S. Highway 127 South
Frankfort, Kentucky 40601
(502)564-7360

Cabinet for Labor
Division of Education & Training
U.S. Highway 127 South
Frankfort, Kentucky 40601
(502)564-6895

Building complaints
Cabinet for Labor
Division of Compliance

(same address as above)
(502)564-7360

Combustion devices
Cabinet for Labor
Division of Compliance
(same address as above)
(502)564-7360

Cabinet for Labor
Division of Education & Training
(same address as above)
(502)564-6895

Ventilation
Department of Housing, Buildings
  & Construction
Division of Building Code
  Enforcement
The 127 Office Building
Frankfort, Kentucky 40601
(502)564-8090

Cabinet for Labor
Division of Education & Training
(same address as above)
(502)564-6895

Cabinet for Labor
Division of Compliance
(same address as above)
(502)564-7360

LOUISIANA
Tobacco smoke
Department of Health & Hospital
P.O. Box 60630
New Orleans, Louisiana 70160
(504)568-5053

Department of Environmental
  Quality
Air Quality Division
P.O. Box 44096
Baton Rouge, Louisiana 70804
(504)342-1201

Biologicals
Department of Health & Hospital
(same address as above)
(504)568-5053

Building complaints
N/A

Combustion devices
N/A

Ventilation
N/A

MAINE
Tobacco smoke
Department of Human Services
Division of Health Education
Statehouse Station 11
Augusta, Maine 04333
(207)289-3201

Biologicals
Department of Human Services
Occupational & Residential Health
Statehouse Station 10
Augusta, Maine 04333
(207)289-3826

Department of Administration
Bureau of Public Improvements
Statehouse Station 77
Augusta, Maine 04333
(207)289-4509

Building complaints
(same addresses and phone
numbers as for biologicals)

Combustion devices
(same addresses and phone
numbers as for biologicals)

Ventilation
(same addresses and phone
numbers as for biologicals)

Office of Energy Resources
Energy Extension Service
233 Oxford Street
Portland, Maine 04101
(207)879-4199

MARYLAND
Tobacco smoke
N/A

Biologicals
Department of the Environment
Center for Environmental Health
201 West Preston Street
Baltimore, Maryland 21201
(301)225-5753

Building complaints
N/A

Combustion devices
N/A

Ventilation
N/A

MASSACHUSETTS
Tobacco Smoke
Department of Public Health
23 Service Center
Northampton, Massachusetts 01060
(617)727-0732

Biologicals
Department of Public Health
Environmental Hygiene
150 Tremont Street
Boston, Massachusetts 02111
(617)727-2660

Department of Environmental
  Quality Engineering
Division of Air Quality Control
One Winter Street
Boston, Massachusetts 02108
(617)292-5593

Building complaints
N/A

Combustion devices
Department of Environmental
  Quality   Engineering
Division of Air Quality Control
(same address as above)
(617)292-5593

Ventilation
Department of Public Safety
Board of Building Regulations &
  Standards
One Ashburton Place, Room 1301

Boston, Massachusetts 02108
(617)727-3200

Department of Public Health
Environmental Hygiene
150 Tremont Street
Boston, Massachusetts 02111
(617)727-2660

MICHIGAN
Tobacco smoke
Department of Public Health
Environmental & Occupational
  Health
3500 North Logan Street
P.O. Box 30035
Lansing, Michigan 48909
(517)373-1356 or 335-9218

Biologicals
Department of Public Health
Bureau of Lab & Epidemiological
  Services
(same address as above)
(517)335-8050

Building complaints
(same address as for biologicals)
(517)335-8352

Combustion devices
Department of Public Health
Environmental Health Sciences
  Center
(same address as above)
(517)335-8350

Ventilation
Department of Public Health
Bureau of Environmental &
  Occupational Health
(same address as above)
(517)335-8250

MINNESOTA
Tobacco Smoke
Department of Health
Regulatory Enforcement
717 S.E. Delaware Street

Minneapolis, Minnesota 55440
(612)623-5336

Department of Health
Center for Non-Smoking
(same address as above)
(612)623-5500

Biologicals
Pollution Control Agency
Division of Air Quality
520 Lafayette Road North
St. Paul, Minnesota 55155
(612)296-7802

Building complaints
N/A

Combustion devices
Department of Health
Health Risk Assessment
717 S.E. Delaware Street
Minneapolis, Minnesota 55440
(612)623-5333

Ventilation
Department of Administration
408 Metro Square Building
St. Paul, Minnesota 55101
(612)296-4639

MISSISSIPPI
Tobacco smoke
Department of Health
Preventive Health Services
P.O. Box 1700
Jackson, Mississippi 39215-1700
(601)960-7725

 Biologicals
Department of Health
(same address as above)
(601)960-7725

Building complaints
N/A

Combustion devices
N/A

Ventilation
Department of Energy &
  Transportation

Energy Conservation/Efficiency
  Branch
Dickson Building, Suite 404
510 George Street
Jackson, Mississippi 39202
(601)961-4733

Bureau of Buildings
1501 Walter Sillers Building
Jackson, Mississippi 39202
(601)359-3621

MISSOURI
Tobacco smoke
Department of Health
Division of Environmental Health
  & Epidemiology
1730 East Elm Street
P.O. Box 570
Jefferson City, Missouri 65102-0570
(314)751-6102

Biologicals
(same address and phone number
as above)

Building complaints
(same address and phone number
as above)

Combustion devices
(same address and phone number
as above)

Ventilation
(same address and phone number
as above)

MONTANA
Tobacco smoke
Department of Health &
  Environmental Sciences
Food & Consumer Health Bureau
Cogswell Building
Helena, Montana 59620
(406)444-2408

Biologicals
Department of Health &
  Environmental Sciences
Occupational Health Bureau

Cogswell Building, Room A113
Helena, Montana 59620
(406)444-3671

Building complaints
(same address and phone number
as for biologicals)

Combustion devices
(same address and phone number
as for biologicals)

Ventilation
(same address and phone number
as for biologicals)

NEBRASKA
Tobacco smoke
Department of Health
Environmental Health & Housing
  Surveillance
301 Centennial Mall South
P.O. Box 95007
Lincoln, Nebraska 68509
(402)471-2541 or 2102

Biologicals
(same address as above)
(402)471-2541

Building complaints
(same address as above)
(402)471-2541

Combustion devices
(same address as above)
(402)471-2541

Ventilation
(same address as above)
(402)471-2541

NEVADA
Tobacco smoke
Department of Human Resources
Division of Health
505 East King Street
Carson City, Nevada 89710
(702)885-4740

Biologicals
Department of Industrial Relations

1390 South Curry Street
Carson City, Nevada 89710
(702)885-3270

Building complaints
Department of Industrial Relations
(same address as above)
(702)885-3270
(same address as for tobacco smoke)
(702)885-4740

Combustion devices
N/A

Ventilation
Office of Community Services
State Energy Office
1100 East William Street, Suite 117
Carson City, Nevada 89710
(702)855-4420

NEW HAMPSHIRE
Tobacco smoke
Department of Health & Human
  Services
Division of Public Health
6 Hazen Drive
Concord, New Hampshire
  03301-6527
(603)271-4549

Biologicals
Department of Health & Human
  Services
Bureau of Environmental Health
6 Hazen Drive
Concord, New Hampshire
  03301-6527
(603)271-4676

Building complaints
N/A

Combustion devices
N/A

Ventilation
Public Utilities Commission
8 Old Suncook Road, Building 1
Concord, New Hampshire
  03301-5185
(603)271-2431

NEW JERSEY
Tobacco smoke
Department of Health
CN 360
Trenton, New Jersey 08625
(609)984-1349

Biologicals
(same address as above)
(609)633-2043

Building complaints
(same address as above)
(609)984-1863

Combustion devices
(same address as above)
(609)633-2043 or 984-1364

Ventilation
Department of Community Affairs
Division of Housing &
   Development
South Broad & Front Streets, CN804
Trenton, New Jersey 08625
(609)633-6060 or 292-7899

NEW MEXICO
Tobacco smoke
Health & Environmental
   Department
Public Health Division
Smoking Prevention & Cessation
P.O. Box 968
Santa Fe, New Mexico 87504-0968
(505)827-2381

Biologicals
N/A

Building complaints
N/A

Combustion devices
N/A

Ventilation
Energy, Minerals & Natural
   Resources Dept.
525 Marquez Place
Santa Fe, New Mexico 87501
(505)827-5908

NEW YORK
Tobacco smoke
Department of Health
2 University Place
Albany, New York 12203-3313
(518)474-0512

Biologicals
Department of   Health
Occupational
   Health/Environmental
   Epidemiology
2 University Place
Albany, New York 12203-3313
(518)458-6433

Building complaints
Department of   Health
Occupational
   Health/Environmental
   Epidemiology
(same address as above)
(518)458-6433

Energy Office
Two Rockefeller Plaza
Albany, New York 12223
(518)474-5227

Department of Health
Bureau of Toxic Substance
   Assessment
2 University Place, Room 240
Albany, New York 12203-3313
(518)458-6376

Combustion devices
N/A

Ventilation
Energy Office
Two Rockefeller Plaza
Albany, New York 12223
(518)474-5227

NORTH CAROLINA
Tobacco Smoke
Department of Human Resources
Division of Health Services
P.O. Box 2091

Raleigh, North Carolina 27602
(919)733-2775

Department of Human Resources
Environmental Epidemiology
  Branch
·225 North McDowell Street
Raleigh, North Carolina 27602
(919)733-3410

Biologicals
Department of Human Resources
Environmental Epidemiology
  Branch
(same address as above)
(919)733-3410

Building complaints
Department of Human Resources
Environmental Epidemiology
  Branch
(same address as above)
(919)733-3410

Combustion devices
Department of Human Resources
Environmental Epidemiology
  Branch
(same address as above)
(919)733-3410

Ventilation
Department of Human Resources
Environmental Epidemiology
  Branch
(same address as above)
(919)733-3410

Department of Insurance
Mechanical Section
410 North Boylan Avenue
Raleigh, North Carolina 27603
(919)733-3901

NORTH DAKOTA
Tobacco smoke
Department of Health
1200 Missouri Avenue
P.O Box 5520
Bismarck, North Dakota 58505-5520
(701)224-2367 or 2493

Biologicals
Department of Health
Division of Environmental
  Engineering
1200 Missouri Avenue
P.O. Box 5520
Bismarck, North Dakota 58505-5520
(701)224-2348

Building complaints
(same address and phone number
as for biologicals)

Combustion devices
(same address and phone number
as for biologicals)

Ventilation
N/A

OHIO
Tobacco smoke
Department of Health
246 North High Street
Columbus, Ohio 43266-0588
(614)466-0277

Biologicals
Department of Health
Bureau of Environmental Health
246 North High Street
Columbus, Ohio 43266-0588
(614)466-1450

Environmental Protection Agency
Division of Air Pollution
P.O. Box 1049
1800 Water Mark Drive
Columbus, Ohio 43266-0149
(614)644-2270

Building complaints
N/A

Combustion devices
N/A

Ventilation
Department of Development
Office of Energy Conservation
30 East Broad Street, 24th Floor

Columbus, Ohio 43266-0413
(614)466-6797

OKLAHOMA
Tobacco Smoke
Department of Health
Radiation & Special Hazards
Service
1000 Northeast Tenth Street
P.O. Box 53551
Oklahoma City, Oklahoma 73152
(405)271-5221

Biologicals
(same address and phone number
as above)

Building complaints
(same address and phone number
as above)

Combustion devices
(same address and phone number
as above)

Ventilation
(same address and phone number
as above)

OREGON
Tobacco Smoke
Department of Human Resources
State Health Division
1400 Southwest Fifth Avenue
Portland, Oregon 97201
(503)229-5272

Biologicals
Department of Human Resources
Office of Health Status Monitoring
1400 Southwest Fifth Avenue
Portland, Oregon 97201
(503)229-5792

Department of Environmental
Quality
811 Southwest Sixth Avenue
Portland, Oregon 97204
(503)229-5713

Building complaints
N/A

Combustion devices
Department of Environmental
Quality
(same address as above)
(503)229-5353

Ventilation
Building Codes Agency
401 Labor & Industries Building
Salem, Oregon 97310
(503)373-7902 or 378-4133

PENNSYLVANIA
Tobacco smoke
Department of Health
Division of Health Promotion
P.O. Box 90
Harrisburg, Pennsylvania 17108
(717)787-5900

Biologicals
Department of Environmental
Resources
Bureau of Air Quality Control
Third & Locust Street, Fulton Bank
Building
P.O. Box 2063
Harrisburg, Pennsylvania 17120
(717)787- 4310

Department of Health
Division of Epidemiology
P.O. Box 90
Harrisburg, Pennsylvania 17108
(717)787-3350

Building complaints
N/A

Combustion devices
N/A

Ventilation
Department of Community Affairs
Division of Manufactured Housing
Forum Building, Room 508
Harrisburg, Pennsylvania 17120
(717)787-9682

PUERTO RICO
Tobacco Smoke

Environmental Quality Board
204 Ramaiada Street
P.O. Box 11488
Santurce, Puerto Rico 00910
(809)725-8898

Biologicals
(same address and phone number
as above)

Building complaints
N/A

Combustion devices
(same address as above)
(809)722-0077

Ventilation
N/A

RHODE ISLAND
Tobacco smoke
Department of Health
75 Davis Street
206 Cannon Building
Providence, Rhode Island 02908
(401)277-1312

Biologicals
(same address as above)
(401)277-2438

Building complaints
(same address and phone number
as for biologicals)

Ventilation
State Building Commission
610 Mount Pleasant Avenue
Building No. 2
North Providence, Rhode Island
  02908
(401)277-3033

SOUTH CAROLINA
Tobacco smoke
Department of Health &
  Environmental Control
2600 Bull Street
Columbia, South Carolina 29201
(803)734-4790

Biologicals
Department of Health &
  Environmental Control
Air Quality Analysis Division
P.O. Box 2202
Columbia, South Carolina 29202
(803)737-7020

Department of Health &
  Environmental Control
Division of Health Hazard
  Evaluation
2600 Bull Street
Columbia, South Carolina 29201
(803)734-5429

Building complaints
Department of Labor
Occupational Safety & Health
  Division
3600 Forest Drive
P.O. Box 22329
Columbia, South Carolina
  29211-1329
(803)734-9644

Combustion devices
Department of Health &
  Environmental Control
Bureau of Air Quality Control
2600 Bull Street
Columbia, South Carolina 29201
(803)734-4750

Ventilation
(same address and phone number
as for building complaints)

SOUTH DAKOTA
Tobacco smoke
Department of Health
Division of Public Health
Joe Foss Building
523 East Capitol Avenue
Pierre, South Dakota 57501
(605)773-3361

Biologicals
(same address as above)
(605)773-3364

Building complaints
(same address and phone number
as for tobacco smoke)

Department of Commerce &
 Regulation
State Fire Marshal
118 West Capitol Avenue
Pierre, South Dakota 57501
(605)773-3562

Combustion devices
(same address and phone number
as for tobacco smoke)

Ventilation
Energy Office
217 1/2 West Missouri
Pierre, South Dakota 57501
(605)773-3603

TENNESSEE
Tobacco smoke
Department of Health &
 Environment
Health Promotion
100 Ninth Avenue, North,
 Fourth   Floor
Nashville, Tennessee 37219-5405
(615)741-7366

Biologicals
Department of Health &
 Environment
Division of Air Pollution Control
Customs House
701 Broadway
Nashville, Tennessee 37219-5403
(615)741-3931

Building complaints
(same address and phone number
as for biologicals)

Combustion devices
(same address and phone number
as for biologicals)

Ventilation
N/A

TEXAS
Tobacco smoke
Department of Health
1100 West 49th Street
Austin, Texas 78756
(512)458-7405 or 7269

Biologicals
Department of Health
Occupational Safety & Health
 Division
1100 West 49th Street
Austin, Texas 78756
(512)458-7254

Building complaints
(same address and phone number
as for biologicals)

Combustion devices
(same address and phone number
as for biologicals)

Ventilation
(same address and phone number
as for biologicals)

Governor's Energy Management
 Center
P.O. Box 12428
Austin, Texas 78711
(512)463-1931

UTAH
Tobacco smoke
Department of Health
Bureau of Drinking Water &
 Sanitation
288 North 1460 West
Salt Lake City, Utah 84116
(801)538-6159

Biologicals
Department of Health
Bureau of Air Quality
288 North 1460 West
P.O. Box 16690
Salt Lake City, Utah 84116
(801)538-6108

Building complaints
N/A

Combustion devices
Energy Office
355 West North Temple
Third Triad Center, Suite 450
Salt Lake City, Utah 84180-1204
(801)538-5428

Ventilation
(same address and phone number
as for combustion devices)

VERMONT
Tobacco Smoke
Department of Health
Division of Epidemiology
60 Main Street
P.O. Box 70
Burlington, Vermont 05402
(802)863-7240

Biologicals
Department of Health
Division of Environmental Health
60 Main Street
P.O. Box 70
Burlington, Vermont 05402
(802)863-7220

Building complaints
(same address and phone number
as for biologicals)

Combustion devices
N/A

Ventilation
Department of Health
Division of Occupational &
  Radiological Health
Administration Building
10 Baldwin Street
Montpelier, Vermont 05602
(802)828-2886

VIRGINIA
Tobacco smoke
Department of Health
James Madison Building
109 Governor Street
Richmond, Virginia 23219
(804)786-3551

Biologicals
Department of Health
Health Hazards Control Division
James Madison Building
109 Governor Street
Richmond, Virginia 23219
(804)786-6029

Building complaints
(same address and phone number
as for biologicals)

Combustion devices
(same address as for tobacco smoke)
(804)786-1763

Ventilation
Department of Mines, Minerals &
  Energy
Division of Energy
2201 West Broad Street
Richmond, Virginia 23220
(804)367-0330

Housing & Community
  Development Department
205 North Fourth Street
Richmond, Virginia 23219-1747
(804)789-1575

WASHINGTON
Tobacco Smoke
Department of Social & Health
  Services
Toxic Substances Section
Mail Stop LD-11
Olympia, Washington 98504
(206)753-2556

Biologicals
(same address and phone number
as above)

Building complaints
(same address and phone number
as above)

Combustion devices
N/A

Ventilation
Energy Office

801 Legion Way, S.E.
Olympia, Washington 98504-1211
(206)586-5021

Department of Community
   Development
Community Services
Mail Stop GH-51
Ninth & Columbia Building
Olympia, Washington 98504
(206)586-8966

WEST VIRGINIA
Tobacco smoke
Department of Health
Indoor Air Quality Program
4873 Brenda Lane
Charleston, West Virginia 25312
(304)348-0644

Biologicals
(same address as above)
(304)348-0696

Building complaints
Fire Marshal's Office
2000 Quarrier Street
Charleston, West Virginia 25305
(304)348-2191

Combustion devices
(same address and phone number
as for building complaints)

Ventilation
(same address and phone number
as for building complaints)

WISCONSIN
Tobacco Smoke
Health & Social Services
   Department
Environmental/Chronic Disease
   Epidemiology
P.O. Box 309
Madison, Wisconsin 53701-0309
(608)267-3835

Biologicals
(same address as above)
(608)266-1253

Department of Natural Resources
Bureau of Air Management
P.O. Box 7921
Madison, Wisconsin 53707
(608)266-1902

Building complaints
Health & Social Services
   Department
Community Health & Prevention
   Bureau
P.O. Box 309
Madison, Wisconsin 53701-0309
(608)266-9337

Combustion devices
(same address as for tobacco smoke)
(608)266-7089

Ventilation
Deputy of Administration
Energy & Intergovernmental
   Relations Division
P.O. Box 7868
Madison, Wisconsin 53707
(608)266-2758

WYOMING
Tobacco smoke
N/A

Biologicals
N/A

Building complaints
N/A

Combustion devices
N/A

Ventilation
N/A

PART TWO

ENVIRONMENTAL HAZARDS OUTSIDE THE HOUSE

8

HAZARDOUS WASTE SITES

"UPSTATE WASTE SITE MAY ENDANGER LIVES." That was the front page headline on *The New York Times* on August 3, 1978. The headline the next day was "HEALTH CHIEF CALLS WASTE SITE A 'PERIL'; ASKS PREGNANT WOMEN AND INFANTS TO LEAVE NIAGARA FALLS SECTOR."

The dateline was Love Canal, New York. Many people read the story. It received national coverage. Lois Marie Gibbs is one of the area residents who lived it.

Lois was 26 at the time, living with her husband and new baby in a modest three-bedroom bungalow in Niagara Falls. When she moved in, in 1972, she did not know that her dreamhouse was next to a toxic dumpsite containing nearly 22,000 tons of chemical wastes, including polychlorinated biphenyls (PCBs), dioxin and long-lasting pesticides.

For years the Hooker Chemical Corporation (along with, to a much lesser degree, the city of Niagara Falls and the U.S.) had dumped those chemicals in what had been the "Love Canal." In 1953 Hooker filled in the dump and sold it to the city for $1. Soon a road was built on top of it and houses sprang up on either side, along with a public school. Parents' complaints of nauseating smells, the appearance of black sludge, and minor burn marks showing up on their children went unheeded until the late '70s when New York state started an investigation.

In 1980, President Jimmy Carter declared a health emergency when an EPA study showed that a third of the Love Canal residents had suffered chromosome damage. Five months later he signed a bill for the permanent evacuation of close to 800 families.

In 1985, 1,300 former Love Canal residents divvied up the $20 million awarded in their class action suit. But the money means little to recipient Marie Pozniak. Her daughter was born with abnormalities and she herself has had several cancer operations. "They could give me 20 million dollars," she said, "and it wouldn't compensate for the mental anguish I face every time I look at my daughter."

As with so many other environmental problems, scant attention was paid to hazardous waste. With virtually no regulation, dumping was widespread, with little concern for its consequences. Love Canal rang the first alarm. It wasn't long after that more toxic sites were discovered, garnering national attention and raising concern among millions of Americans who found themselves wondering if their town would make the next headline.

THE PROBLEM

Hazardous waste is produced at the rate of 100,000 tons a day, or *36 million tons a year* in the United States. While actually a small part of the six billion tons of garbage generated annually in this country, it represents the most significant part—polluting our water and air. Industrial waste, which is the most common source of hazardous substances, accounts for 6.4% of the total volume of waste regulated by the EPA. (The other very toxic hazardous waste, radioactive waste, is regulated

Aerial view in 1982 of Western Processing Inc., a hazardous waste handling and disposal firm in Kent, Washington, with storage tanks, liquid, wastepits and ponds. EPA/MSL/Las Vegas.

by the Nuclear Regulatory Commission.) The sources of the rest of the waste subject to EPA regulations are agriculture, 50.3%; mining/milling, 39%; municipal, 3.1%; utility, 1.2%

Hazardous wastes are primarily industrial chemicals that pose a threat to the environment and to the health of people exposed to them. Vegetation and wildlife can be endangered as well by pollutants like metals and organic solvents. The EPA has identified over 4,000 "extremely hazardous" substances.

Different chemicals have different effects. The impact of the hazardous waste site depends on a number of factors including: the toxicity of the chemical or chemicals, its concentration, and its location. Groundwater is most frequently contaminated, followed by surface water and air. Many of the waste sites are in locations where they seep into underground waters, nearby streams and lakes. At some sites, toxic vapors rise from evaporating liquid wastes and pollute the air. Or the air becomes contaminated from uncontrolled chemical reactions.

The chemical and petroleum industries are responsible for many of the waste sites. Some are municipal landfills, the result of an accumulation of pesticides, cleaning solvents and other household chemicals discarded in the household trash. Other sites are the result of accidents or transportation spills.

More than 25,000 hazardous waste sites have been reported to the EPA. It's been projected that as many as 10%, or 2,500, will require cleanup by the Superfund program.

SUPERFUND—WHAT THE GOVERNMENT IS DOING

In 1980 the federal government took its first major step in regulating toxic wastes. Congress passed the Comprehensive Environmental Response, Compensation, and Liability Act (CERCLA) to, among other things, develop priorities for cleaning up the worst sites. The Act set up a $1.6 billion Hazardous Waste Trust Fund, which became known as "Superfund." The money in Superfund was to be used to clean up the worst existing sites and to respond in emergency situations.

After CERCLA, two more acts were passed: the Toxic Substances Control Act (TSCA) and the Resource Conservation and Recovery Act (RCRA). TSCA provided for the identification and control by the EPA of chemical products that pose a risk to humans or the environment through their manufacture, distribution, use or disposal. The purpose of RCRA was to create guidelines for the management of toxic waste and its disposal.

In 1985, the EPA developed the Chemical Emergency Preparedness Program (CEEP) to help states and local communities prepare for, and respond to, chemical accidents.

The following year, Congress passed the Superfund Amendments and Reauthorization Act (SARA), which increased the Superfund pot to $8.5 billion. Included in SARA is Title III: The Emergency Planning and Community Right to Know Act of 1986, which requires federal, state and local governments and industry to work together in developing emergency plans and "community right to know" reporting on chemical hazards.

With thousands of reported hazardous waste sites, a National Priorities List (NPL) was set up to identify the sites posing the biggest threat. The first NPL was printed in September of 1983. It contained 407 sites. The NPL is updated at least once a year. In 1989 there were over 1,200 final or proposed sites on the list. At the end of 1989, 115 of these sites were at federal facilities.

Sites are placed on the NPL on the basis of their scores on the Hazard Ranking System. At the time of printing the cutoff point for making the list was 28.50. The higher the number, the greater risk posed by the site, and the higher that site is placed on the NPL.

The following 9th NPL of final and proposed sites, by state, was issued in July of 1989:

NATIONAL PRIORITIES LIST OF WASTE SITES/1989

	Final		Proposed		
State/Territory	Non-Fed	Fed	Non-Fed	Fed	Total
Alabama	8	2	2	0	12
Alaska	1	0	1	4	5
Arizona	5	0	3	3	9
Arkansas	10	0	0	0	10
California	44	8	33	13	98
Colorado	12	1	2	2	17
Connecticut	8	0	6	0	14
Delaware	11	1	8	0	20
District of Columbia	0	0	0	0	0
Florida	32	0	15	4	51
Guam	1	0	0	0	1
Georgia	6	1	6	1	14
Hawaii	0	0	6	1	7
Idaho	4	0	3	2	9
Illinois	19	4	16	0	39

State/Territory	Final		Proposed		
	Non-Fed	Fed	Non-Fed	Fed	Total
Indiana	30	0	7	0	37
Iowa	9	0	15	1	25
Kansas	9	0	2	1	12
Kentucky	12	0	5	0	17
Louisiana	8	1	2	0	11
Maine	5	1	2	1	9
Maryland	7	0	1	2	10
Massachusetts	21	0	1	3	25
Michigan	65	0	16	0	81
Minnesota	39	1	0	1	41
Mississippi	2	0	1	0	3
Missouri	12	2	8	1	21
Montana	8	0	2	0	10
Nebraska	2	1	2	0	5
Nevada	0	0	0	0	0
New Hampshire	15	0	0	1	16
New Jersey	97	3	6	3	109
New Mexico	5	1	3	1	10
New York	72	1	0	3	76
North Carolina	15	0	6	1	22
North Dakota	2	0	0	0	2
Ohio	29	0	2	3	34
Oklahoma	7	1	3	0	11
Oregon	5	1	1	0	7
Pennsylvania	68	2	24	2	96
Puerto Rico	8	0	0	1	9
Rhode Island	8	0	1	2	11
South Carolina	14	0	7	1	22
South Dakota	1	0	0	0	1
Tennessee	9	1	3	1	14
Texas	23	1	3	2	29
Utah	3	2	5	2	12
Vermont	4	0	4	0	8
Virginia	11	1	9	0	21
Washington	21	4	10	10	45
West Virginia	5	0	1	0	6
Wisconsin	35	0	4	0	39
Wyoming	1	0	1	1	3
TOTAL	767	32	348	30	1177

Of the top 50 sites, which are the most hazardous, 10 are in New Jersey, followed by Texas with five and Massachusetts with four. The other states in the first 50 are: New Hampshire (3), Pennsylvania (3), Florida

(3), Montana (3), Minnesota (3), New York (2), Michigan (2), Delaware (2), and with one site each, Iowa, Arkansas, South Dakota, Ohio, Colorado, Alabama, California, Maine, Washington, Iowa, and Wisconsin.

WHAT YOU CAN DO

Although it may seem like there is nothing you can do, you do have some options. If you know you live near a hazardous waste site, the first thing

A student wearing a self-contained breathing apparatus and fully encapsulating "moon suit" at the EPA Hazardous Materials Incidence Response Training Center in Cincinnati, Ohio. The exercise over an obstacle course helps the trainee to become accustomed to moving in the cumbersome gear. Tom Sell/EPA.

you'll want to do is make sure your local health department knows it as well and has reported it to the EPA. If you suspect that an area near you may be a toxic waste site call the RCRA Hotline at 1-800-424-9346 and ask if that location is listed. If it isn't check with your health department. You can also call the EPA's National Response Center at 1-800-424-8802 and report the site. That is also the number to call if you see, or suspect, illegal dumping, or if there is a spill of chemicals or an accident.

As public awareness of toxic waste sites has grown, so has legislation and government programs to deal with it. SARA permits citizens to sue any person or any governmental entity for alleged violation of a provision of the Superfund law. It also authorizes technical assistance grants so that citizens can hire experts to explain the complexities of hazardous waste problems and the Superfund program.

It is also possible to obtain information about contaminants that may be coming your way from a nearby manufacturing plant or business. Any facility manufacturing hazardous chemicals is required to file Material Safety Data Sheets (MSDS) with the Occupational Safety and Health Administration (OSHA). Starting in 1987, companies that prepared MSDS were also required to submit the list to the local emergency planning committee, the state emergency response commission and the local fire department on a yearly basis. Under the Emergency Planning and Community Right to Know Act of 1986, which is known as Title III and is part of SARA, you have access rights to that information.

Title III requires other action as well. Under its Emergency Release Notification provision, the release of hazardous chemicals and substances must be reported immediately to state and local officials. In addition, every year businesses with 10 or more employees, which make or process more than 25,000 pounds of a single specified chemical or 10,000 pounds of combined specific toxic chemicals, must report to the EPA their routine emission of toxic chemicals to the air, land or water. You can get this information, as well, from your local emergency planning board or the state.

In your own home, you can test water to find out if it's been contaminated by the hazardous waste site nearby. If you have a pond or stream on your property, it is a good idea to check that as well, especially if you do any swimming or fishing there. (See Chapter 4, for information on testing.)

Another option you have is to take on the polluter yourself. In Chicago, a resident phoned the Northwest Community Organization (NCO), a local community advocacy group, and asked if they knew what the guys in the "moon suits who were digging up soil in his neighborhood" were doing. The organization didn't, but investigated quickly and found out the crews were cleaning up PCBs that had spilled out of Commonwealth Edison equipment. Under a Freedom Information query, NCO discovered that there were 14 PCB spill sites in its area. The first public meeting that NCO was finally able to set up with Commonwealth Edison was with low level management, who were "not authorized" to do anything. It took phone calls to local government officials before a public meeting with top management from the utility was arranged. After three public meetings, and *lots of publicity in the local media*, Commonwealth Edison agreed to speed up the clean up. David del Valle, the NCO staff member who worked on the problem, says in 10 months all 14 sites were cleaned up, and so were the other 50 sites in the rest of the city. He contends that if they hadn't put pressure on Commonwealth Edison, the cleanup could have gone on for years.

NCO won its battle with Commonwealth Edison. It took quite a bit of work and perseverance but NCO and residents think it was worth the effort. Out of frustration and desperation, Lois Gibbs founded the Love Canal Homeowners Association. It took years, tremendous effort and lots of publicity, but eventually she and other residents succeeded in getting government action and a $20 million settlement in their class action suit. Even though it is sometimes difficult to take on large companies, with persistence you can make your environment safer and healthier!

EPA REGIONAL OFFICES FOR
HAZARDOUS WASTE SITES

ALABAMA—4	KENTUCKY—4	OHIO—5
ALASKA—10	LOUISIANA—6	OKLAHOMA—6
ARIZONA—9	MAINE—1	OREGON—10
ARKANSAS—6	MARYLAND—3	PENNSYLVANIA—3
CALIFORNIA—9	MASSACHUSETTS—1	PUERTO RICO—2
COLORADO—8	MICHIGAN—5	RHODE ISLAND—1
CONNECTICUT—1	MINNESOTA—5	SOUTH
DELAWARE—3	MISSISSIPPI—4	CAROLINA—4
DISTRICT OF	MISSOURI—7	SOUTH DAKOTA—8
COLUMBIA—3	MONTANA—8	TENNESSEE—4
FLORIDA—4	NEBRASKA—7	TEXAS—6
GEORGIA—4	NEVADA—9	UTAH—8
GUAM—9	NEW HAMPSHIRE—1	VERMONT—1
HAWAII—9	NEW JERSEY—2	VIRGINIA—3
IDAHO—10	NEW MEXICO—6	VIRGIN ISLANDS—2
ILLINOIS—5	NEW YORK—2	WASHINGTON—10
INDIANA—5	NORTH	WEST VIRGINIA—3
IOWA—7	CAROLINA—4	WYOMING—8
KANSAS—7	NORTH DAKOTA—8	WISCONSIN—5

REGION 1
JFK Federal Building
Boston, Massachusetts 02203
(617)565-3425

REGION 2
26 Federal Plaza
New York, New York 10007
(212)264-0949

REGION 3
6th & Walnut Streets
Philadelphia, Pennsylvania 19106
(215)597-9905

REGION 4
245 Courtland Street, N.E.
Atlanta, Georgia 30308
(404)347-3004

REGION 5
230 South Dearborn Street
Chicago, Illinois 60604
(312)353-1325

REGION 6
1201 Elm Street
Dallas, Texas 75270
(214)655-6720

REGION 7
1735 Baltimore Avenue
Kansas City, Missouri 64108
(913)236-2803

REGION 8
1860 Lincoln Street
Denver, Colorado 80203
(303)293-1698

REGION 9
215 Fremont Street
San Francisco, California 94105
(415)974-8026

REGION 10
1200 6th Avenue
Seattle, Washington 98101
(206442-2100

EPA SOLID AND HAZARDOUS WASTE AGENCIES

ALABAMA
Land Division
Department of Environmental
  Management
1751 Federal Drive
Montgomery, Alabama
  36130
(205)271-7730

ALASKA
Air and Solid Waste Management
Department of Environmental
  Conservation
Pouch O
Juneau, Alaska 99801
(907)465-2666

AMERICAN SAMOA
Environmental Quality Commission
Government of American Samoa

Pago Pago, American Samoa 96799
overseas operator
call 663-2304

ARIZONA
Office of Waste & Water Quality
  Management
Department of Environmental
  Quality
2005 N. Central Avenue, Room 304
Phoenix, Arizona 85004
(602)257-2305

ARKANSAS
Hazardous Waste Division
Dept. of Pollution Control &
  Ecology
P.O. Box 9583
Little Rock, Arkansas 72219
(501)562-7444, ext. 504

CALIFORNIA
Department of Health Services
714/744 P Street
Sacramento, California 95814
(916)323-2913

Toxic Substances Control Division
Department of Health Services
714/744 P Street
Sacramento, California 95814
(916)324-1826

State Water Resources Control
  Board
P.O. Box 100
Sacramento, California 95801
(916)445-1553

COLORADO
Waste Management Division
Department of Health
4210 East 11th Avenue
Denver, Colorado 80220
(303)320-8333, ext. 4364

CONNECTICUT
Hazardous Material Management
  Unit
Department of Environmental
  Protection
State Office Building
165 Capitol Avenue
Hartford, Connecticut 06106
(203)566-4924

Resource Recovery Authority
179 Allyn Street, Suite 603
Professional Building
Hartford, Connecticut 06103
(203)549-6390

DELAWARE
Hazardous Waste Management
  Section
Division of Air and Waste
  Management
Dept. of Natural Resources
  and Environmental Control
P.O. Box 1401, 89 Kings Highway

Dover, Delaware 19903
(302)736-4764

DISTRICT OF COLUMBIA
Pesticides and Hazardous
  Materials Division Superfund
Dept. of Consumer Affairs &
  Regulatory Affairs
5010 Overlook Avenue, S.W.
Room 114
Washington, D.C. 20032
(202)767-8414

FLORIDA
Solid & Hazardous Waste
Underground Storage Tanks
Dept. of Environmental Regulations
Twin Towers Office Building
2600 Blair Stone Road
Tallahassee, Florida 32301
(904)488-0300

GEORGIA
Land Protection Branch
Industrial & Hazardous Waste
  Management Program
Floyd Towers East
205 Butler Street, S.E.
Atlanta, Georgia 30334
(404)656-2833

GUAM
Environmental Protection Agency
P.O. Box 2999
Agana, Guam 96910
overseas operator call 646-8863

HAWAII
Department of Health
Hazardous Waste Program
P.O. Box 3378
Honolulu, Hawaii 96801
(808)548-6410

IDAHO
Hazardous Materials Bureau
Department of Health & Welfare
Idaho State House

Boise, Idaho 83720
(208)334-5879

ILLINOIS
Division of Land Pollution Control
Environmental Protection Agency
2200 Churchill Road
Springfield, Illinois 62706
(217)782-6760

INDIANA
Dept. of Environmental
  Management
105 S. Meridian St., P.O. Box 6015
Indianapolis, Indiana 46225
(317)232-3210

IOWA
Hazardous Materials Branch
U.S. EPA Region VII
726 Minnesota Avenue
Kansas City, Kansas 66101
(913)236-2888

KANSAS
Bureau of Waste Management
Dept. of Health and Environment
Forbes Field, Building 321
Topeka, Kansas 66620
(913)862-9360, ext. 290

KENTUCKY
Division of Waste Management
Dept. of Environmental Protection
Cabinet for Natural Resources and
  Environmental Protection
Fort Boone Plaza, Building #2
Frankfort, Kentucky 40601
(502)564-6716, ext. 214

LOUISIANA
Hazardous Waste Division
Office of Solid & Hazardous Waste
Dept. of Environmental Quality
P.O. Box 44307
Baton Rouge, Louisiana 70804
(504)342-9079

Groundwater Division
Dept. of Environmental Quality
P.O. Box 44274
Baton Rouge, Louisiana 70804
(504)342-8950

MAINE
Bureau of Oil & Hazardous
  Materials Control
Department of Environmental
  Protection
State House Station #17
Augusta, Maine 04333
(207)289-2651

MARYLAND
National Resources Planner
Hazardous & Solid Waste
  Management
201 W. Preston Street, Room 212
Baltimore, Maryland 21201
(301)225-5647

MASSACHUSETTS
Division of Solid & Hazardous
  Waste
Dept. of Environmental Quality
  Engineering
One Winter Street, 5th Floor
Boston, Massachusetts 02108
(617)292-5589

MICHIGAN
Waste Management Division
Environmental Protection Bureau
Department of Natural Resources
Box 30038
Lansing, Michigan 48909
(517)373-2730

MINNESOTA
Solid & Hazardous Waste Division
Pollution Control Agency
520 Lafayette Road, North
St. Paul, Minnesota 55155
(612)296-7282 or 296-7444

MISSISSIPPI
Division of Solid & Waste
  Management
Bureau of Pollution Control
Department of Natural Resources
P.O. Box 10385
Jackson, Mississippi 39209
(601)961-5062

MISSOURI
Waste Management Program
Department of Natural Resources
Jefferson Building
205 Jefferson Street. (13/14 fls.)
P.O. Box 176
Jefferson City, Missouri 65102
(314)751-3176

MONTANA
Solid and Hazardous Waste Bureau
Department of Health &
  Environmental Sciences
Cogswell Building, Room B-201
Helena, Montana 59620
(406)444-2821

NEBRASKA
Hazardous Waste Management
  Section
Department of Environmental
  Control
State House Station
P.O. Box 94877
Lincoln, Nebraska 68509
(402)471-2186

NEVADA
Waste Management Program
Division of Environmental
  Protection
Dept. of Conservation & Natural
  Resources
Capitol Complex
201 South Fall Street
Carson City, Nevada 89710
(702)885-4670

NEW HAMPSHIRE
Division of Public Health Services
Office of Waste Management
Department of Health and Welfare
Health and Welfare Building
6 Hazen Drive
Concord, New Hampshire 03301
(603)271-4662

NEW JERSEY
Division of Waste Management
Department of Environmental
  Protection
32 East Hanover Street, CN-027
Trenton, New Jersey 08625
(609)292-1250

NEW MEXICO
Groundwater and Hazardous
  Waste Bureau
Environmental Improvement
  Division
Health and Environmental
  Department
P.O. Box 968
Santa Fe, New Mexico 87504-0968
(505)827-2924

NEW YORK
Division of Hazardous Substance
  Regulation
Department of Environmental
  Conservation
50 Wolfe Road, Room 209
Albany, New York 12233
(518)457-6603

NORTH CAROLINA
Solid and Hazardous Waste
Management Branch
Division of Health Services
Department of Human Resources
P.O. Box 2091
Raleigh, North Carolina 27602
(919)733-2178

NORTH DAKOTA
Division of Hazardous Waste

Management and Special Studies
Department of Health
1200 Missouri Avenue, Room 302
Bismarck, North Dakota 58502-5520
(701)224-2366

OHIO
Division of Solid & Hazardous
    Waste Management
Environmental Protection Agency
361 East Broad Street
Columbus, Ohio 43215
(614)466-7220

OKLAHOMA
Waste Management Service
State Department of Health
P.O. Box 53551
1000 Northeast 10th Street
Oklahoma City, Oklahoma 73152
(405)271-5338

OREGON
Hazardous and Solid Waste
    Division
Department of Environmental
    Quality
811 Southwest 6th Avenue
Portland, Oregon 97204
(503)229-5356

PENNSYLVANIA
Bureau of Waste Management
Dept. of Environmental Resources
P.O. Box 2063
Harrisburg, Pennsylvania 17120
(717)787-9870

PUERTO RICO
Environmental Quality Board
Santurce, Puerto Rico 00910-1488
(809)725-0439

RHODE ISLAND
Solid Waste Management Program
Department of Environmental
    Management
240 Cannon Building

75 Davis Street
Providence, Rhode Island 02908
(401)277-2797

SOUTH CAROLINA
Bureau of Solid Waste Management
Dept. of Health and Environmental
    Control
2600 Bull Street
Columbia, South Carolina 29201
(803)758-5681

SOUTH DAKOTA
Office of Air Quality and Solid
    Waste
Department of Water and Natural
    Resources
Joe Foss Building, Room 217
523 East Capitol Street
Pierre, South Dakota 57501-3181
(605)773-3153

TENNESSEE
Division of Solid Waste
    Management
Department of Public Health
701 Broadway
Customs House, 4th Floor
Nashville, Tennessee 37219-5403
(615)741-3424

TEXAS
Division of Solid Waste
Department of Health
1100 West 49th Street
Austin, Texas 78756-3199
(512)458-7271

Hazardous and Solid Waste
    Division
Water Commission
P.O. Box 13087, Capitol Station
Austin, Texas 78711-3087
(512)463-7760

UTAH
Bureau of Solid and Hazardous
    Waste Management

Department of Health
P.O. Box 16700
288 North 1460 West Street
Salt Lake City, Utah 84116-0700
(801)533-4145

VERMONT
Waste Management Division
Agency for Environmental
  Conservation
103 South Main Street
Waterbury, Vermont 05676
(802)244-8702

VIRGIN ISLANDS
Department of Conservation &
  Cultural Affairs
P.O. Box 4399, Charlotte
St. Thomas, Virgin Islands 00801
(809)774-6420

VIRGINIA
Division of Technical Services
Department of Waste Management
Monroe Building, 11th Floor
101 North 14th Street
Richmond, Virginia 23219
(804)225-2667

WASHINGTON
Solid and Hazardous Waste

Management Division
Department of Ecology
Mail Stop PV-11
Olympia, Washington 98504
(206)459-6316

WEST VIRGINIA
Waste Management Division
Department of West Virginia
  Natural Resources
1260 Greenbrier Street
Charleston, West Virginia 25311
(304)348-5935

WISCONSIN
Bureau of Solid Waste
Department of Natural Resources
PO Box 7921
Madison, Wisconsin 53707
(608)266-1327

WYOMING
Solid Waste Management Program
Department of Environmental
  Quality
122 West 25th Street
Herschler Building
Cheyenne, Wyoming 82002
(307)777-7752

9

NUCLEAR POWER PLANTS AND WEAPONS PLANTS

"U.S. AIDES SEE A RISK OF MELTDOWN AT PENNSYLVANIA
NUCLEAR PLANT; MORE RADIOACTIVE GAS IS RELEASED"
 New York Times, March 31, 1979
"SOVIETS REPORTING ATOM PLANT 'DISASTER'
SEEK HELP ABROAD TO FIGHT REACTOR FIRE"
 New York Times, April 30, 1986

The first headline was from Three Mile Island; the second, from Chernobyl in the Soviet Union.

Dr. Elizath Whelan, Executive Director of the nonprofit Council on Science and Health says, "The health risks from nuclear power, while highly publicized, are inconsequential when compared to everyday risks such as cigarette smoking, driving in automobiles or flying in aircraft."

Scott Peters, media services manager for the U.S. Council for Energy Awareness (the trade organization for nuclear energy) has told me, "I don't believe that the presence of nuclear power plant should be any considera- tion in buying a home." Though it may not be the deciding factor, I doubt that, given the choice, many folks would choose to live near one.

Of course, there are many people who *do* live near power plants. Maybe you are one of them. You bought your home way before anyone thought of building a nuclear power plant in your neighborhood; or you bought your home before the first commercial nuclear power plant went on line; or you bought your home before those frightening headlines.

A BRIEF HISTORY

In 1946, Congress passed the Atomic Energy Act. It transferred control of the atom from the military to civilian hands. The Atomic Energy Commission (AEC) was created to oversee and develop every aspect of nuclear technology, for both military and peaceful uses; and the first electricity generated by nuclear power was produced by a government breeder reactor in 1951.

In 1954 the Atomic Energy Act was amended to allow private industry to build and operate nuclear facilities. The world's first full-scale nuclear generating plant, for commercial use, was designed by Westinghouse, financed by the federal government and built in Shippingport, Pennsylvania, in 1954.

In 1957 Congress passed the Price Anderson Act, which protects utility companies from full financial liability for a serious nuclear accident—virtually a no-fault insurance plan. Between 1965 and 1967 utility companies in the United States ordered 50 nuclear power plants. Near the end of the 1960s, the AEC predicted that there would be 1,000 nuclear power plants operating by the year 2000.

Commonwealth Edison's Braidwood Nuclear Power Plant in Braidwood, Illinois. U.S. Council for Energy Awareness.

In 1974 Congress did away with the AEC and replaced it with the Nuclear Regulatory Commission (NRC), to protect public health and safety, and the Energy Research and Development Administration (ERDA), to study and promote all kinds of energy.

By the late '70s the nuclear power industry was in a decline. No new reactor has been ordered since 1978 and all reactors ordered since 1974 have been cancelled.

There is a lot of controversy on the industry's demise. The Department of Energy (DOE) and the nuclear industry blame over-regulation and public intervention in licensing procedures. The Union of Concerned Scientists (UCS), a nonprofit, major public policy organization, and others say it is "misregulation" and the restriction of public oversight that have led to the industry's problems.

NUCLEAR POWER MISHAPS

The worst accident in the commercial nuclear power program in the United States happened in March 1979. A core meltdown (something the nuclear industry said could never happen) nearly took place at the Three Mile Island Nuclear Power Plant (TMI) in Middletown, Pennsylvania, just 12 miles from Harrisburg, the state capital. The Nuclear Regulatory Commission's report stated that TMI came within 30 to 60 minutes of a full meltdown.

Another close call was at the Browns Ferry nuclear plants in Alabama in 1975. A fire, caused by workers using a candle to test for air leaks, destroyed many of the safety system cables. The potential disaster was averted but raised concerns about what would happen the next time there was an accident at a nuclear power plant.

According to the UCS there have been more than 200 precursors to core meltdown accidents in the commercial nuclear power industry. There have been many other incidents that have increased public concern.

In 1974, the Zion Station plant near Chicago had to be closed a year after it opened when it was discovered that its emergency core cooling system was incorrectly wired and would have been ineffective in an accident. The same year leaks were found in two reactors and cracks were found in a third when the Atomic Control Commission examined 21 of the 50 plants on line in the United States at that time.

In 1981, days before the Diablo Canyon plant in California was to be issued a license to operate, the NRC discovered several crucial construction flaws. One of the flaws was floor supports in the plant, which were not adequately reinforced against seismic stress. The Diablo Canyon plant is near an active, offshore earthquake fault!

Nuclear power has generated a great many questions and tremendous, seemingly endless controversy. Highly acclaimed scientists can be found to support both sides of the issue.

NUCLEAR POWER: SOME PROS AND CONS

Opponents of nuclear power say that there is no doubt that nuclear accidents can happen. No matter how sophisticated the safety mechanisms are, mechanical and human failure simply can never be predicted or totally prevented. The Union of Concerned Scientists calls nuclear power "an inherently dangerous technology requiring the highest standards of care and performance." It charges the Nuclear Regulatory Agency with not resolving some of the most serious safety problems at nuclear power plants. In a position paper in November 1988, it stated that "the present generation of nuclear power plants now in operation throughout the United States has been plagued by poor management, poor design, and excessive cost. There is a significant risk that a major accident will occur resulting in a substantial release of radiation."

Dr. Karl Morgan, a former director of the Health Physics Division at the Oak Ridge National Laboratory in Tennessee, warns that radiation safety standards may be as much as 10 times too lax. He charges that general negligence in the nuclear industry has resulted in the deaths of some 200 uranium miners due to radon levels that were too high, the exposure of thousands of people to radiation from uranium sludges left over from mining operations in the Rocky Mountains and Midwest, and the plutonium contamination of hundreds of square miles from the government's weapons facility at Rocky Flats, Colorado.

Proponents argue that nuclear power plants are highly regulated and are not a threat. Many scientists believe that the chance of a meltdown is so small that the average person is at a greater risk from coal pollution, a hydroelectric dam burst or a gas explosion. In 1974 the Atomic Energy Commission issued the Rasmussen report on the safety of nuclear reactors. Dr. Norman Rasmussen of M.I.T. calculated that the worst accident could kill 3,300 people and cause cancer in another 45,000. However, he also said that the likelihood of such a meltdown was once in a billion reactor years. (A reactor year is one reactor operating for one year.)

Another major problem is the disposal of nuclear waste from power plants and weapons factories. Thousands of tons of spent fuel from commercial power plants are stored at each reactor site. Millions of tons of highly radioactive military waste and uranium mill tailings are stored in temporary locations. At least nine states have banned the burial of radioactive wastes. Many people are concerned about having truckloads of radioactive waste drive through their neighborhoods.

Unit 2 of Pacific Gas and Electric Company's Diablo Canyon Nuclear Power Plant, midway between Los Angeles and San Franciso. U.S. Council for Energy Awareness.

Opponents of nuclear power contend that not enough is known about the safe disposal of waste that will remain radioactive for tens of thousands of years. They say no one can really predict whether buried containers will eventually disintegrate because of the intense heat generated by the radioactivity, and what effect that would have on geologic stability. Supporters of nuclear power contend that the problem is really political; that sites can be found where the waste can be buried safely and that measures can be taken to prevent the intense heat buildup that could lead to the disintegration of the buried containers.

Nuclear waste from power plants (and weapons factories) continues to pile up. Today, about 18% of the electricity in the United States is generated by nuclear power plants.

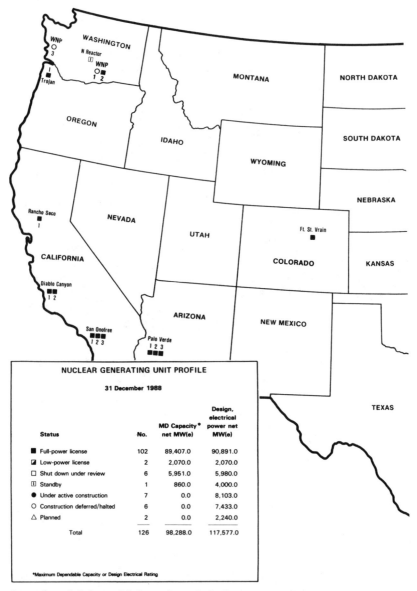

NUCLEAR GENERATING UNIT PROFILE

31 December 1988

Status	No.	MD Capacity* net MW(e)	Design, electrical power net MW(e)
■ Full-power license	102	89,407.0	90,891.0
◪ Low-power license	2	2,070.0	2,070.0
□ Shut down under review	6	5,951.0	5,980.0
⊡ Standby	1	860.0	4,000.0
● Under active construction	7	0.0	8,103.0
○ Construction deferred/halted	6	0.0	7,433.0
△ Planned	2	0.0	2,240.0
Total	126	98,288.0	117,577.0

*Maximum Dependable Capacity or Design Electrical Rating

Because of space limitations, symbols do not reflect precise locations.

Commercial nuclear power reactor sites in the United States as of December 31, 1988. EPA. U.S. Department of Energy.

Office of Scientific and Technical Information
U.S. Department of Energy

Revised December 31, 1988
from *Nuclear Reactors Built,
Being Built, or Planned* (DOE/OSTI-8200-R52)

But while there are 109 nuclear plants on-line in this country, 14 other countries get a greater percentage of their energy from nuclear power plants than the United States. France has 49 reactors producing 70% of its electricity. Belgium gets 67% of its electricity from nuclear power plants, Sweden gets 50%, Taiwan 44%, South Korea 44%, Switzerland 39%, Finland 38%, Bulgaria 30%, West Germany 29%, Japan 25%, Czechoslovakia 21%, Britain and Hungary over 18%. The United States ranks 15th and the Soviet Union ranks 19th with 10%.

Indian Point.   U.S. Council for Energy Awareness.

NUCLEAR POWER PLANT LOCATIONS AND STATUS

As of January 1, 1988, there were 109 nuclear power plants licensed to operate and produce nuclear power in 34 states in the United States. The 110th, Seabrook in New Hampshire, was licensed only to load fuel, which means it could install the fuel rods for low-level testing.

Following is a list of the plants, by state, location, name of plant, name of utility company, whether it has an operating license (OL) or a construction permit (CP), and when it began commercial operation:

PLANT LOCATION AND STATUS

SITE	PLANT	UTILITY	STATUS	COMMENCED COMMERCIAL OPPERATION
ALABAMA				
Decatur	Browns Ferry-1	Tennessee Valley Authority (TVA)	OL	1974
	Browns Ferry-2	TVA	OL	1975
	Browns Ferry-3	TVA	OL	1977
Dothan	Joseph M. Farley Unit 1	Alabama Power Co.	OL	1977
	Joseph M. Farley Unit 2	Alabama Power Co.	OL	1981
Scottsboro	Bellefonte 1	TVA	CP	1993
	Bellefonte 2	TVA	CP	1995
ARIZONA				
Wintersburg	Palo Verde 1	Arizona Public Service Co.	OL	1986
	Palo Verde 2	Arizona Public Service Co.	OL	1986
	Palo Verde 3	Arizona Public Service Co.	OL	1988
ARKANSAS				
Russelville	Arkansas Nuclear One-1	Arkansas Power & Light	OL	1974
	Arkansas Nuclear Two-1	Arkansas Power & Light	OL	1980
CALIFORNIA				
San Clemente	San Onofre 1	So. Cal. Edison & San Diego Gas & Elec. Co.	OL	1968
	San Onofre 2	So. Cal. Edison & San Diego Gas & Elec. Co.	OL	1983
	San Onofre 3	So. Cal. Edison & San Diego Gas & Elec. Co.	OL	1984
Avila Beach	Diablo Canyon 1	Pacific Gas & Elec. Co.	OL	1985
	Diablo Canyon 2	Pacific Gas & Elec. Co.	OL	1986
Herald	Rancho Seco 1	Sacramento Municipal Utility District	OL	1975
COLORADO				
Platteville	Fort St. Vrain	Pub. Ser. Co. of Col.	OL	1979

SITE	PLANT	UTILITY	STATUS	COMMENCED COMMERCIAL OPPERATION
CONNECTICUT				
Haddam Neck	Haddam Neck	Conn. Yankee Atomic Power Co.	OL	1968
Waterford	Millstone 1	Northeast Utilities	OL	1971
	Millstone 2	Northeast Utilities	OL	1975
	Millstone 3	Northeast Utilities	OL	1986
FLORIDA				
Florida City	Turkey Point 3	Florida Power & Light	OL	1972
	Turkey Point 4	Florida Power & Light	OL	1973
Red Level	Crystal River 3	Florida Power Corp.	OL	1977
Fort Pierce	St. Lucie 1	Florida Power & Light	OL	1976
	St. Lucie 2	Florida Power & Light	OL	1983
GEORGIA				
Baxley	Edwin I Hatch 1	Georgia Power	OL	1975
	Edwin I Hatch 2	Georgia Power	OL	1979
Waynesboro	Alvin W. Vogtle, Jr. 1	Georgia Power	OL	1987
	Alvin W. Vogtle, Jr. 2	Georgia Power	CP	1989
ILLINOIS				
Morris	Dresden 2	Commonwealth Edison	OL	1970
	Dresden 3	Commonwealth Edison	OL	1971
	Zion 1	Commonwealth Edison	OL	1973
	Zion 2	Commonwealth Edison	OL	1974
Cordova	Quad-Cities 1	Comm. Ed. Co-Ill. Gas & Elec.	OL	1973
	Quad-Cities 2	Comm. Ed. Co-Ill. Gas & Elec.	OL	1973
Seneca	LaSalle 1	Commonwealth Edison	OL	1984
	LaSalle 2	Commonwealth Edison	OL	1984
Bryon	Bryon 1	Commonwealth Edison	OL	1985
	Bryon 2	Commonwealth Edison	OL	1987
Braidwood	Braidwood 1	Commonwealth Edison	OL	1988

SITE	PLANT	UTILITY	STATUS	COMMENCED COMMERCIAL OPPERATION
	Braidwood 2	Commonwealth Edison	OL	1988
Clinton	Clinton 1	Illinois Power	OL	1987
IOWA				
Pala	Duane Arnold	Iowa Elec. Power & Light	OL	1975
KANSAS				
Burlington	Wolf Creek	Kansas Gas & Elec.	OL	1985
LOUISIANA				
Taft	Waterford 3	La. Power & Light	OL	1985
St. Francisville	River Bend	Gulf States Utilities	OL	1986
MAINE				
Wiscasset	Maine Yankee	Maine Yankee Atomic Power	OL	1972
MARYLAND				
Lusby	Calvert Cliffs 1	Baltimore Gas & Elec.	OL	1975
	Calvert Cliffs 2	Baltimore Gas & Elec.	OL	1977
MASSACHUSETTS				
Rowe	Yankee	Yankee Atomic Elec.	OL	1961
Plymouth	Pilgrim 1	Boston Edison	OL	1972
MICHIGAN				
Big Rock Point	Big Rock Point	Consumers Power	OL	1963
South Haven	Palisades	Consumers Power	OL	1971
Laguna Beach	Enrico Fermi 2	Detroit Edison	OL	1988
Bridgman	Donald C. Cook Unit 1	Indiana & Mich. Elec.	OL	1975
	Donald C. Cook Unit 2	Indiana & Mich. Elec.	OL	1978
MINNESOTA				
Monticello	Monticello	Northern State Power	OL	1971
Red Wing	Prairie Island 1	Northern State Power	OL	1973

SITE	PLANT	UTILITY	STATUS	COMMENCED COMMERCIAL OPPERATION
	Prairie Island 2	Northern State Power	OL	1974
MISSISSIPPI Port Gibson	Grand Gulf 1	Miss. Power & Light	OL	1985
MISSOURI Fulton	Callaway 1	Union Electric	OL	1985
NEBRASKA Fort Calhoun	Fort Calhoun 1	Omaha Public Power District	OL	1973
Brownsville	Cooper	Nebraska Public Power District	OL	1974
NEW HAMPSHIRE Seabrook	Seabrook 1	Public Service of N.H.	OL*	Indef
	Seabrook 2	Public Service of N.H.	CP	Indef
NEW JERSEY Toms River	Oyster Creek 1	GPU Nuclear Corp.	OL	1969
Salem	Salem 1	Pub. Serv. Elec. & Gas	OL	1977
	Salem 2	Pub. Serv. Elec. & Gas	OL	1981
	Hope Creek 1	Pub. Serv. Elec. & Gas	OL	1986
NEW YORK Buchanan	Indian Point 2	Consolidated Edison	OL	1974
	Indian Point 3	NYS Power Authority	OL	1976
Scriba	Nine Mile Point 1	Niagara Mohawk Power	OL	1969
	Nine Mile Point 2	Niagara Mohawk Power	OL	1988
	James A. FitzPatrick	NYS Power Authority	OL	1975
Ontario	R. E. Ginna 1	Rochester Gas & Elec.	OL	1970

* has license to load fuel/conduct precritical testing

SITE	PLANT	UTILITY	STATUS	COMMENCED COMMERCIAL OPPERATION
NORTH CAROLINA				
Southport	Brunswick 1	Carolina Power & Light	OL	1975
	Brunswick 2	Carolina Power & Light	OL	1977
Cowans Ford Dam	William McGuire Unit 1	Duke Power	OL	1981
	William McGuire Unit 2	Duke Power	OL	1984
Bonsal	Shearon Harris 1	Carolina Power & Light	OL	1987
OHIO				
Oak Harbor	Davis-Besse 1	Toledo Edison-Cleveland Electric Illum.	OL	1977
North Perry	Perry 1	Toledo Edison-Cleveland Electric Illum.	OL	1987
	Perry 2	Toledo Edison-Cleveland Electric Illum.	CP	1977
OREGON				
Prescott	Trojan 1	Portland General Elec.	OL	1976
PENNSYLVANIA				
Peach Bottom	Peach Bottom 2	Philadelphia Elec.	OL	1974
	Peach Bottom 3	Philadelphia Elec.	OL	1974
Pottstown	Limerick 1	Philadelphia Elec.	OL	1986
	Limerick 2	Philadelphia Elec.	OL	1990
Shippingport	Beaver Valley 1	Duquesne Light/Ohio Ed.	OL	1976
	Beaver Valley 2	Duquesne Light/Ohio Ed.	OL	1987
Goldsboro	Three Mile Island 1	GPU Nuclear Corp.	OL	1974
Berwick	Susquehanna 1	Pa. Power & Light	OL	1983
	Susquehanna 2	Pa. Power & Light	OL	1985
SOUTH CAROLINA				
Hartsville	H.B. Robinson 2	Carolina Power & Light	OL	1971
Seneca	Oconee 1	Duke Power	OL	1973
	Oconee 2	Duke Power	OL	1974
	Oconee 3	Duke Power	OL	1974
Broad River	Virgil Summer 1	So. Carolina Elec. and Gas	OL	1984

SITE	PLANT	UTILITY	STATUS	COMMENCED COMMERCIAL OPPERATION
Lake Wylie	Catawba 1	Duke Power	OL	1985
	Catawba 2	Duke Power	OL	1986
TENNESSEE				
Daisy	Sequoyah 1	TVA	OL	1981
	Sequoyah 2	TVA	OL	1982
Spring City	Watts Bar 1	TVA	CP	1988
	Watts Bar 2	TVA	CP	1989
TEXAS				
Glen Rose	Comanche Peak 1	Texas Utilities	CP	1988
	Comanche Peak 2	Texas Utilities	CP	1989
Bay City	South Texas Project 1	Houston Lighting & Power	OL*	1987
	South Texas Project 2	Houston Lighting & Power	CP	1989
VERMONT				
Vernon	Vermont Yankee	Vermont Yankee Nuclear Power Corp	OL	1972
VIRGINIA				
Gravel Neck	Surry 1	Va. Electric & Power	OL	1972
	Surry 2	Va. Electric & Power	OL	1973
Mineral	North Anna 1	Va. Electric & Power	OL	1978
	North Anna 2	Va. Electric & Power	OL	1980
WASHINGTON				
Richland	WPPSS 1	Wash. Public Power	CP	Indef
	WPPSS 2	Wash. Public Power	OL	1984
Satsop	WPPSS 3	Wash. Public Power	CP	Indef
WISCONSIN				
Two Creeks	Point Beach 1	Wisconsin Elec. Power	OL	1970
	Point Beach 2	Wisconsin Elec. Power	OL	1972
Carlton Township	Kewaunee	Wisconsin Public Ser. Corp.	OL	1974

* has low power operating license

NUCLEAR WEAPONS PLANTS

While the location of commercial plants is public information, many people have lived near a plant involved in the manufacture of nuclear weapons—and never knew it. The plant in Fernald, Ohio, was the first. It started operating in 1951. Because of its name, the "Feed Materials Production Center," many people assumed the plant was making some kind of livestock feed.

Charles Zinser of Fernald is convinced that his three- and eight-year-old sons' cancer was caused by leaking uranium. Some 14,000 residents filed a $300 million lawsuit against the company that ran the plant in Fernald.

HAZARDS AT WEAPONS PLANTS

In December 1988, the Department of Energy (DOE) released a report on hazards at 16 facilities making nuclear weapons in the United States. According to that report, radioactive and toxic chemicals have migrated beyond some plants and contaminated public water supplies.

Pollution from plants in Ohio and Texas and from two national labs in Northern California were said to pose serious threats to public health and the environment. Areas in Amarillo, Texas; Twin Falls, Idaho; and Denver, Colorado could eventually be affected.

Before the report came out, the Federal Government had consistently maintained that the weapons plants posed no threat because since World War II contaminants were contained on huge reservations in remote parts of the country.

Following is a list of the plants, the location of each, a brief description of what each does, and the main hazards with which each is associated.

WEAPONS PLANTS: LOCATION, FUNCTION AND HAZARDS

CALIFORNIA
Lawrence Livermore National Laboratory, Livermore, 1952. This is one of the principal national weapons labs. It has leached toxic contamination from other operations into the groundwater. The contamination is expected to migrate to nearby residential communities, which depend on groundwater.
Sandia National Laboratories, Livermore, 1949 (also in Albuquerque, N.M., and north of Las Vegas, Nevada). Hazardous materials used at the laboratories since the early 1940's have contaminated miles of desert

near the Las Vegas site. Underground storage tanks have leaked. Open lagoons are receiving contaminated wastes and may be leaking.

COLORADO
Rocky Flats Plant, near Golden, 1953. The plant processes plutonium for weapons. It is leaking volatile, cancer-causing organic chemicals into underground water north of Denver. Storage tanks have leaked chemicals into the soil. The soil around the site is contaminated with plutonium at elevated levels.

FLORIDA
Pinellas Plant, Largo, 1956. The plant produces mechanical components for weapons. Underground storage tanks containing chemical compounds are believed to be leaking.

IDAHO
Idaho National Engineering Laboratory, near Idaho Falls, 1949. The plant reprocesses nuclear fuel and operates experimental reactors. It has discharged radioactive and toxic wastes into unlined waste lagoons. From there the waste has leached into the Snake River Aquifer, a giant underground reservoir. In the report it is called one of the most contaminated sites in the weapons industry.

MISSOURI
The Kansas City Plant, Kansas City, 1949. The plant produces electronic components for weapons. It has contaminated soil and sewer lines with PCBs by discharging carcinogenic chemicals into pits. The plant has also released 240 tons of toxic chemicals into the water.

NEVADA
Nevada Test Site, near Las Vegas, 1950. Nuclear weapons were tested at this site, above ground, until 1961, and below ground since then. About 75 square miles of the site is thoroughly contaminated with radioactive materials from those tests, including plutonium, cesium and strontium.
Sandia National Laboratories, north of Las Vegas (see California).

NEW MEXICO
Los Alamos National Laboratory, Los Alamos, 1943. Test firings of high explosives have contaminated the test area with uranium. Chemicals and radioactive particles have been found on the site.
Sandia National Laboratories, Albuquerque (see California).

OHIO

Feed Materials Production Center, Fernald, 1951. This plant turns uranium hexafluoride, a liquid or gas, into uranium metal that is further processed for use in nuclear weapons or fuel for government reactors. It has two silos, which are filled with 390,000 cubic feet of radioactive wastes that emit radon. The plant has also emitted more than 300,000 pounds of uranium oxide and has contaminated drinking wells.

Mound Facility, Miamisburg, 1947. The plant makes high explosives and plutonium components for satellites. Waste pits are believed to be leaching toxic chemicals into soil. Officials are concerned about plutonium leaching into groundwater.

Portsmouth Uranium Enrichment Complex, Piketon, 1952. The plant's cooling system is daily releasing 30 to 40 pounds of carcinogenic and toxic hexavalent chromium, used in the process of enriching uranium for reactor fuel. The compound mixes with drops of water, forming a mist, which the DOE report said could travel a great distance, ending up on plants and soils in the surrounding area.

SOUTH CAROLINA

Savannah River Plant, near Aiken, 1950. The plant produced radioactive tritium and plutonium for nuclear weapons. It has released millions of curies of tritium gas into the atmosphere from accidents. A primary aquifier in the area has been contaminated with solvents. This plant has been criticized by Congress and environmental groups in recent years for mishandling radioactive and toxic wastes and contaminating underground water supplies.

TENNESSEE

Y-12 Plant, Oak Ridge, 1943. The plant fabricates weapon components. It has polluted streams with mercury. A pond at the plant containing arsenic, boron and sulfate is leaking into surface streams. Crops and livestock may be contaminated by poisonous releases into the atmosphere. Like the plant in Texas, the Y-12 has been criticized for mishandling radioactive and toxic wastes and contaminating underground water supplies.

TEXAS

Pantex Facility, Amarillo, 1951. The plant, 17 miles northeast of Amarillo, is the final assembly point for nuclear warheads. Thousands of gallons of toxic solvents from the plant were discharged into a giant unlined waste pit from 1954 to 1980. It's believed that the chemicals are leaking into the Ogallala Aquifer, the primary drinking source for Amarillo. It is also the principal source of water for irrigation on the Texas High Plains. Radioactive wastes have also contaminated soil around the plant. Winds on the high plains can blow contaminated dust onto nearby grain fields.

WASHINGTON
The Hanford Reservation, near Richmond, 1944. Since 1944 and into the early '80s liquid radioactive and toxic wastes were dumped in trenches. They have contaminated large underground reservoirs used for drinking water and irrigation.

In 1989, the $5.4 billion Shoreham Nuclear Power Plant in New York was permanently shut down before ever becoming fully operational. At least part of the reason for the plant's demise was the unceasing opposition by local residents and anti-nuclear groups. The nuclear energy controversy is far from over.

A low-level nuclear waste disposal site in Barnwell, South Carolina.
Nuclear Regulatory Commission.

PUBLIC DOCUMENT ROOMS

Copies of most Nuclear Regulatory Commission (NRC) documents are available in the commission's Public Documents Room (PDR) at 1717 H

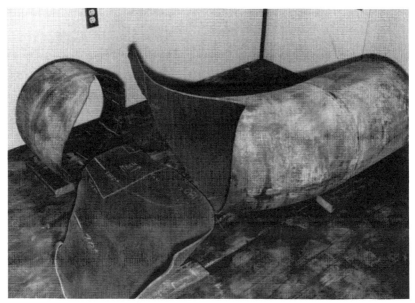

A ruptured 18-inch main feedpipe at the Surrey Unit 2 power plant at Gravel Neck, Virginia. Four people were killed and four were injured when it ruptured in 1986. Nuclear Regulatory Commission.

Street, N.W., Washington, D.C., for public inspection. Documents relating to licensing procedures or the operation of specific facilities are available in local PDRs in the vicinity of each proposed or existing nuclear facility. Following is a list of PDRs by state:

ALABAMA
Browns Ferry Nuclear Power Station
  & Low Level Waste Storage
Athens Public Library
South Street
Athens, AL 35611

Joseph M. Farley Nuclear Plant
Houston-Love Memorial Library
212 West Burdeshaw Street
P.O. Box 1369
Dothan, AL 36302

Bellefonte Nuclear Plant
Scottsboro Public Library
1002 South Broad Street
Scottsboro, AL 35768

ARIZONA
Palo Verde Nuclear Station
Phoenix Public Library
12 East McDowell Road
Phoenix, AZ 85004

ARKANSAS
Arkansas Nuclear One
Tomlinson Library
Arkansas Tech. University
Russelville, AR 72801

CALIFORNIA
Humboldt Bay Power Plant
Eureka-Humboldt County Library
636 F Street
Eureka, CA 95501

UCLA Training Reactor
West Los Angeles Regional Library
11360 Santa Monica Boulevard
Los Angeles, CA 90025

Rancho Seco Nuclear Generating Plant
Sacramento Public Library
828 I Street
Sacramento, CA 95814

San Onofre Nuclear Station
University of California General
 Library
P.O. Box 19557
Irvine, CA 92713

Diablo Canyon Nuclear Power Plant
Robert Kennedy Library
California Polytechnic—State
 University
San Luis Obispo, CA 93407

COLORADO
*Fort St. Vrain Nuclear
 Generating Station*
Greeley Public Library
City Complex Building
919 7th Street
Greeley, CO 80631

CONNECTICUT
Haddam Neck Plant
Russell Library
123 Broad Street
Middletown, CT 06457

Millstone Nuclear Power Station
Waterford Public Library
49 Rope Ferry Road
Waterford, CT 06385

FLORIDA
Crystal River Nuclear Plant
Coastal Region Library
8619 W. Crystal Street
Crystal River, FL 32629

St. Lucie Plant
Charles Miley Learning
 Resources Center
Indian River Community College

3209 Virginia Avenue
Fort Pierce, FL 33450

Turkey Point Plant
Miami-Dade Public Library
Homestead Branch
700 North Homestead Boulevard
Homestead, FL 33030

Urban and Regional
 Documents—Collection Library
Florida International University
University Park
Miami, FL 33199

GEORGIA
Edwin I. Hatch Nuclear Plant
Appling County Public Library
301 City Hall Drive
Baxley, GA 31513

Alvin W. Vogtle Nuclear Plant
County Library
412 4th Street
Waynesboro, GA 30830

ILLINOIS
Byron Station
Byron Public Library
109 N. Franklin Street
Byron, IL 61010

Founder's Memorial Library
Northeastern Illinois University
DeKalb, IL 60115

Rockford Public Library
215 North Wyman Street
Rockford, IL 61101

Clinton Power Station
University of Illinois Law Library
504 East Pennsylvania Avenue
Champaign, IL 61820

Vespasian Warner Public Library
120 West Johnson Street
Clinton, IL 61727

*Quad Cities Station & Sheffield
 Low-level Waste Burial Site*
Dixon Public Library

221 Hennepin Avenue
Dixon, IL 61021

*Dresden Nuclear Power Station &
  Morris Spent Fuel Storage Facility*
Morris Public Library
604 Liberty Street
Morris, IL 60450

LaSalle County Station
Jacobs Memorial Library
Illinois Valley Community College
Rural Route 1
Oglesby, IL 61348

Braidwood Station
Wilmington Public Library
201 South Kankakee Street
Wilmington, IL 60481

Zion Nuclear Power Station
Waukegan Public Library
128 N. County Street
Waukegan, IL 60085

Kerr-McGee West Chicago
West Chicago Public Library
332 E. Washington St.
West Chicago, IL 60185

IOWA
Duane Arnold Energy Center
Cedar Rapids Public Library
500 1st Street, S.E.
Cedar Rapids, IA 52401

KANSAS
Wolf Creek Generating Station
William Allan White Library
Emporia State University
1200 Commercial Street
Emporia, KS 66801

Washburn University School of
  Law
Topeka, KS 66621

LOUISIANA
River Bend Station
Troy Middleton Library

Louisiana State University
Baton Rouge, LA 70803

Waterford Generating Station
Earl Long Library
University of New Orleans
Lakefront Drive
New Orleans, LA 70418

MAINE
Maine Yankee Atomic Power Plant
Wiscasset Public Library
High Street, P.O. Box 367
Wiscasset, ME 04578

MARYLAND
Calvert Cliffs Nuclear Power Plant
Calbert County Public Library
Fourth Street, P.O. Box 450
Prince Frederick, MD 20678

MASSACHUSETTS
Yankee Rowe Nuclear Power Station
Library/Learning Resource Center
Greenfield Community College
One College Drive
Greenfield, MA 01301

Pilgrim Nuclear Power Station
Plymouth Public Library
11 North Street
Plymouth, MA 02360

MICHIGAN
Palisades Nuclear Plant
Van Wylen Library
Hope College
Holland, MI 49423

Big Rock Point Nuclear Plant
North Central Michigan College
1515 Howard Street
Petoskey, MI 49770

Enrico Fermi Atomic Power Plant
Monroe County Library System
Monroe, MI 48161

Donald C. Cook Nuclear Power Plant
500 Market Street
St. Joseph, MI 49085

MINNESOTA
Monticello Nuclear Generating Plant
Minneapolis Public Library
300 Nicollet Mall
Minneapolis, MN 55401

MISSISSIPPI
Grand Gulf Nuclear Station
George McLendon Library
Hinds Union College
Main Street
Raymond, MS 39154

MISSOURI
Callaway Plant
County Public Library
710 Court Street
Fulton, MO 65251

John Olin Library
Washington University
Skinker and Lindell Boulevards
St. Louis, MO 63130

NEBRASKA
Cooper Nuclear Station
Auburn Public Library
1118 15th Street
P.O. Box 324
Auburn, NE 68305

Fort Calhoun Station
W. Dale Clark Library
215 S. 15th Street
Omaha, NE 68102

NEVADA
Yucca Mountain High-Level Waste
  Geologic Repository Site
James Dickinson Library
University of Nevada-Las Vegas
4505 Maryland Parkway
Las Vegas, NV 89154

NEW JERSEY
Hope Creek Nuclear Station
Pennsville Public Library
190 S. Broadway
Pennsville, NJ 08070

Salem Nuclear Generating Station
Salem Free Public Library
112 West Broadway
Salem, NJ 08079

Oyster Creek Nuclear Power Plant
Ocean County Library
101 Washington Street
Toms River, NJ 08753

NEW YORK
James Fitzpatrick Nuclear Power Plant
  & Nine Mile Point Nuclear Station
Penfield Library
State University of New York
Oswego, NY 13126

Robert Emmet Ginna Nuclear Plant
Rochester Public Library
115 South Avenue
Rochester, NY 14610

West Valley Demonstration Project
Buffalo & Erie County Public
  Library
Lafayette Square
Buffalo, NY 14203

Indian Point Station
White Plains Public Library
100 Marine Avenue
White Plains, NY 10601

NORTH CAROLINA
William B. McGuire Nuclear Station
J. Murrey Arkins Library
University of North Carolina at
  Charlotte-UNCC Station
Charlotte, NC 28223

Sheaton Harris Nuclear Power Plant
Richard Harrison Library
1313 New Bern Avenue
Raleigh, NC 27610

Brunswick Steam Electric Plant
William Madison Randall Library
University of North Carolina at
  Wilmington
601 S. College Road
Wilmington, NC 28403-3297

OHIO
Perry Nuclear Power Plant
Perry Public Library
3753 Main Street
Perry, OH 44081

Davis-Besse Nuclear Power Station
William Carlson Library
University of Toledo
2801 West Bancroft Avenue
Toledo, OH 43606

OKLAHOMA
Kerr-McGee Sequoyah
Sallisaw City Library
101 E. Cherokee Street
Sallisaw, OK 74955

OREGON
Trojan Nuclear Plant
Portland State University
P.O. Box 1151
10th & Harrison
Portland, OR 97207

PENNSYLVANIA
Beaver Valley Power Station
B.F. Jones Memorial Library
663 Franklin Avenue
Aliquippa, PA 15001

Three Mile Island Nuclear Station &
  Peach Bottom Atomic Power Station
State Library of Pennsylvania
Walnut Street & Commonwealth
  Avenue
Box 1601
Harrisburg, PA 17105

Babcock & Wilcox Parks Township &
  B & W Apollo
Apollo Memorial Library

219 N. Pennsylvania Avenue
Apollo, PA 15613

Limerick Generating Station
Free Library of Philadelphia
19th & Vine Street
Philadelphia, PA 18103

Pottstown Public Library
500 High Street
Pottstown, PA 19464

Saxton Nuclear Experimental Facility
Saxton Community Library
911 Church Street
Saxton, PA 16678

Beaver Valley Power Station &
  Susquehanna Steam Electric Station
Pattee Library
Room C 207
Pennsylvania State University
University Park, PA 16802

Susquehanna Steam Electric Station
  & Low-Level Waste Storage
Osterhout Free Library
71 South Franklin Street
Wilkes-Barre, PA 18701

RHODE ISLAND
Wood River Junction
Cross Mill Public Library
Old Post Road
Charleston, RI 02813

SOUTH CAROLINA
Barnwell Reprocessing Plant & Low-
  Level Waste Burial Site
Barnwell County Public Library
Hagood Avenue
Barnwell, SC 19812

Catawba Nuclear Station
South Carolina State Library
1500 Senate Street
Columbia, SC 29201

York County Library
138 East Black Street
P.O. Box 10032
Rock Hill, SC 29730

H.B. Robinson Plant & Robinson Independent Spent Fuel Storage
Hartsville Memorial Library
220 N. Fifth Street
Hartsville, SC 29550

Oconee Nuclear Plant
Oconee County Library
501 W. South Broad Street
Walhalla, SC 29691

Virgil C. Summer Nuclear Station
Fairfield County Library
Garden & Washington Streets
Winnsboro, SC 29180

TENNESSEE
Sequoyah Nuclear Plant, —Watts Barr Nuclear Plant & TVA Sequoyah Low-Level Waste Storage
Chattanooga-Hamilton County Library
1001 Broad Street
Chattanooga, TN 37402

TEXAS
Comanche Peak Steam Electric Station
University of Texas at Arlington Library
701 South Cooper
P.O. Box 19497
Arlington, TX 76019

Glen Rose-Somervell Library
Barnard & Highway 144
P.O. Box 417
Glen Rose, TX 76043

South Texas Project
Austin Public Library
810 Guadalupe Street
P.O. Box 2287
Austin, TX 78701

San Antonio Public Library
203 St. Mary's Street
San Antonio, TX 78205

Wharton County Junior College
J.M. Hodges Learning Center

911 Boling Highway
Wharton, TX 77488

VERMONT
Vermont Yankee Nuclear Power Station
Brooks Memorial Library
224 Main Street
Brattleboro, VT 05301

VIRGINIA
North Anna Power Station
Alderman Library
University of Virginia
Charlottesville, VA 22901

Surry Power Station & Independent Spent Fuel Storage
Swem Library
College of William & Mary
Wiliamsburg, VA 23185

WASHINGTON
WPPSS Nuclear Project 3 & 5
W.H. Abel Memorial Library
125 Main Street South
Montesano, WA 98563

WPPSS Nuclear Projects 1, 2 & 4, Basalt Waste Isolation Project & Richland Low-Level Waste Burial Site
Richland Public Library
Swift and Northgate Streets
Richland, WA 99352

WISCONSIN
Kewaunee Nuclear Power Plant
Library Learning Center
University of Wisconsin
2420 Nicolet Drive
Green Bay, WI 54301

LaCrosse Nuclear Power Plant
LaCrosse Public Library
800 Main Street
LaCrosse, WI 54601

Point Beach Nuclear Plant
Joseph Mann Library
1516 16th Street
Two Rivers, WI 54241

PART THREE

BUYING AN ENVIRONMENTALLY SOUND HOUSE

$\boxed{10}$

SHOPPING FOR A HOME: USING YOUR EYES, EARS AND NOSE ... AND REALTOR, INSPECTOR, LAWYER ETC. ETC.

Until now we've focused on the environmental health hazards you can encounter in the home you own or rent, and how they can be resolved. This chapter will tell you what to look for when buying a home to avoid these dangers.

STEP ONE: YOUR OWN, PERSONAL INSPECTION

The real estate agent has just taken you through a house that seems perfect. Maybe it is too good to be true. On the other hand, maybe it is as great as it seems. *Now is the time to find out.*

INSIDE THE HOUSE

On the first walk-through most people really aren't looking that carefully for problems. Some problems, of course, may be very obvious. Others may take a little more sleuthing and be discovered only on your follow-up visit.

Even if you plan to have an inspection done (highly recommended) there are some initial, basic steps everyone should take, slowly ... and through the house. And let me emphasize the word *slowly*. There are all kinds of warning signs you should look for. You want to take your time and observe everything very carefully using the tools you have at your disposal: your eyes, ears and nose. Take a pad with you to make a note of things that you see and have a question about. Don't rely on your memory. Your own preliminary inspection could save you time, money and a lot of disappointment.

Make yourself conscious of how the house smells. Are there unpleasant odors anywhere? They could signal a problem. Does the basement smell or feel damp? If instead of a basement there is just a crawl space, check it out. Usually the floor of a crawl space is the ground. Is there any standing water on that ground? Especially around the walls and in the corners?

You also want to check for dampness around appliances. Do you see any mold, mildew or efflorescence (white, fuzz-like powder that forms on basement walls when moisture is present behind the walls).

Ask for a glass of water (even if you're NOT thirsty). If the homeowner is heading for the refrigerator you can say something like, "I really don't like water from the refrigerator, it's too cold." Make sure the water you're getting is from the tap. You can be very discreet as you check it out. First of all, does it look like water you want to drink? Does it have any odor? How does it taste? If the water looks great, smells great (doesn't smell), and tastes great—it doesn't necessarily mean that it is great. But there is certainly a better likelihood that it is OK.

Look at the walls, the ceilings, the woodwork. Is paint chipping or flaking? If the house was built before 1977 the paint used was probably lead-based. Even if the house was repainted after 1977 with lead-free paint, the earlier layers of paint can be hazardous. (The condition of the walls, ceilings and woodwork can also be an indication of how well the house was cared for by the current occupants.)

Look at the windows, all the windows. Can they be opened? Is there a wind whistling through, even though the windows are shut? (This may *not* be evident on a pleasant day when there is no wind blowing.)

Go into the attic, even if it is difficult to get into. Look for water stains, especially around a chimney (if there is one), vent pipes and along the roof line. Look for any indication (droppings) of uninvited visitors such as mice or squirrels. Check on what kinds of vents are in the attic for ventilation.

If there are pipes in the basement encased in insulation, is that insulation flaking? Those flakes could be asbestos.

These are all things that sound obvious, simple. And they are. But you'd be surprised at the people who put on those old rose-colored glasses as they look at something that is one of the biggest investments of their lives. With some forethought and careful observation you may spot a potentially big problem and not want to proceed any further with that house.

If you've detected anything wrong, you may want to ask the owner, or occupant, about some of those things you've taken notes on, but remember: Your concerns and the concerns of the person trying to sell the house—the owner and/or broker—may be pretty far apart!

OUTSIDE THE HOUSE

You've been through the house. It smells fine. The water tastes great. There are no small, colorful particles on your head or coat sleeves from flaking paint. You step outside.

Take a deep breath. How does the air smell? It is not supposed to smell bad!

How do the grass and plant life around the house look? You don't have to be a botanist to recognize plants that just don't look healthy. How does the soil look? Does it have any odors? Are there any vacant lots near the house where an industrial plant could suddenly spring up, *after* you're comfortably settled in your house?

Note how close the house is to the street and how big that street is. Are there many cars driving by? Are there any trucks, any BIG trucks passing by? What may seem like a lazy, quiet country road on a weekend or in the middle of a weekday (when most people look for a house), may present a very different picture during a weekday morning rush hour. I once bought a house on a lake. I saw it in the fall, in the middle of the week. On one side there was a house—on the other side a very small private beach. The real estate agent assured me that it was just as quiet on the weekend, that during the summer few people used the small beach because the lake had a much larger, well appointed beach and there were few motorboats because the lake wasn't that big. It was fall and there was really no way I could see what it would be like on a typical, hot summer weekend. But I could have tried to track down some neighbors to ask about use of the small, private beach and the prevalence of motor boats. I could also have talked with the Lake Association. I did neither. I took the real estate agent at her word. That summer, the noise on the weekend from the people using the very small private beach and the motor boats reminded me too much of the noise and congestion in New York City that I was trying to escape. I sold the house two years later. Was the real estate agent lying when she told me how quiet it would be? Maybe—or perhaps she didn't know, or perhaps what is unbearable noise to me, would not bother her at all. I may have been unable to find out what I'd be up against on a typical summer weekend, but I certainly could have made a greater effort.

If the house you're looking at is on a lake, stream or river, look at the water and smell it. Someone who wants to fish or take a daily dip will have different concerns and will be looking for different things than the person who just wants to have "a nice view."

IN THE NEIGHBORHOOD

The house looks good, the bushes look healthy, the water is clear, the air smells sweet. So how's the neighborhood?

Take a leisurely drive around the area. Look for industrial plants, factories, an airport. Is smoke coming out of the factory? Does the air smell bad? Again, if it's a weekend you may not be getting a true picture. And if it's at a time when planes aren't flying, or the wind is blowing in the wrong direction, you may not hear the distracting and stressful noise that neighborhood residents are regularly subjected to.

Do you see a large number of "for sale" signs on houses in the neighborhood? Is there some reason all those people are getting out, something that would make you want to leave as well?

"CONCLUSIONS"

Chances are you will not come to a definitive conclusion after just one visit, but after making a very careful inspection (and you may want to return on the weekend or during the morning rush hour to do a little more sleuthing) you may realize that the house is not for you. That will save you time and money and enable you to continue your search. At the very least, your own personal inspection can make you aware of possible problems that you want to look into more deeply or have a professional check out.

STEP TWO: CHECKING THE HOUSE OUT, FOR REAL

On the surface, the house looks terrific. Now it's time to *thoroughly check out* the house, the neighborhood, the town. You don't want to be surprised, once you move in, by a zoning law that will allow a shopping mall (and all that additional traffic, auto emissions and noise) or nuclear power plant to be built on the vacant lot next door. And you don't want to find out, after you move in, as a good friend of mine did, that the house is filled with asbestos. You can get some answers from the real estate salesperson and the owner, but the bottom line is that the major footwork is up to you, to make sure you are getting all the answers you need.

There's nothing wrong with buying a house with a problem or two. Sometimes you can even get a great buy if the house needs work. But you want to buy that house with your eyes wide open. You want to know what problems exist, what problems may develop and what you will have to do to resolve them. You may well have to go to more than one person to get the answer to one seemingly simple question. Following are some of the environmental/health issues of concern when buying a new house—and some of the people and places where you may find answers.

THE REAL ESTATE BROKER / THE OWNER

Your Real Estate Broker
The first thing you want to do is get a little background information on the person who will be showing you homes and very possibly selling you one. A broker is licensed by the state. A real estate salesperson is licensed to work under the supervision of a licensed broker and can show you a house, but only the broker can enter into a contract. If the broker is a member of the National Association of Realtors trade organization, he or she subscribes to the association's code of ethics. That means, the real estate broker should disclose any known material defects. In California, this is mandated by law, but most states do not have a law like that on the books. In New York, for example, there is no law to that effect at the time of publication of this book, but there have been some lawsuits against a realtor or homeowner for not disclosing a known defect. You may want to call the state branch of the National Association of Realtors to find out what laws, if any, your state has.

There are a number of things you may want to consider when using a broker or real estate agent: how long they've been licensed, how long they've been working as a broker, how long they've been selling houses and/or living in the area where you're looking; how many homes they've sold in the last three months; and if this is a full-time job. The longer the real estate agent has been selling homes where you're looking, the more knowledgeable the agent is likely to be. You might also ask for recommendations from friends or people in the area who have recently purchased (or sold) a home.

You should always remember that the real estate agent is working for the owner, who pays the commission. And you should also bear in mind that the owner or realtor may not volunteer information that might turn off a potential buyer. So it is important to ask questions!

There is some basic information that a professional, competent real estate broker should have available for every house you look at, including the age of the house, the year it was built, the source of drinking water and the types of heating, ventilating and air conditioning systems.

Next are the less obvious, but just as important questions—zoning regulations and laws regarding any renovations you might want to do on your house or a neighbor might want to do on his or her house. This should definitely be checked with the local planning board. There have been many horror stories. In Hauppauge, New York, in 1981 a company that shreds cars was suddenly installed over the Labor Day Weekend, according to Marion DiNicole, one of the many unhappy residents. A group of homeowners has been in court since, trying to get the company to shutdown. The residents claim that toxic fumes permeate the neighborhood and explosions shake their homes and rattle their windows. Another resident, Janice Scanziani, is worried that the health of her children may be endangered. She's also angry because she says she is unable to enjoy her house or yard, and now she can't sell the house because the shredder has caused property values to go down.

Ask the real estate agent, or owner, why the house is being sold. If the reason is a job transfer or an upscale move to a bigger house there should be no hesitancy about giving the reason. Perhaps there has been talk of building a nuclear power plant nearby. You may not want to face that prospect either. On the other hand, it is important to remember that something that the seller may find unacceptable, may not bother you.

Owner/Seller

There are a number of things you want to find out from the owner, things that the real estate agent may not know. Following are some of the questions to ask the owner:

- Are you the original owner and, if not, how long have you owned it?
- When was the house last painted, inside and out, and what kind of paint was used?
- What kind of insulation is in the house, around pipes; has any insulation been put in and, if so, what kind?
- Do you have documentation on the insulation work done?
- Does the house have lead pipes?
- Have any plumbing repairs or renovations been done, and if so, what kind of piping was used; was lead solder used?
- Do you have documentation on the plumbing work done?
- Have you done any minor or major renovation or construction, and if so, what materials did you use?
- Do you have documentation of what was done?

- Have you tested for radon, and if so, what were the results and how have you resolved any problem.
- Do you have the radon test results and documentation on the work done?
- Do you know what kind of flooring is under the carpeting? (Is it particleboard?)
- Do you know what kind of tiles are on the floor? (Are they asbestos?)
- Do you know what kind of paneling is on the walls? (Is it particleboard?)
- Do you have the architectural plans for the house?

The owner may not be able to answer all the questions or may plead ignorance because he or she does not want to make certain revelations.

NEIGHBORS

People in the neighborhood can be a great source of information. You might approach someone you see outside and explain that you are looking at a house nearby. Very often people love to talk about their neighborhood (the great things about it) and the things that are driving them crazy—like the fact they lost the fight to keep a gas station from opening on the corner. Sometimes people don't think of something as a problem, so you may have to ask some questions that are a little more probing, once you are engaged in conversation. You might ask if there has been any problem in the neighborhood, any odd recurring illnesses among area residents; any problems with the drinking water; any problems with the water at the nearby swimming hole, pond, lake or stream; any problems with the local vegetation (have trees or bushes suddenly started dying); have they, or anyone they know, tested for radon in their homes and what were the results. You may end up doing one of them a favor—for example, making them aware of radon and the reason for doing a radon test. A problem that you discover in this way could be something that would not matter a whole lot to you. On the other hand, it may be something that you would find totally unacceptable. In either case, you simply want to eliminate as many surprises as possible before buying any house and moving in.

GOVERNMENT AGENCIES

Local Town Government
First off, find out who you should be contacting about specific questions. If the town is very small you may have to go one step up, to the county

level or even to the state government for some answers. Ask your real estate agent what the local government is responsible for and who would be the best person to contact. If the town is very small your real estate agent may tell you, for example, the name of the person to call about health information as well as the home phone number of that person! (I called a fair number of local officials at home in my quest for answers!) The bigger the town, the more unlikely that is. However, whatever the size of the town, the real estate agent should at least be able to point you in the direction of a local government official or office. Call that person and ask where and who you can call for all the other questions you have.

Local Health Department

Many things come under the health department. But if you have questions about something that it doesn't have jurisdiction over, it should be able to advise you as to who does.

The local health department may be able to tell you if there have been any reports of an abnormally high incidence of a particular illness in the area. For example, in New Jersey a study by the state has shown that people living within a mile of the Lipari landfill, one of the nation's most toxic Superfund waste sites, are more likely to get adult leukemia or produce babies with low birth weights than people living outside the area. Ask if there have been any calls about symptoms experienced by a cluster of people in one area—symptoms for which there is no immediate explanation.

Check on any reports of contaminated water—drinking or recreational. When I was looking for a house in upstate New York there were a lot of houses for sale, at what seemed to me very reasonable prices, on a lovely lake. I was surprised and thrilled until I did a little research. Residents were being told not to fish and/or swim in the lake! There were several stories about the polluted lake in the local paper. I certainly didn't buy one of the reasonably priced homes on that lake!

Find out if the health department has any information on testing for radon in the area and what the results were.

Local Planning Board

You surely want to speak to someone on the planning board, which decides on zoning changes and renovation and construction guidelines. The best person to speak with is the head of the group. Again, you want to find out the current zoning regulations for the area where you are considering the purchase of a house, and if any changes have been proposed.

Check also on any restrictions on renovating or repairing your home and/or putting on additions. For example, does any addition have to be a certain distance from your property line? The same rules, of course, apply to the house next door. Does construction work, inside or outside, have to be done at specific times? Even if you may not be planning any renovations or additions, the people in the house next door may be.

Check, as well, on who owns the vacant lot next to the house, or the lovely woods in the back. Find out whether any plans have been filed, or approved, for construction of a new building, shopping mall, power plant, dumpsite etc., in the area, how far along the plans are, when the actual construction will take place, and how long it is expected to take until completion.

Are there any zoning regulations regarding the transport of toxic substances? That wouldn't be an issue on a dirt road in a rural area, however, it could be a concern if the house is on, or near, a major roadway.

THE LOCAL NEWSPAPER

Call the local paper or, better yet, just walk right in (this is *not advised* for large metropolitan daily newspapers like the *New York Times* and *Washington Post*) and ask who covers environmental or controversial issues. (Reporters love to show how smart they are, how much they've uncovered!) Ask about any problems in the area with unexplained outbreaks of illness, with toxic waste dumps, with an industrial plant or a proposal, perhaps, to build a nuclear power plant etc.

LOCAL COMMUNITY GROUPS AND ORGANIZATIONS

Local community groups and organizations are another excellent source of information. The local newspaper should be able to provide a list of organizations as well as members of the community who are active (aka activists and/or troublemakers). If you do have concerns about a particular issue, call the group or person working on that issue. You should be able to get a lot of information on the extent of the problem, what can be done about it, what, if anything, is currently being done about it, and future prospects. You'll also get an idea as to how concerned the local citizenry is about problems, how effective they are, and how well they might work together to solve future problems.

THE HOUSE INSPECTION

Most people do have an inspection of the house done before buying it. It is usually required by the bank if you are applying for a mortgage. If you are paying for the house with cash you do not have to have an inspection done—but that could prove foolish. The question is not whether you will get an inspection but rather who will do it and what it will cover.

To find a building inspector, ask the bank where you are trying to get a mortgage for suggestions. Its best interests will be served by recommending an honest, conscientious inspector. You can check the yellow pages under "Building Inspection Services," or if you know someone in the area who has just purchased a house, ask who they used. You can also ask your real estate agent. Get the names of several inspectors, so that you'll have a choice.

Ask the inspector how long he or she has been doing house inspections, how long in that particular area, and what his or her qualifications are. Do they guarantee their work in any way? A call to the better business bureau is an additional way to be as sure as possible that you are using a reliable, competent company and/or inspector.

Next, find out just what the inspector will be examining and be prepared to tell your specific concerns, what you want to know about the house. Besides the general condition of the house, will it be checked for asbestos? termites? Will the ventilation system be assessed? Will there be testing for radon, leaded paint; will the water be tested; what kind of pipes and solder are in the plumbing system; will the heating system be checked (the furnace, air conditioning unit, humidifier etc.); will appliances be checked for leaks?

If possible, be present at the inspection. This is a place where, conceivably, you and your family will be spending a lot of time. Ask questions. If, for example, the inspector notices something he says "could be asbestos," ask precisely what he means. Would it be wise to call in an expert on asbestos?

You may want to go a step further and call in a professional engineer for a structural inspection.

If the termite test is positive, and the owner is going to take care of the problem before the closing, find out exactly that will be done, what kind of pesticide will be used and how it will be applied.

LEGAL ISSUES OR "CAVEAT EMPTOR"

Disclosure by the Seller/Broker

Before the 19th century, the general rule was "caveat emptor" or let the buyer beware. And while that is still a good edict to bear in mind, you should also be aware that you do have, at the very least, some basic rights if you are buying a home anywhere in the United States.

A more updated warning from the California Association of Realtors is: "A real estate broker is qualified to advise on real estate. If you desire legal advice, consult your attorney." That appears on the second, and last, page of California's Real Estate Disclosure Statement form, required by California's Real Estate Transfer Disclosure Statement law, in effect since January 1987. It is something like a lemon law for houses, requiring the seller and real estate agent to make specific information available to the buyer. The seller is required to fill out a two-page form, which includes information on such concerns as source of the water supply (city, well or private utility), type of water heater and the condition of virtually every part of the house from the electrical system and plumbing to the driveways and sidewalks. The real estate agent is also required to make a diligent visual inspection of the accessible areas of the property and then make a statement about it, disclosing material defects. (For more information on the law call the California Association of Realtors at [213]739-8200.)

California's law, when it went into effect, was the most inclusive in the United States in terms of formalizing and spelling out what the seller and broker must do in terms of disclosing problems in the house. But today there are many case laws or statutory laws in other states that, while maybe not as far reaching as California's laws, require more disclosure than ever before from the seller or broker or both.

At the very least, the seller or broker cannot "actively conceal" (hide) a major defect from you or not tell the truth when you ask a direct question about the structural part of the building. That is basic common law, violation of which is grounds for a lawsuit. Regardless of what laws are on the books in your state, you are protected by the common law of fraud and misrepresentation.

Many states have taken that common law much further through case and statutory laws. It is no longer sufficient in many states to "not conceal defects." The seller and/or broker is required to inform you about known problems, without your even asking. With all the attention being paid to, and concern over, environmental hazards, it appears that more and more states are going for greater and greater disclosure requirements.

To find out what legal obligation the seller or broker or both have to you, the potential buyer, call the state association of realtors (if you have any difficulty the National Association of Realtors can give you the number—the NAR number is [312]329-8200), a local law official—perhaps a city council member or a state official—or a local real estate lawyer. Even though these laws are changing fairly rapidly, you should be able to find out what information the seller and broker are required to make available to you.

Signing the Contract

When you do find the house you think you want to purchase, it's a good idea to hold off on signing a contract until the inspection is completed. That way, if something in the inspection dissuades you from purchasing the house, you do not have to pay the lawyer's fee for drawing up the contract.

If you have to have the contract in place before the inspection can take place, be sure to have contingencies in the contract. Among other things, you may want to have the purchase contingent on the outcome of a radon test. Or you may want to have a clause that will guarantee that all the plumbing, heating and electrical systems will be in good working condition at the time of closing. Go over this thoroughly with your lawyer. Most states do have a standard contract for the sale of real estate, but that won't necessarily protect your interests. Again, take nothing for granted.

Non-disclosures/Legal Remedies

You have purchased a home and suddenly there is an unexpected major problem—for example, you find out that there is a Superfund toxic waste site two blocks away, or the house does contain asbestos (and lots of it) or the water is contaminated. You do have some recourse. While you may have a clear-cut case of fraud, what's more likely is that your problem will fall in a gray area, for any number of reasons.

What you consider a major problem, the seller of the house or real estate broker may not. For example, after talking with neighbors you find that there was a time when the house was thought to be haunted. While this may be of major concern to you, and if you had known you would never have bought the house, neither the seller nor broker may consider that a material defect. They may contend that they haven't hidden anything—they just didn't think the information was relevant. And you never asked.

If you have purchased a home and suddenly find a problem that you had no idea existed and have reason to believe the previous owner or the broker knew of its existence, you have some legal recourse. The first thing you should do is talk with someone at the state real estate commission, preferably an attorney there, and/or a private real estate lawyer.

You may find out that the owner and/or broker is under no obligation to have informed you about the house's history. You may find out that the owner and/or broker was obliged to tell you about the toxic waste site in the area. Your best bet is to consult with an attorney on what course of action to take. You may want to simply file a complaint with the state real estate commission against the broker. Or you may want to file a lawsuit for damages.

Winning the lawsuit can bring you different awards in different states. Following are a number of possibilities. The state you live in may do one of them, some of them, or all of them.

If the court rules in your favor, the original contract of sale may be voided. You, the buyer, would be entitled to monetary compensation commensurate with the financial position you were in before the sale.

The court may award you the cost of repairing the problem.

You may be awarded the monetary difference between the value of the property with the defect and what you paid for it, with the value being determined, usually, by the price of similar properties.

The above fall under "contract damages." Many states also award punitive damages if there was a cover-up or intent to deceive. A finding of fraud will justify a punitive damage award in most states. In addition to contract damages, you can sue if you have suffered personal injury as a result of the seller not abiding by the law. Compensation could include doctor fees, lost wages and a monetary award for pain and suffering.

Ending up in a courtroom is the last place most people want to find themselves. You bought a home for you and your family. You want to enjoy it, live in it comfortably, feel safe and secure. You are naturally concerned about the health and welfare of your family and the large financial investment the house represents. The bottom line is that you are the person who has the most at stake in finding out every last detail that you can about the house—before you buy.

You may be fortunate and hook up with a thorough, competent and conscientious real estate broker who will track down every possible problem and answer all your questions accurately and precisely. You may be purchasing your home from a scrupulously honest homeowner. However, you cannot count on either. An omission by the real estate broker, or even the seller, may be unintentional or on purpose. That omission, whether unintentional, careless or intentional, could turn living in your new home into a nightmare, eventually costing you time, aggravation and money, not to mention your health.

Your responsibility as the person buying the home, and the person who will be living in it, is to do everything in your power to find any of those possible omissions. There may very well be none or, diligent as *you* are, you may miss something. But chances are that after that extra effort you will not have any surprises once you take possession of your dreamhouse and move in. And your home, as long as you're in it, will be a safe haven and a source of pleasure for you and your family.

APPENDIX A
BUYING A HOUSE -
ENVIRONMENTAL
CHECKLIST

Go over this checklist before you start looking at houses and become as familiar as possible with what you want to be on the lookout for. Take a copy of this checklist with you. Check off the items as you see them. Make notes on what you want to ask the owner, broker or others. Be polite but don't be afraid to ask questions!

PART ONE - INITIAL VISIT

Inside the House

Walls:
Is the paint chipping or peeling?
Are their any water stains?
Are the walls cracked?
Are there any water stains on
  wallpaper?
Where are the electrical outlets?
Do any of the electrical outlets
  have any obvious problems?
Are any of the walls paneled?

Ceilings:
Is paint chipping or peeling?
Are there any cracks?
Are there lighting fixtures?
Are there vents?
Are there any suspended
  ceilings with panels?

Floors:
What kind of floor is in the
  kitchen?
In the bathroom?
In the basement?
In the attic?
What kinds of floor are in the
  other rooms?
Do you see any vents in the
  floor?
Are there any obvious water
  stains on the carpet?
Is there any smell coming from
  the carpet?
Can you tell what is under the
  carpet?

Windows:
Is paint chipping or peeling
  from window frames?

Can you feel any breeze coming through windows that are closed?

If it is an old house, do the windows look like they are the original ones?

Do the windows look like they close tightly?

Woodwork:

Is paint chipping or peeling from woodwork?

Kitchen:

Is there any kind of device on the faucet that could indicate a problem with the water?

How does the water run when you turn it on?

Does it look like water you'd want to drink?

Does it smell like water you'd want to drink?

Is there any mold or mildew around any of the appliances?

Is there any dampness in the basement?

In the attic?

Near appliances?

Bathrooms:

Is there any mold or mildew?

How well does the water run in the sink and in the shower/bath?

How does the water look?

Does it have any odor?

Basement:

Is it a full basement or a crawl space?

Is there any unpleasant odor?

Do you see any mold or mildew on the walls, floor, around appliances?

Do the walls feel damp?

Can you see any cracks in the walls or floor?

Are there pipes with insulation around them?

What kind of condition is it in?

Is it flaking, ripped or coming apart?

Are there windows in the basement and, if there are, what are they like?

Attic:

Can you see the insulation in the attic?

If there are closets in the attic, can you see the insulation there?

Can you tell what kind it is?

Are there vents?

Is the attic noticeably hotter or stuffier than the rest of the house?

Is there any unpleasant smell?

Are there any droppings on the floor from mice or squirrels?

Are there any water stains or moisture?

NOTES:

Outside the House

The outside of the house:
What is on the outside of the house? (Paint? Shingles? Siding?)
What condition is it in?
If it is painted, is the paint chipping or peeling?
If there is a chimney, can you see any cracks in it?
Do the trees and grass look healthy?
How does the soil look?
How does the air smell?

Noise:
What kind of noise do you hear? (Sounds and volume can vary greatly on different days and at different times.)
How close is the road?
How many lanes does the road have?
How busy is the road? (This too can vary greatly by day and time.)
Are there any trucks on the road?

The neighborhood:
How close are the houses on either side and across the street?
Is there a vacant lot next door, behind the house, across the street, farther down the street?
Is the lot big enough for a factory, dumpsite, nuclear power plant?

Water:
Is there a pond or stream on the property?
Does it look clean?

Does it have any smell?
Would you want to swim in it? or have your kids swim in it?
If the house is on a lake, or has lake rights, does the lake look clean, smell okay, would you want to swim in it?

NOTES:

In the Area

Nuclear power industry:
Is there a nuclear power plant in the area?
How close to the house is it?
Is there an industrial plant nearby?
How large is it?
What does it produce?

Water:
Is the house near a river, lake, stream?
Does the water look clean?
Does it have an odor?

NOTES:

PART TWO - CONSIDERING PURCHASE

The Inspection

What are the qualifications of
the inspector?
Is any guarantee given?
Can the company or inspector
provide references? (Check
these out.)
What will the inspection cover?
Will the inspector look for
asbestos? lead pipes? the
ventilation system? proximity
of well to septic system (if
appropriate)?

NOTES:

NOTES:

What to Ask the Broker

How old is the house?
Why is it being sold?
What kind of plumbing does it
have?
What kind of heating does it
have?
What is the source of the
drinking water?

NOTES:

Tests to Consider

Termite—a must
Water—a must, if the source of
water is a well
Lead—if the house is old
enough to have lead paint
Radon—can be misleading if
not done correctly or if
testing device is placed in the
wrong part of the house.

What to Ask the Owner

Is he/she the original owner?

How long has he/she owned the house?

When was it last painted—inside and outside—and what kind of paint was used?

What kind of insulation has been used?

Did he/she put in any insulation, and if so, what was it?

What are the water pipes made of?

Have any repairs or renovations of the plumbing been made, and if so, what were they?

Was lead solder used?

Is the paperwork for the repairs/renovations available?

What is under the carpeting?

What is under the tiles on the floor?

What kind of paneling is on the walls?

What is under the paneling?

Has the house ever been treated for termites, and if so, what termiticide was used?

Is there any paperwork for the extermination?

Is there documentation for any tests that have been done such as radon, water test, lead, formaldehyde, asbestos?

NOTES:

What to Ask the Neighbors? (Diplomatically)

If the wind is blowing the wrong way, are there any unpleasant odors?

How is the water? Does it always taste okay? Has anyone had any problems with it?

How is that lake down the road for swimming?

Have there been any odd, recurring illnesses in the neighborhood?

How's your garden doing?

Have they or any of the neighbors tested for radon in their homes, and if so, what were the results?

Have there been any problems with termites in the neighborhood?

NOTES:

What to Ask the Local Health Department

Have there been any reports of an abnormally high incidence of a particular illness?

Have there been calls about unexplained symptoms experienced by a cluster of people in one area?

Are there any known toxic dumpsites?

Have there been any complaints about foul odors from factories, industrial sites or dumpsites?

Have there been any problems with the water?

Has testing for radon been done in the area, and if so, what were the results?

NOTES:

What to Ask the Planning Board

What are the zoning regulations where the house is located?

Are any attempts being made to change the regulations, and if so, what are they?

Are there any requirements/restrictions for repairing, renovating or putting additions on the house?

Have any plans been filed for the large vacant lot next door? down the road? in the area?

Have any plans been filed, or approved for a factory, dumpsite, power plant, etc., and if so, when will work begin and how long is it scheduled to take?

Are there any regulations regarding the transport of hazardous wastes?

NOTES:

What to Ask the Local Newspaper

(First find out who covers environmental or controversial issues.)

Have there been any unexplained outbreaks of illness or health problems in the area?

Are there any toxic waste dumps in the area?

Who are the community activists, and what are the names of the active community groups and how can they be contacted?

NOTES:

What to Ask the Local Activist/Community Group

What needs to be done about a particular problem?

What is being done about the water problems, the toxic dumpsite, etc.?

How health conscious/receptive is the area and how difficult has it been to get any action?

NOTES:

APPENDIX B
OTHER HELPFUL PHONE NUMBERS

The following numbers can provide additional information on various environmental hazards. Some have free publications, which may be helpful. Others have "experts" with access to the latest information in a particular area. There are some toll-free 800 numbers available. They have been underlined. Others that don't fall into a particular category are in the last section of 800 numbers.

SOURCES FOR SPECIFIC PROBLEMS

Included here are federal agencies and organizations that deal with the problem. Some of the organizations are trade associations or advocacy groups.

Asbestos:

TSCA Assistance Information Service (EPA Asbestos Hotline)—(202)554-1404; in operation 8:30 A.M.-5:00 P.M. EST; or write TSCA Industry Assistance Office, EPA, TS-799, 401 M Street S.W., Washington, D.C. 20460; information and publications on regulations under the Toxic Substances Control Act and EPA's asbestos programs.

ASHRAE—see Indoor Air Pollution.

National Asbestos Council—(404)633-2622; 1777 Northeast Expressway, Suite 150, Atlanta, Georgia 30329; has technical specialists on staff who can answer consumer questions; free asbestos handbook; nonprofit.

White Lung Association—(301)727-6029; 1114 Cathedral Street, Baltimore, Maryland 21201; working on rights of those exposed to asbestos; organization for asbestos-related disease victims.

Safe Buildings Alliance—(202)381-1815; Metropolitan Square, 655 15th Street N.W., Suite 12, Washington, D.C. 20005; free pamphlet "Asbestos in Buildings: What Owners and Managers Should Know"; SBA is an association of leading building products companies that formerly manufactured asbestos-containing materials for building construction.

Asbestos Information Association/North America—1725 Jefferson Davis Highway, Arlington, Virginia 22202.

Hazardous Waste Sites:

RCRA/Superfund Hotline—1-800-424-9346; in operation weekdays 8:30 A.M. to 7:30 P.M. E.S.T. in Washington, D.C., only, call (202)382-3000; information and publications on regulations under both the Resource Recovery Act (including solid and hazardous waste issues) and the Superfund law; can report hazardous waste sites in your area; operated by EPA.

EPCRA (Emergency Planning and Right to Know Act)—1-800-535-0202; for information on toxic chemicals use in maufacturing; operated by EPA.

National Response Center—1-800-424-8802; to report an oil or hazardous waste spill, or illegal dumping; in operation 24 hours; under the EPA.

Citizens for a Better Environment—(312)939-1984; 59 East Van Buren, Suite 1600, Chicago, Illinois 60605; research, information, free publications; nonprofit advocacy group.

Indoor Air Pollution:

(Many of these organizations will have information on all the indoor pollutants, including asbestos, radon, formaldehyde, pesticides, etc.)

American Lung Association—(212)315-8700; 1740 Broadway, New York, New York 10019; or your local Lung Association; free publications.

American Society of Heating, Refrigeration, and Air-Conditioning Engineers, Inc. (ASHRAE)—(404)636-8400; 1791 Tullie Circle N.E., Atlanta, Georgia 30329; over 150 branches in the United States; information on all aspects of indoor air pollution; limited information for the general public, mostly technical information for professionals; call main number and ask for "technology"; nonprofit.

American Institute of Architects—(202)626-7493 (reference line); 1350 New York Avenue N.W., Washington, D.C. 20006; information and free pamphlet on indoor pollution; nonprofit professional organization.

American Gas Association—(703)841-8400; 1515 Wilson Boulevard, Arlington, Virginia 22209; information and publications available; nonprofit trade association.

Centers for Disease Control-Office on Smoking and Health—(301)443-2610; Park Building, Room 1-16, Rockville, Maryland 20857; information on environmental tobacco smoke; under the U.S. Department of Health and Human Services.

Edison Electric Institute—(202)778-6593; 1111 19th Street N.W., Washington, D.C. 20036; publications available on energy (for a charge); not for profit trade association representing investor-owned electric utilities.

National Coalition for Clean Indoor Air—(202)797-5436; 316 Pennsylvania Avenue S.E., Suite 400, Washington, D.C. 20003.

U.S. Department of Energy—free pamphlet, "Air to Air Heat Exchangers," available by writing to: Renewable Energy Information, P.O. Box 8900, Silver Spring, Maryland 20907.

U.S. Department of Health and Human Services—(513)841-4382; 4676 Columbia Parkway (Mail Drop R2), Cincinnati, Ohio 45226; for help with indoor air quality problems.

World Health Organization-Publications Center—(518)436-9686; 49 Sheridan Avenue, Albany, New York 12210; free list of available publications.

Lead:

Conservation Law Foundation of New England—(617)742-2540; 3 Joy Street, Boston, Massachusetts 02108; has a Lead Poisoning Project.

Centers for Disease Control—(404)329-3286; 1600 Clifton Road N.E., Atlanta, Georgia 30333; under the U.S. Department of Health & Human Services.

ASHRAE—see Indoor Air Pollution.

Nuclear Power Plants:

The Union of Concerned Scientists—(617)547-5552; 26 Church Street, Cambridge, Massachusetts 02238; information and literature on nuclear power safety; independent nonprofit agency.

U.S. Council for Energy Awareness—(202)293-0770; Suite 400, 1776 I Street N.W., Washington, D.C.; information and literature on nuclear power plants; a nonprofit trade organization.

Pesticides:

National Pesticides Telecommunications Network (Pesticides Hotline)—toll-free number: 1-800-858-PEST; in Texas only: (806)743-3091; in operation 24 hours a day, every day for information about pesticides; under the EPA.

EPA—number for information on pesticides: (202)382-2902.

National Coalition Against the Use of Pesticides (NCAUP)—(202)543-5450; 530 7th Street S.E., Washington, D.C. 20003; information on research, health effects and alternatives; nonprofit advocacy group.

Public Citizen—see General Consumer Groups.

Concern—see General Consumer Groups.

Radon:

ASHRAE—see Indoor Air Pollution.

EPA-public information center for radon information—(202)382-2080; 1-800-SOS-RADON for free publications.

Radon Technical Information Services-Research Triangle Institute—(919)541-7131; P.O. Box 12194, Research Triangle Park, North Carolina 27709; information on Radon/Radon Progeny Measurement Proficiency Program.

American Association of Radon Scientists and Technologists—(201)664-7070; 50 Van Buren Avenue, Westwood, New Jersey 07656; has free publications; a nonprofit trade organization.

Public Citizen—see General Consumer Groups.

Concern—see General Consumer Groups.

Water Hotline—1-800-426-4791; information on radon in water (see Water).

Water:

Safe Drinking Water Hotline—1-800-426-4791; in operation weekdays, 8:30 A.M.-5:00 P.M. EST; information on regulations under the Safe Drinking Water Act and radon in drinking water; free publications; under the EPA.

The Water Quality Association (WGA)—(708)505-0160; 4151 Naperville Road, Lisle, Illinois 60532; information on home water treatment devices; nonprofit trade association.

National Sanitation Foundation—(313)769-8010; 3475 Plymouth Road, P.O. Box 1468, Ann Arbor, Michigan 48106; ratings for water treatment units; nonprofit.

National Water Well Association—(614)761-1711; 6375 Riverside Drive, Dublin, Ohio 43017; has free publications; nonprofit trade and professional organization.

Citizens for a Better Environment—see Hazardous Waste Sites.

GENERAL CONSUMER GROUPS:

Concern—(202)328-8160; 1794 Columbia Road N.W., Washington, D.C. 20009; community action guides for drinking water, groundwater and pesticides, at $3 each; nonprofit environmental and educational organization.

United States Public Interest Research Group—(202)546-9707; 215 Pennsylvania Avenue S.E., Washington, D.C. 20003; call for local or regional branch; publications approximately $1 to $10; nonprofit advocacy group.

Consumer Federation of America—(202)387-6121; 1424 16th Street N.W., Suite 604, Washington, D.C. 20036; subscription to newsletter, $25 per year; nonprofit public interest group.

Public Citizen—(202)293-9142; 200 P Street, Washington, D.C. 20036; publications on nuclear power plants, pesticides, radon; nonprofit consumer research and advocacy group.

American Council on Science and Health—(212)362-7044; 1995 Broadway, New York, New York 10023; publications; nonprofit consumer education assistance.

OTHER INFORMATION GROUPS

National Association of Realtors—(312)329-8200; 430 N. Michigan Avenue, Chicago, Illinois 60611; information regarding your rights as a homebuyer; phone numbers for state branches.

National Association of Home Builders (NAHB)—1-800-368-5242; in Maryland: (301)249-9400; 400 Prince Georges Boulevard, Upper Marlboro, Maryland 20772; NAHB National Research Center ([301]249-4000) for home building publications ranging in price from $5 to $30.

American Medical Association—(312)464-4818 (information desk); 535 North Dearborn Street, Chicago, Illinois 60610.

FEDERAL AGENCIES

U.S. Environmental Protection Agency—(202)554-1404 (publications office) for free publications; 401 M Street S.W., Washington, D.C.

U.S. Food & Drug Administration—(301)443-3170; 5600 Fishers Lane, Rockville, Maryland 20857; publications available.

National Bureau of Standards—(301)975-5851; Building 226, Room B306, Gaithersburg, Maryland 20899; for lab accreditation program for bulk and air samples call: (301)975-4017.

National Voluntary Laboratory Accreditation Program (NVLAP)—(301)975-4016; U.S. Department of Commerce, Gaithersburg, Maryland 20899; to get accredited status of laboratories dealing with asbestos, building sealants, carpet, construction related materials (concrete, cement, soil, rock), paint and related coatings, solid-fuel room heaters, thermal insulation materials.

U.S. Department of Energy—(202)586-5373 (Office of Consumer Affairs); 1000 Independence Avenue S.W., Washington, D.C. 20585; information on energy.

800 NUMBERS

EPA Pesticide Hotline—1-800-858-PEST (7378); see Pesticides.

EPA Water Hotline—1-800-426-4791; operates weekdays 8:30 A.M.-5:00 P.M. EST; free publications.

National Jewish Lungline—1-800-222-LUNG (1-800-222-5864); in operation 8:00 A.M.-5:00 P.M. Rocky Mountain Time; information on lung diseases from chemical exposure.

Cancer Information Service—1-800-4-CANCER (1-800-422-6237); information on cancer; free publications; federally funded by National Cancer Institute.

Consumer Product Safety Commission—1-800-638-2772; 5401 Westband Avenue, Bethesda, Maryland 20207; recorded information and publications available 24 hours a day when calling from a touchtone phone; operators are on duty weekdays 10:30 A.M.-4:00 P.M. EST to take complaints about unsafe consumer products.

Superfund—1-800-424-9346; see Hazardous Waste Sites.

Chemical Manufacturers Association—1-800-262-8200.

American College of Physicians—1-800-523-1546.

American Academy of Pediatrics—1-800-433-9016.

APPENDIX C
WHERE TO CALL IN
CANADA

Since the home environmental hazards discussed in this book are also commonly found in Canada, a list of places to call for assistance in Canada is included. The two main agencies dealing with these problems on a national level are Environment Canada and Health and Welfare Canada. As with the United States, the federal government in Canada has jurisdiction in some areas and provincial and local governments in Canada have jurisdiction in other areas. The phone numbers listed will provide access either to the "right" person to talk to (first choice!), or to the person who can direct the caller to the specific person for a specific problem.

Environment Canada

Inquiries Center
Environment Canada
351 St. Josefs Blvd., 6th Floor
Hull, Quebec K1A 0H3

(819)997-3743 - 24-hour
  environment emergency hotline
(819)997-6822 - Communications
  Directorate that can direct callers
  to the appropriate federal or local
  number

Environment Canada Regional Offices

Atlantic
Environment Canada
45 Alderney Drive
Dartmouth, Nova Scotia   B2Y 2N6
(902)426-7155

Quebec
Environment Canada
3 Buade Street
P.O. 406
Quebec, Quebec G1R 4V7

Ontario
Environment Canada
25 St. Clair Avenue East
Toronto, Ontario M4T 1M2
(416)973-6467

Western and Northern
Environment Canada
2nd Floor, Twin Atria 2
4999-98 Avenue
Edmonton, Alberta T6B 2X3
(403)468-8075

Pacific and Yukon
Environment Canada
3rd Floor
Kapilano 100 - Park Royal South
West Vancouver, British Columbia
V7T 1A2
(604)666-5900

Health and Welfare Canada

Health and Welfare Canada
Health Protection Branch
Tunney's Pasture
Ottawa, Ontario K1A OL2
(613)957-2990

The following numbers at Health and Welfare Canada are for specific problems:

Radon (613)954-6676
Asbestos (613)957-1881
Formaldehyde (613)957-1881
Lead (613)957-1501
Water (613)957-3128

Pesticides (613)957-1852
Hazardous Waste Sites
  (613)957-1876
Indoor Air Quality (613)957-3128

The following numbers are for the Health and Welfare Canada Provincial Offices and Territories:

British Columbia (604)387-5394
Alberta (403)427-3665
Saskatchewan (306)787-7345
Manitoba (204)945-3731
Ontario (416)965-2421
Quebec (418)643-3160
New Brunswick (506)453-2581
Nova Scotia (902)424-4310

Prince Edward Island
  (902)368-4903
Newfoundland (709)576-3124
Yukon Territories (403)667-5120
Northwest Territories
  (403)873-7128

The following numbers are for other federal agencies that may be helpful:

Agriculture Canada
Sir John Carling Building
930 Carling Avenue
Ottawa, Ontario K1A 0C5
(613)995-5222

Atomic Energy Control Board
270 Albert Street
P.O. Box 1046
Ottawa, Ontario K1P 5S9
(613)995-5894

Transport Canada
Department of Transport
Place de Ville
330 Sparks Street
Ottawa, Ontario K1A 0N5
(613)990-2309

Consumer and Corporate Affairs
  Canada
Ottawa, Ontario K1A 0C9
(819)997-2938

Canadian Environmental Network

The Canadian Environmental Network has a comprehensive list of environmental organizations in Canada. The national office has national organizations and the regional offices have local branches of the national organizations and local organizations for specific problems. Some of the regional offices have printed directories available; eventually all are scheduled to have directories available.

*Canadian Environmental
Network/Reseau Canadien de
L'Environment*
M. Martin Theriault

P.O. Box 1289
Station B Ottawa, Ontario K1P 5R3
(613)563-2078
FAX: (613)232-4354

Regional offices for the Canadian
Environmental Network
Alberta Environmental Network
10511 Saskatchewan Drive
Edmonton, Alberta T6E 4S1
(403)433-9302

British Columbia Environmental
  Network
952 West 21st Street
Vancouver, British Columbia V5Z 1Z1
(604)733-2400

Northern Environmental Network
Site 12, Compartment 28
RR #1
Whitehorse, Yukon Y1A 4Z6
(403)668-6407 or 667-5030

Reseau Quebecois Des Groupes
  Ecologiques
C.P. 1480, Succ, Place D'Armes

Montreal, Quebec H2Y 3K8
(514)982-9444

Atlantic Environmental Network
3115 Veith Street, 3rd Floor
Halifax, Nova Scotia B3K 3G9
(902)454-7828

Manitoba Environmental Network
P.O. Box 3125
Winnipeg, Manitoba R3C 4E6
(204)956-1468

Ontario Environmental Network
P.O. Box 3125, Station P
Toronto, Ontario M5S 2Z7
(416)925-1322

Saskatchewan Eco-Network
205-219 22nd Street East
Saskatoon, Saskatchewan S7K 0G4
(306)665-1915

GLOSSARY

abatement—When referring to asbestos, its control beyond a special operations and maintenance program.

acceptable air quality—Air in which there are no known contaminants at harmful concentrations; air that a substantial percentage of people (usually 80%) do not express discomfort with when they are exposed to it.

acid aerosol—Acidic liquid or solid particles that are small enough to become airborne.

ACM—Asbestos-containing material.

adsorbent—A porous solid that traps pollutants in the numerous pores on its surface.

air changes per hour (ACPH)—A way to measure the movement of a volume of air; for example, if all the air in a house is replaced with fresh air in one hour, the house has 1 ACPH. Air changes also may be expressed in cubic feet per minute.

air to air heat exchanger—A mechanical ventilation device that exhausts stale air and supplies fresh air to an enclosed space, while at the same time transferring most of the heat from the air being exhausted to the fresh air supply.

allergen—A substance that can cause an allergic reaction in a person sensitive to that substance.

allergic rhinitis—Inflammation of the mucous membranes of the nose.

alpha particle—A positively charged subatomic particle emitted during radioactive decay; indistinguishable from a helium atom nucleus, and consisting of two protons and two neutrons. Alpha particles do not penetrate the skin but can damage the lungs when inhaled and, over time, cause cancer.

alpha-track detector—A device used to test for radon progeny levels; it is a small container with a sheet of special plastic. Alpha particles strike the plastic and produce tracks. The tracks can be related to the concentration of radon.

ammonia (NH_3)—A pungent, suffocating, gaseous compound that is a common indoor pollutant; its source may be cleaning products or the metabolic activity of occupants.

aquifer—A geological formation supplying water for wells.

asbestos—A group of naturally appearing mineral fibers found in rocks; used in various building materials, including pipe insulation, fire board, woodstove gaskets and some plaster products.

asbestosis—A usually fatal disease where lung tissue becomes scarred by the inhalation of asbestos fibers.

ASHRAE—The American Society of Heating, Refrigerating, and Air-Conditioning Engineers.

biological organisms (biologicals)—Bacteria, molds and their spores, pollen, viruses and other biological materials.

biological pesticide—A pesticide having a living organism as one of its active ingredients, such as insect-infecting bacteria, fungi and viruses.

block walls—See hollow-block walls.

building-related illness (BRI)—A discrete, identifiable disease or illness that can be traced to a specific pollutant or source within a building.

carbon dioxide (CO_2) —An odorless, colorless gas that is a minor part of the atmosphere, formed whenever carbon-containing substances are burned.

carbon monoxide (CO)—An odorless, highly toxic, flammable gas produced by the incomplete combustion of natural gas, oil, wood, coal, tobacco and other materials. Inhalation prevents normal oxygen intake and distribution to the body, and can cause death.

caulk—To fill or close a seam or joint with a sealant to prevent leaks.

cementitious—Cement-like; friable materials that are densely packed and non-fibrous.

CDC—Centers for Disease Control, federal agency in Atlanta, Georgia, under the U.S. Department of Health and Human Services.

CERCLA—The Comprehensive Environmental Response Compensation and Liability Act of 1980, established to develop priorities for cleaning up the worst toxic waste sites.

channel drain—See French drain.

chemical sensitivity—Having an allergic reaction, such as dizziness, eye and throat irritation, chest tightness and nasal congestion, to certain chemicals.

charcoal canister (CC)—A device, containing activated charcoal, that absorbs radon gas; used to test for radon levels in a specific location in the home.

chlorine—A chemical used to purify water.

chlorination—Adding chlorine to water to disinfect it.

coliform bacteria—A bacteria that when found in water is an indication that human or animal wastes are getting into the water.

containment—The isolation of the work area from the rest of the building to prevent hazardous substances like lead or asbestos fibers from getting into the rest of the house.

contaminant—A pollutant in the air that reduces its acceptability.

continuous monitoring—A method of sampling and measuring the concentration of pollutants in the air over a period of time.

continuous working level monitor (CWLM)—A way to describe the measurement of radon progeny levels over a period of time. (See working level.)

corrosion—A dissolving and wearing away of metal caused by a chemical reaction.

CPSC—Consumer Product Safety Commission.

crawl space—An area beneath some types of houses where there is limited access to utilities and other services.

cubic feet per minute (CFM)—A measurement of air movement: the amount, in cubic feet, of indoor air that is exchanged with outdoor air in one minute.

cumulative working level months (CWLM)—The total lifetime exposure to radon working levels expressed in total working months. (See working level month.)

Curie (Ci)—A quantitative measure of radioactivity; one curie equals 3.7 x 10 to the tenth power disintegrations per second.

decay series—The consecutively produced products in the progressive decay of a radioactive substance. Series commences with a long-lived parent such as U-238 and ends with a stable element such as Pb206.

dehumidifier—Device used to lower the moisture in the air.

depressurization—In housing, a condition that occurs when the air pressure inside a house is lower than the air pressure outside.

dioxin—A toxic by-product of chemical processes such as the manufacture of pesticides or paper bleaching.

distillation—The process of changing water into a vapor through heat, and then allowing it to condense back into liquid form to rid the water of impurities.

drain tiles—Perforated pipes that drain water away from the foundation of the house.

duct—Any tube or pipe that carries air, liquid or wiring; usually hidden above the ceiling, behind the walls or under the floor.

efflorescence—In housing, white, fuzzy-like powder that can form on basement walls when moisture is behind the walls.

effluent—The discharge from waste water treatment plants, which can be human waste, trace elements, organic and inorganic compounds from industrial sewers.

encapsulant—See sealant.

electromagnetic fields (EMF)—A combination of electric fields and magnetic fields that rotates from electric cables, wires, fixtures, and everyday appliances. Preliminary studies indicate EMF may cause cancer and reproduction problems.

encapsulation—Covering or sealing any surface so that no hazardous material can escape.

EPA—Environmental Protection Agency, the federal agency that regulates contaminants in the environment in cooperation with state and local governments.

exfiltration—Uncontrolled air leakage out of a building through cracks, gaps, holes or other openings.

exhaust fan—A mechanical device (fan) used to eliminate air from a building.

exposure (human)—The presence of people in an area where levels of an airborne contaminant are elevated; amount of airborne contaminant inhaled by a person, typically a factor of the concentration and length of time.

exposure (material)—The amount or fraction of a contaminant that is visible.

fibrous—Containing or consisting of long strands of fibers; spongy, fluffy.

footing—A concrete or stone base that supports a foundation wall and is used to distribute the weight of the house over the soil or subgrade underlying the house.

forced ventilation—See mechanical ventilation.

formaldehyde (HCHO)—A colorless, gaseous compound with a detectable, pungent smell at high concentrations.

french drain (also channel drain)—A water drainage technique installed in basements of some houses during initial construction, consisting typically of a one- or two-inch gap between the basement block wall and the concrete floor slab around the entire perimeter inside the basement.

fresh air—Outside air that is generally assumed to be sufficiently uncontaminated to be used for ventilation.

friable—Something that is easily crumbled or reduced to powder.

fungi—Parasitic lower plants that lack chlorophyll, including molds and mildew.

gamma radiation—A true ray of energy, in contrast to beta and alpha radiation, with properties similar to X rays and other electromagnetic waves.

gaskets—The fibrous material used in airtight stoves to make doors fit tightly when closed; frequently made of asbestos, which can pose a hazard.

grab sampling—A way of collecting an air sample to measure contaminant levels. An air sample is drawn into a plastic bottle or glass tube. This method of testing is commonly used to measure radon, carbon monoxide, gases and organic compounds.

granite—A crystalline rock that can contain uranium; a source of radon and radon progeny.

groundwater—Water below the soil level contained by a rock formation or aquifer.

gypsum—A very common mineral, soft enough to be scratched by the fingernail, found in crystals and masses.

half-life—The time required for half of the atoms of a radioactive element to undergo decay. For example, Plutonium 238 has a half life of about 50 years.

hard water—Water containing a relatively high number of dissolved solids, mostly magnesium and calcium; the harder the water the less suds from soap.

heat exchanger—A device used to transfer heat from one medium to another.

heat recovery ventilation (HRV)—Ventilating a house by using an air to air heat ventilator in order to save as much as 80% of the heat (or cool air in the summer) that is lost in natural or mechanical ventilation.

heat recovery ventilator—See heat exchanger.

heavy metals—Metals having a high density or specific gravity, such as cadmium, lead and mercury.

HEPA vacuum—A vacuum with a special filter that can pick up very small fibers that cannot be picked up by a regular household vacuum cleaner; HEPA stands for high efficiency particulate air.

hollow-block walls (block walls)—A wall built of hollow rectangular masonry units arranged to provide an air space within the wall between the facing and backing tiers of the individual blocks.

humidity—The water vapor content of the air.

hydrocarbons—Air pollutants resulting from the use of paints, solvents and wood preservatives.

hypersensitivity pneumonitis—A group of respiratory diseases that involve inflammation of the lungs; thought to be caused by an allergic reaction to biological contaminants.

indoor air—Air that occupies the space within the interior of a house or other building.

indoor air pollution—The contamination by noxious gases or airborne particles, from any source, that makes indoor air unpleasant or unfit to breathe.

infiltration—Uncontrolled air leakage into a building through cracks, gaps, holes and other openings.

inorganics—Compounds such as barium, cadmium, chromium, lead, mercury, silver, sodium, beryllium, cobalt, copper, magnesium, manganese, molybdenum, nickel, potassium, tin, vanadium and zinc that do not have the structure or characteristics of living organisms.

joist—Any of the parallel horizontal beams set from wall to wall to support the boards of a floor or ceiling.

lead—A heavy, soft, malleable, bluish-gray metal that, when absorbed by the body, can result in an acute toxic condition.

liquid scintillation spectrometer—A device for measuring radon in water that emits light when stuck by a nuclear particle.

mainstream smoke—Smoke drawn through tobacco during inhalation and then exhaled.

MCL—Maximum contaminant levels.

mechanical ventilation—Ventilation by a mechanical device such as a fan or blower.

mesothelioma—Cancer of the pleura (membrane lining the chest or lung) or abdominal cavity.

mg/1—Milligram per liter.

microbes—Most microscopic particles and organisms, including fungi, pollen, bacteria and viruses.

micron—Approximately 1/25,000th of an inch (used to measure suspended particles).

mildew—A cottony, usually whitish coating on a surface; caused by fungi when the surface is exposed to moisture.

millirem—1/1000th of a rem.

mold—A growth of minute fungi on vegetable or animal matter, often as a downy or furry coating and associated with decay.

natural ventilation—The unaided movement of air into and out of an enclosed space through intentionally provided openings such as windows, doors, vents or other openings (occasionally incorrectly referred to as "infiltration" or "exfiltration").

NIH—National Institutes of Health, federal agency concerned with health issues affecting Americans.

NIOSH—The National Institute for Occupational Safety and Health is under the U.S. Department of Health and Human Services; concerned with air pollution and other hazards in the workplace.

NPL—National Priorities List of worst hazardous waste sites in the United States, which is updated yearly by CERCLA.

nitric oxide (NO) —A colorless gas formed during combustion that can be irritating to the skin, eyes and respiratory tract.

nitrogen dioxide (NO2) —A gas that is a by-product of any high temperature combustion, such as by gas ranges and unvented space heaters.

organics—Compounds, natural or synthetic, that are based on carbon, including chloroform, PCBs, herbicides and pesticides.

particleboard—A building panel made of small pieces of wood bonded together with resins; frequently a source of formaldehyde.

passive smoking (also referred to as secondhand smoking or involuntary smoking)—Exposure to other people's tobacco smoke, which has been linked to the same diseases and side effects as smoking.

pathogen—Any disease-causing organism.

PCBs—Polychlorinated biphenyls, chemicals that were widely used for insulators and flame retardants.

peak levels—The highest levels of airborne contaminants (much higher than average) that occur for short periods of time as a result of the sudden release of the contaminant.

personal monitors—A miniaturized air sampler that an individual can wear to sample and measure the concentrations of a pollutant the individual is exposed to over a period of time.

pesticide—A chemical for killing pests like insects or fungi.

pH—A scale, from 1 to 14, used for measuring the degree of acidity or alkalinity of compounds in water.

picocurie (pCi)—A unit of measurement of radioactivity; it is one-trillionth of a curie; radon is typically measured in picocuries per liter (pCi).

picocuries per liter (pCl)—See picocurie.

plenum—A space filled with a gas (usually air) that has greater pressure than the atmospheric pressure.

plywood—A wood panel made from a number of thin layers of wood glued together with resins, which can be a source of formaldehyde.

polyethylene—A plastic polymer of ethylene used chiefly for containers, electrical insulation and packaging.

polymer—A chemical compound of high molecular weight.

polyurethane—A light polymer used for padding and insulation in furniture, clothing and packaging, and in the manufacture of resins for adhesives and fillers.

portland cement—A type of hydraulic cement usually made by burning a mixture of limestone and clay in a kiln.

potable—A term used for water, which means it is fit or suitable for drinking.

pressed wood—A building material made of wood veneers, particles or fibers bonded together with an adhesive under heat and pressure.

prevalent levels—Levels of airborne contaminants occurring under normal conditions.

progeny—See radon daughters.

radiation—The transmission of energy from one source to another source through an intervening medium or space.

radioactivity—The spontaneous release of energy by the nucleus of an atom, which results in a change in mass.

radon—An invisible, naturally occurring, inert, radioactive gas that comes from uranium; formed in the decay chain of uranium, with an atomic weight of 222 and a half-life of 3.82 days.

radon daughters, radon progeny—A term used to refer collectively to the intermediate products in the radon decay chain. Each "daughter" is an ultrafine radioactive particle that decays into another radioactive daughter until finally a stable nonradioactive lead molecule is formed and no further radioactivity is produced. The daughters can attach to dust particles and, if inhaled, can cause lung cancer.

radon progeny integrating sampling unit (RPISU)—A device for measuring radon levels using an air pump, which constantly pulls air through.

RCRA—Resource Conservation and Recovery Act, established to create guidelines for the management of toxic waste and its disposal.

rem—Roentgen equivalent in man, the measure of biological damage to human tissues caused by a certain amount of radiation.

respirable suspended particulates (RSP)—Tiny particles formed during the combustion of such things as tobacco, coal and wood, which can be inhaled and result in a rise in blood pressure, allergic reactions, reduced respiratory capacity and/or lung cancer.

risk—The likelihood of developing a disease as a result of exposure to a contaminant.

SARA—The 1986 Superfund Amendments and Reauthorization Act.

SDWA—The Safe Drinking Water Act (1974), sets standards for safe drinking water and provides assistance to states.

sealant—A liquid (such as paints, chemicals or soft substances) that can be applied to surfaces, or circulated through pipes, to form a hard, watertight coating (seal) when dry.

sediment—Loose solid material that settles to the bottom of a liquid, such as dirt in water.

sick building syndrome (SBI)—A term that is used when a number of building occupants have the same symptoms—which disappear when the leave the building.

sidestream smoke—Smoke from smoldering tobacco; accounts for most of gases and particles in environmental tobacco smoke (96%), the rest coming from mainstream smoke.

slab-on-grade construction—A term describing the construction of a house on a flat bed of concrete, generally without a basement or crawl space.

softener—A device to artificially soften water.

soft water—Water that has relatively fewer dissolved minerals in it; suds more easily but is thought to be less healthy than hard water.

soil gas—Gaseous elements and compounds that occur in the small spaces between particles of earth and soil; depending on air pressure changes, can travel through, or leave, the soil or rock.

source—The point of emission of a contaminant or pollutant.

spring—Groundwater on the earth's surface that comes from a crack or fault in the earth.

sub-slab suction—Using a fan to blow radon away from the house through pipes that are under the foundation.

sulfur dioxide (SO2)—A common air pollutant that can result from the combustion of sulfur-containing fuel in kerosene heaters, or of oil or coal containing sulfur in other combustion appliances.

sump pump—A pump or vertical-lift that will drain water from a pit or hole in a basement designed to collect the water.

Superfund—The popular name for the $8.5 billion Hazardous Response Waste Fund, set up in 1980 primarily to cleanup the most dangerous hazardous waste sites.

tensile strength—The resistance of a material to longitudinal stress.

termiticide—A pesticide used to control termites.

trace elements—Minute quantities of naturally occurring metallic substances.

trowel—A flat-bladed tool.

TSCA—Toxic Substances Control Act, set up to identify and control chemical products that pose a risk to humans or the environment.

turbidity—A term used to describe cloudy or murky water, caused by the presence of undissolved solids, particles and other types of sediment; can interfere with disinfection efforts.

ug/dl—Micrograms per deciliter.

ug/l—Micrograms per liter.

uranium—A radioactive metallic element that, during its decay chain, becomes radon.

ventilation—The process of supplying fresh air, or removing household air, or both, by natural or mechanical means in any enclosed space.

ventilation rate—The rate at which air enters and leaves a building; it can be expressed as the number of changes of outside air per unit of time (air changes per hour, or ach) or the rate at which a volume of outside air enters per unit of time (cubic feet per minute, or cfm).

volatile organic compounds (VOC)—Organic compounds that vaporize at room temperature or pressure and are found in many household products and building materials.

WQA—Water Quality Association.

working level (WL)—A measurement for radioactive exposure to radon decay products. One WL is the amount of radioactive energy an individual is exposed to from 200 pCi/l of radon.

working level month (WLM)—A measurement of exposure to radon over one month; one WLM is exposure to 200 pCi/l of radon for 173 hours—the usual number of working hours in one month.

INDEX